WHEN I SAW TIRUPATI BALAJI !!!!
(Naaham Karta)

WHEN I SAW TIRUPATI BALAJI

(Naaham Karta)

P.V.R.K. Prasad

GYAN

Published by

GYAN

Gyan Publishing House
5, Ansari Road
Daryaganj, New Delhi-110002
Phone: 011-47034999, 9811692060
E-mail: books@gyanbooks.com

Distribution Network
gyanbooks.com
India, USA, Canada, UK, Australia, France

ISBN: 978-81-212-0933-5 (HB)

Reprint in India, 2024
First Published, 2008

Printed at: Gyan Press, Delhi.

When I Saw Tirupati Balaji: Naaham Karta
Author: P.V.R.K. Prasad

CONTENTS

BLESSINGS

Srihari is a personification of bliss, which Lord Brahma and other Devatas found elusive. Peerless among Gods, He is the savior of those who constantly chant His name.

Srihari rids chosen devotees of their sins and puts them on the right path. His advent as Lord Venkateswara at Tirumala was to fulfill the wishes of millions of His devotees in Kaliyuga. Tirumala, His abode, is verily the heaven on earth.

Lakhs of devotees throng the Seven Hills at Tirumala to this day to worship Lord Balaji and experience fulfillment in their lives. One gets immense reward for even a small act of service rendered in this holy land.

It is here that our affectionate disciple PVRK Prasad rendered yeoman service as Executive Officer of the Tirumala Tirupathi Devasthanams. In fact, he transformed Tirumala into a heaven on earth by ensuring that no devotee has anything to complain about. He launched many programmes to meet the diverse needs of devotees. Integrity and high standards are the characteristic hallmarks of all he does. Still, *'naham karta'* (I am not the doer) is an article of faith with him.

Lord Venkateswara's miraculous powers, highlighted in scriptures, can be witnessed by people in their day-to-day lives as well. Prasad has captured and chronicled devotees' pleasant encounters with the Lord. He narrates how Srihari used him as an instrument for getting certain things done. The book now in your hands, *When I Saw Tirupati Balaji*, is the English version of *'Naham Karta.'* It is an invaluable work that reflects several individuals' inscrutable experiences with Lord Balaji.

We pray that our revered Guru should bless Prasad with a long life, robust health, prosperity, wisdom, devotion and detachment so that he continues to render such services.

FOREWORD

In this book, I have read the experiences of Mr. P.V.R.K. Prasad, IAS, pertaining to mostly his tenure as Executive Officer, Tirumala Tirupati Devasthanams, Tirupati, Andhra Pradesh.

Every episode whetted my curiosity to go to the next episode. They are exciting and full of devotion.

He has not given any spiritual message. Yet, the miracles through which he narrated the visible effect of the Invisible Power keeps the reader enthralled.

Narration is simply engrossing.

My compliments to Mr. Prasad.

May God bless him.

P.V. NARASINAHARAO

HUMBLE OFFERING

The grace of 'guru' and the Lord are absolutely necessary, if any good work is to be started and successfully completed.

With the blessings of my Guru Sri Satya Pramoda Thirtha of Uttaradi Math, who was responsible for my taking an absolute 'U' turn in my lifestyle as well as attitudes, and the blessings of the present Pithadhipathi Sri Satyatma Thirtha, I penned my experiences with the Lord and His work. Through my Gurus, I submit this flower at the feet of Lord Balaji as a humble offering.

(Sri Venkateswara of Tirupati is the advent of Lord Vishnu, who has thousands of names including Balaji, Srinivasa, Lord of the Seven Hills, Tirumalesa, Tirupativasa, Srivaru.)

WHEN I SAW TIRUPATI BALAJI

Discerning readers of 'Sarva Sambhavam' column in 'Swati', who read my memoirs serialized by the Telugu weekly, wrote letters crediting me for the many projects and policies that took shape when I was the Executive Officer of Tirumala Tirupati Devasthanams (TTD).

Regardless of what I did in the interests of devotees or TTD, I believe that all my actions stemmed from my innate belief: "Naham Karta, Harih Karta" (I am not the doer, Srihari is). I treated both commendations and condemnations as 'prasadam' from Lord Srinivasa.

I merely recorded the events as they took place, without imposing my views on readers. My experiences—some wonderful, some strange and some incredible - trigger conflicting emotions in atheists and theists.

I don't know how my experiences impacted rationalists who question, "Is there God? If there is, how does He look? Have you seen Him?" or the seekers of truth who ask, "How much of faith one should repose in God to earn His support for human endeavors ?"

This book has answers for all such questions.

My own belief in 'Naham Kartha, Hari Kartha' has only grown stronger over the years.

P.V.R.K. Prasad

ACKNOWLEDGEMENTS

I got the inspiration for coming out with 'When I saw Tirupati Balaji', an English version of 'Naham Karma Hari Kartha' mainly from my dear friends— Mr. G. Valliswar, Chief Editor, Andhra Pradesh, and Mr. Ch. S. Madhava Rao, formerly of the U.S. Consulate, Chennai. Both spent considerable time with me not only in preparing the draft but also in modifying the text during subsequent readings. I am indebted to them for their deep involvement.

I am thankful to Dr. Ramanarayan, Professor in Indian School of Business, and Mr. Vasantha Kumar Parigi for their valuable suggestions.

Mr. D. Bhujanga Rao, Mr. Mahadev and Mr. M.V.V. Giri Kiran were very helpful in DTP work and support services.

1

WHEN I WAS BROUGHT DOWN TO MY KNEES

One may experience knee pain when one climbs the Seven Hills to have '*darshan*' of Lord Srinivasa at Tirumala. But when knee pain strikes even before one sets out on a journey to Tirumala, it is a mystery. I had to witness the agony when I tried to scotch the very idea of going to Tirumala.

× × ×

My postings in the districts, as trainee Assistant Collector in West Godavari district, Sub-Collector, Bhuvanagiri and Project Officer, Small Farmers' Development Agency, Nalgonda district, and District Collector, Khammam (for three years), had almost ended. In 1977, the Government appointed me Managing Director of the Andhra Pradesh Irrigation Development Corporation with its headquarters at Hyderabad.

With the stints in the districts over, my wife and I had been planning to seek admission for children in good schools and settle down in our own home coming up in Hyderabad. There was a call from the office of the Chief Secretary, Mr. I. J. Naidu. When I called on him, he told me that I should pack up and go back to the districts once again. But this time I should go as Executive Officer of the Tirumala Tirupati Devasthanams (TTD), as suggested by Chief Minister Dr. M. Channa Reddy.

The tradition of the Chief Minister hand-picking IAS officials for some prestigious positions had just begun. The Chief Minister shortlisted a few candidates from out of those suggested by the Chief Secretary. From among them, I was given the first choice for the TTD position. Explained the Chief Secretary: "For one to work in a religious institution, one should have total faith in the institution and the Lord and one should be eager and willing to work there. The Chief Minister has selected you. Posting orders will be given only if you give your consent".

I was not inclined to take a decision on the spot either way. Conflicting emotions crossed my mind. I was not reconciled to leaving Hyderabad so soon after having planned to settle down. But could I say that I was not interested in going as it might mean spurning a call from the Lord? In this context, I was reminded of what a friend of mine had told me: when an IAS official working as West Godavari District Collector declined to be posted as TTD Executive Officer, the Government had to cancel the orders already issued. Two or three weeks later, he got into serious trouble resulting in suspension from service.

I, therefore, felt that my wife and I should seriously consider the pros and cons and resolve the dilemma. The Chief Secretary agreed to grant me two days to make up my mind.

Returning home, I discussed the matter at length with my wife Gopi. We had been on the move in the districts for more than a decade. Daughter Madhavi had already moved from school to school at three different places, even before she entered the first class. The new posting would once again disrupt her studies. I was not too keen on moving out. At the same time, I was in no mood to tell the Chief Secretary that I was not interested as it was a call from the Lord. We, therefore, hit upon the idea of leaving the matter to the Government. We thought it was a clever move on our part. I informed the Chief Secretary accordingly. But Mr. I. J. Naidu was not prepared to accept the proposal. He told me point-blank: "Look Prasad, unless you agree to go there willingly, posting orders cannot be given. The CM is particular that the person posted as EO should be keen to go there and work there willingly". After a pause, Mr. I. J. Naidu added, "Anyway, I will convey your viewpoint to the Chief Minister. Let us see what he has to say". I uttered a sigh of relief as I felt the posting would not take place and the issue had been resolved to our satisfaction. But we did not realise then that the decision of not going to Tirumala would end up in my going through a period of agony and anguish. The decision had its fallout that very evening when we went for a movie. - - - - -

As our entire family watched the movie, daughter Madhavi developed pain in her right knee. By the time the movie ended, her knee had swollen and pain increased. We had to carry her to the car. The next morning we took her to a doctor. The doctor suspected it to be a case of an insect bite and prescribed some drugs. But she had no relief either from swelling or pain. The pain was severe when she tried to fold her leg. Two or three days passed by. She underwent many tests, including x-rays, but the cause could not be established. The girl was made to gulp drugs. She stopped going to school as she could not walk or bend her leg. Doctors suspected rheumatoid arthritis. She was then subjected to a rosemary test. The result was the same: "Everything is all right. No abnormalities". With half of her leg bandaged, Madhavi was immobilised. As days rolled by with tests and medication, we could not reply to her plaintive cry, "How long should I suffer? When will I go back to school? ".

It had already been a month since Madhavi stopped going to school. Deep down, I felt that I was overlooking something. What could it be? Could it be a consequence of my stratagems to avoid the TTD posting? Gopika and I reviewed the sequence of events — the call from the Chief Secretary, our decision to leave the matter to the Government, Madhavi developing knee pain in the movie theatre on the very day I conveyed my decision to the Chief Secretary and her forced absence from school from the next day. All the developments fell in place like the pieces in a jigsaw puzzle and seemed to provide an answer to our nagging question as to why she developed the knee problem all of a sudden. - - - - - Preferring good schooling for the child to my serving the Lord. The first thing I did the next morning was to meet the Chief Secretary and give my consent for the TTD posting.

Mr. I. J. Naidu told me very coolly: "The subject came up for discussion with the Chief Minister twice or thrice. I informed him about your lukewarm response. But he is yet to decide on as to who should be posted. Anyway, I will broach the matter again with the Chief Minister at the appropriate time and find out his reaction".

Mr. I. J. Naidu, however, did not assure me of the posting as he was aware of Dr. Channa Reddy's interest in the TTD. I confided in the Chief Secretary, "I had said a 'no' when Lord Srinivasa beckoned me. I was foolish in not jumping at the idea and giving my consent". I told him about my daughter also. "Now I am very eager to go. Please help me in getting the posting". The Chief Secretary merely nodded, giving me the impression that he appreciated my plight.

Surprisingly, what ultimately happened vindicated my interpretation of the events. That evening the Chief Secretary called me to hand over the posting orders. I was overwhelmed with joy. Straight I returned home with the orders. I could not believe what I saw.

Transfixed, I watched our daughter Madhavi come running shouting, "Daddy, Daddy", and encircling me in excitement. "See, I have peeled off the inconvenient half plaster myself. See, how well I am walking. The swelling is gone, the pain is gone..." So saying, in ecstasy, she folded and stretched her leg, skipped and jumped and sprinted. Madhavi's joy soared to the skies. Who pulled us out of the 40-day ordeal?

× × ×

2

DO PRAYERS PRECIPITATE RAINS?

One day, well past midnight, the giant bells in Lord Srinivasa's temple began to toll long after the temple doors had been shut.

The unprecedented and inconceivable event shook Tirumala residents as well as visiting pilgrims out of their sleep and made them sprint towards the temple. Surprise, suspicion and concern were writ large on their faces as they thronged the temple.

They were drowned in a sea of doubts and suspicions at a time Tirumala was thirsting for water.

× × ×

In 1979, a year after I had taken over as TTD Executive Officer, Tirumala went through a terrible water crisis. By August the drought was so severe that water sources — the Gogarbham reservoir and the two tanks – the Alwar tank and the other on the way to Srivari feet - had almost dried up. The present Papanasanam dam was still under construction. The three or four wells, which supplemented water supply, too, had dried up. As a result, severe restrictions had been imposed on water supply and usage in Tirumala. The south-east monsoon had failed.

We were expecting inflows into the reservoirs, tanks and wells in September and October, when cyclones triggered rains during the north-west monsoon. The available water was being judiciously and economically used as rains could get delayed up to October. But that year, the rain Gods had not showered compassion even until the beginning of November. TTD engineers concluded that the available water might last a maximum of four weeks and the prospect of rains was grim.

Tirumala, with an enumerated population of 6000, attracted 25000 every day pilgrims on an average and many more on holidays and festive days. Unlisted vendors and hawkers running into thousands were also either permanent or temporary residents of Tirumala. The water needs of every one had to be met. I started examining the available options. One option was to transport water from Tirupati to Tirumala by tankers and the other was to appeal to pilgrims not to visit water-starved Tirumala. Further restrictions on water supply were out of the question as steep cuts had already been enforced. How could we ask pilgrims not to come? Would it be proper for TTD trustees to ask pilgrims not to visit the Lord as they could not provide water? Whoever were the TTD Trust Board members, it was the Executive Officer who had to look after day-to-day management. After making a number of calculations, I ordered for supply of water by tankers. The tanker water was adequate to meet the temple needs and help maintain basic sanitation levels. I realised that meeting the water needs of the town and pilgrims for the next eight to ten months was impossible, even if funds were not a constraint.

I, therefore, desperately started exploring whether ancient "*sastras*" offered any solution. I called on the TTD Asthana Vidvan and Advisor - the renowned vedic scholar Sri Uppuluri Ganapathi Sastry (90). (The Government of India later conferred on him the "Padma Vibhushan" title).

I asked him whether "*japas*" (prayers) and "*yagnas*" *(offerings through sacred fire to Gods)* would provide a solution to drought and, if so, to what extent. His reply was unambiguous. He said, "The Vedas offer solutions to all such problems. But any Vedic ritual will be effective only when one undertakes it with perfect faith in God and sincerity in thought, word and deed. Competent Vedic scholars, who can undertake such great tasks, are fading out because people, carried away by their craze for modern civilisation, have lost interest in following Vedic traditions. The Vedas are a treasure-house of knowledge and offer a solution to every problem – spiritual as well as temporal".

His tremendous faith in the Vedas offering solutions to even mundane problems moved me. I was certain that he could come up with a solution to the water problem. This 90-year-old erudite scholar had spent 48 years of his life in serious studies, mastering the Vedas and Vedangas. It is not possible to interpret the Vedas correctly unless one is proficient *in "vyakarnana, tarka, vedanta, mimasa, nyaya and nirukta"*. Sri Ganapati Sastry was a stalwart in all the subjects. I was keen on tapping his scholarship and commitment. My single point programme was provision of water to pilgrims, however complex the means might be. Therefore, I was ready to follow in thought, word and deed whatever the *"sastras"* ordained.

Sri Ganapati Sastry pointed out that the rain Gods would shower their blessings if *"Varuna japa"* was performed. He explained in detail as to how I should go about it. He would not be able to lead it, plagued as he was with old age and ill health. However, he named scholars from all over the country who could undertake the ritual.

We decided to launch *"Varuna japa"* from November 1. But it could not take off because of some reason or the other. One scholar after another faced problems in responding to our invitation for reasons ranging from ill health to a death in the family (making him ineligible to take part in the sacred task). As the water level in the Gogarbham reservoir plummeted further, the engineers feared they could not supply water for more than a week. Despite all out efforts, a few more days passed by without the launching of *"Varuna japa"* on which we had pinned all our hopes. In my silent prayers, I asked the Lord, "What is this ordeal? How long is this going to last? Won't *"Varuna japa"* take place properly? Have you approved of it or not?" The final deadline for starting the three-day *"Varuna japa"* was November 8 as we had only three days of water supply.

As if in answer to the question whether the Lord had approved of *"Varuna japa"* or not, the Tirumala hills reverberated to the tolling of bells at *"Banguru Vakili"* in Srivari temple around 2 on the night of November 7. Tirumala was startled. People took to the streets wondering how the bells tolled at that unusual hour. I was woken up to be informed of the strange phenomenon. We could not believe our ears. How could the bells ring when the temple doors had been shut and locked after the midnight *"ekanta seva"*?

Those given to rational thinking reasoned that some pilgrims stuck inside the temple might have rung the bells to get the temple doors opened. But when the temple doors were finally opened as usual for the *"suprabhata seva"* at 3 a.m., and every nook and corner searched to find out who could have rung the bells, none could be found.

The bells that rang in the midnight prior to starting of Varuna Japam

I felt the ringing signified God's clearance for *"Varuna japa"*.

"Varuna japa" was to start early in the morning. The Vedic scholars, who had excused themselves earlier, turned up that day in full strength.

"Varuna japa" comprises many rituals. Some scholars stand for hours in chest deep water in the temple tank, *"pushakarini"*, (recycled unpotable water), to chant *'mantras'*. Some perform *"abhisehka"* to the Lord's processional deities. Some conduct *"homam"* to propitiate the rain Gods, while many others do *'japas'* or recite *'Vedas'* and *'sastras'*. After three days of such activities, the programme concludes with the conduct *of* *"snapana tirumanjanam"* (holy bath to the Lord) in *the* *"pushakarini mantap"*. At 7 a.m. on the fourth day, *"sahasra kalasabhishekam"* (sacred bath to the Lord with water from one thousand vessels) is performed to mark the smooth conclusion of the ceremony – by way of thanks giving.

The entire three-day programme went off without any hiccups smoothly. Even as the *"snapana tirumanjanam"* neared completion on the evening of the third day, the sun shone brightly and the sky was clear. Utterly disappointed, we consoled ourselves saying, "We have done our job. What else could we have done?"

After the sacred bath to the processional deities in the *"pushkarini Mantap"*, the priests, Vedic scholars and other temple employees including me were taking the deities back to the temple. Technically, the *'varuna japa'* was over. *'Abhisekham'*, to be performed the next morning was part of thanksgiving and not part of *'varuna japa'*. Press reporters, who had been closely watching the developments were heard commenting that the *"Varuna japa"* produced only tears but no showers. Could rituals produce rains? commented some in derision. The naïve and gullible Executive Officer would have to explain away a lot of things. The atheists openly ridiculed the Executive Officer's superstition resulting in huge wastage of funds. I was deeply hurt.

Prasad performing Puja at Gogarbham dam prior to the rains.

Where did we go wrong? Was I foolish enough to have believed what all Sri Sastry had told me. Had I been gullible? Had I failed to follow the instructions properly? Had we committed any indiscretion?....As such questions plagued my mind, a large raindrop on my head jolted me. There were claps of thunder and flashes of lightning. There was a sudden heavy downpour. The priests had to run into the temple with the deities to ensure that the deities did not get wet. As a matter of precaution, a special *"chatram"* (umbrella) was normally brought on such occasions along with the deities. The *"chatram"* was not brought that day as the weather was so clear. No one ever even thought of rain though we were performing *'Varuna Japa'* for rains. We

Gogarbham Dam (full) after the rain

virtually had to run into the temple, a few yards away. All of us were completely drenched. The rain continued unabated the whole night until the beginning of *"sahasra kalasabhishekam"* at 7 a.m. the next day.

As the *"sahasra kalasabhishekam"* was to begin, the Chief Engineer came running to announce jubilantly that, "the Gogarbham reservoir is overflowing". Fanstastic, that meant sufficient water for one full year. As tears of joy rolled down my cheeks and the beard (which I had been growing as a vow to get the rains), I prostrated before the Lord Srinivasa involuntarily, and commenced the thanksgiving ceremony.

Significantly, there was no rain anywhere nearby - at Tirupati or Renigunta or Kalahasti or Chandragiri or Railway Kodur. The rain battered only the Tirumala Hills.

Was it a mere coincidence? Or was it the outcome of the *'Vedic'* ritual? Was it the Lord's benediction?

× × ×

3

A JINXED PLANE GROUNDS THE PRESIDENT

All of a sudden the aircraft started swaying in the skies. And moments later, it crashed, ploughed through the ground for a few hundred yards and screeched to a halt. Its nose and tail had fallen apart, while the engines spewed sparks and smoke. Yet, the aircraft did not burst into flames. As a passenger, I missed many a heartbeat but thankfully survived.

× × ×

As I took part in the Padmavathi *'teppotsavam'* (float festival) at Tiruchanur in the middle of July 1981, I received a phone call from the Chief Secretary. The gist of the call was that President Sri Neelam Sanjiva Reddy, then spending his summer at Rashtrapati Nilayam at Bolarum in Secunderabad, would like to visit Tirumala and spend 10-15 peaceful days atop the Hills, the abode of the Lord.

The message was unusual. Normally, the President visits Tirumala for a day or two. Even then the TTD found it taxing to make all the arrangements for the sojourn of the President. Making security arrangements for the President, providing accommodation and food to the President and his personal staff, security personnel, the Minister-in-waiting from the State Government and his staff and VIPs calling on the President, was a Herculean task.

The day-to-day administration naturally suffered on such occasions. If the President, that too a former Chief Minister of Andhra Pradesh, were to stay for 10-15 days at Tirumala, the TTD had to shoulder a great burden. Good cottages had to be reserved in large numbers in advance, putting common pilgrims to hardship in the process. In addition, whenever the President chose to visit the Temple, the *'darshan'* for common pilgrims had to be halted, much to their annoyance and inconvenience. The President might spend ten days peacefully, but, what about others visiting Tirumala in quest of peace?

I explained all these aspects to the Chief Secretary and finally requested him: "Please draw the President's attention to the attendant problems". The Chief Secretary told me that he had already briefed and reasoned with the President. Yet the President was keen on spending two weeks atop the Hills quietly as an ordinary pilgrim, without inconveniencing anybody and without entertaining visitors. Would it be possible? I expressed my misgivings to the Chief Secretary. The Chief Secretary, however, assured me that he would speak to the President once again, at my request.

The very next morning, the Chief Secretary called me over the phone to say, "I have told him everything. But the President insists on staying atop the Hills. He says that he would like to worship the Lord not as the President of India but as an ordinary pilgrim. He wants the arrangements to be made without any pomp and show. 'If you can arrive here today, I will take you to the President. Try if you can convince him". He put down the telephone. What else could I have done? I rushed to the airport to catch the only flight to Hyderabad in the afternoon.

Those days, an 'Avro' flight used to leave Tirupati at 3-30 p.m. and land in Hyderabad around 5-00 p.m. As I left for Renigunta airport, I sought from Additional Superintendent of Police Ravulapati Seetarama Rao (working with the TTD) and TTD Vigilance Officer Janardhan Naidu, details about the Presidents' earlier visits. I also asked for some information on the security plans for the President's visit. They turned up at the airport as I got into the plane. The aircraft took off after a brief delay caused by our discussions.

I was seated in the aisle seat of the ninth row. Seated beside me by the window was the then Cultural Affairs Minister, Mr. Bhattam Srirama Murthy. We briefly spoke to each other about the President's visit. As the aircraft took off thoughts also took a flight. How could I convince the President that his stay for 10-15 days would cause a lot of inconvenience to pilgrims? He might say that no attention be paid to him and that he would like to stay as a common pilgrim. Was it possible? He was a great devotee of the Lord. In two years during my tenure as Executive Officer, he had already visited Tirumala four times for short stays. Even then, in the name of security, transport, medical and health arrangements etc. 500 to 600 officials and staff were put on the job. How about his relatives, friends and political leaders? How could we look after all of them and provide accommodation, food, *'darshan'*, security for so many days? Oh God what would happen to pilgrims? I was jolted out of my thoughts by the turbulence in the flight. The aircraft swayed as it had lost balance.

Mr. P.V.R.K. Prasad with Dr. Neelam Sanjeev Reddy, President of India

Suddenly, the aircraft seemed to be coming down very fast. We felt emptiness in the stomach. Many were shouting in panic. In a couple of moments, the flight seemed to regain its balance. We heaved a sigh of relief. But, soon we experienced that peculiar feeling once again, as the aircraft lost altitude rapidly and swayed violently. Pillows and papers were flying all over. All of us were still wearing our seat belts. The plane seemed to be tilting to the right with the tail portion going up. The passengers, crying and shouting in fright, clung to their seats like lizards. The plane, which had hitherto been gliding sideways, seemed to hit something with a loud thud. The impact was stunning. Shutting my eyes and clutching the seat in front of me, I prayed to the Lord. The plane did not halt. It was now moving with an angled swerve. Suddenly, there was absolute silence and calm all over. The plane had come to a halt. I looked back at the rear portion from where the air was gushing in. To my shock, I noticed a big hole behind our seats. Dust and mud, gushing into the aircraft through the hole, had already smeared the roof inside. I realised that the plane had crash-landed.

Confused and traumatised, I shouted. I unbuckled the seat belt and sprinted to the rear exit door. An airhostess and a passenger followed me. The jammed door would not open when we turned the handle. We kicked it with all our might. As the door opened, we realised that the plane was on the ground and it was raining. We almost walked out of the plane.

Fearing for life, all the passengers rushed out of the plane within a few seconds, shouting, "Govinda, Govinda". Only then we noticed the billowing smoke emanating from the left wing of the plane. The fire that set off the smoke did not look ominous as the downpour had been dousing it. I noticed that I was not wearing spectacles and had only one 'chappal'. Involuntarily, I rushed into the plane to search for my 'specs' even as some passengers shouted against my move. I found my 'specs' as well the missing chappal under the seat and rushed back. The vision was blurred because of the heavy downpour. All of us stood outside, getting drenched in the rain, but not daring to go in and sit. The rain stopped a few minutes later. The smoke emanating from the plane had also completely stopped. The sky had cleared and there was visibility. We noticed that the nose and the tail portions of the plane were lost somewhere. Parts of the propellers lay scattered. One of the engines was missing. We found ourselves in the bed of a partly dried up tank. There were telltale signs of the plane ploughing the ground and skidding for about 200-300 yards.

The rain-drenched soft soil had acted as a shock absorber. All the 29 passengers escaped unscathed, with none shedding even a drop of blood. Once again, I thanked Lord Srinivasa for his compassion. The confused pilots could not explain the crash. Before they realised as to what was happening, the plane was on the ground. All of us found it difficult to believe that we had survived a crash.

Ecstatic over our survival, the passengers congratulated one another, each trying to work out ones' own version of what had happened. As we were all locked in such discussions, some one spotted people approaching us. They were the Additional SP Mr. Seetarama Rao and the TTD Security Officer, Mr Naidu, who had met me at the airport. The heavy gales and sharp showers had prevented them from getting out of the airport. They observed a parked jeep moving away on its own and hitting a tree because of the impact of the gale. Airport officials informed them that the aircraft had lost contact with the control tower. There was the possibility of the plane crashing. They, along with airport officials, wasted no time and took off in the direction the plane had taken and reached the site of the crash. The plane had crashed in a tank five miles west of the Renigunta airport. Seeing them was a great relief.

Being the seniormost officer locally, and having access to resources as Executive Officer, TTD, I took the initiative and formed a security ring around the aircraft. I arranged for the transport of all the passengers to Tirupati in TTD vehicles and their overnight stay. I saw to it that all of them got their baggage. I ensured that the passengers called up their homes over phone even before the news was broadcast over radio. I informed the Chief Secretary and the President's office about my inability to come to Hyderabad.

The next day, accompanied by the Collector, Sub-Collector and the Superintendent of Police, airport officials and air crew, I visited the site of the accident. The pilot and the airport officials tried to reconstruct what had happened and why. Buffeted by high velocity gales, the aircraft travelling between two mountain ranges, had swayed in the skies defying the pilots' attempts to control it. The gales had pushed the plane off course and out of control. It glided sideways into the tank. The plane had brushed against the top of the trees on the tank bund. There was a strip of 15-20 feet stretch of water within the tank adjoining the bund. The rest of the tank bed was dry. Clearing the trees on the tank bund and the waterline, the plane had crashed sideways in the tank bed.

Fortunately, the plane did not plunge into water or hit the huge boulders a little distance away. Had either happened, perhaps none of the 29 passengers would have survived.

As the plane hit the ground, its two engines took the impact. The undercarriage wheels remained drawn up. The crash severed the right engine block which in turn the belly of the plane and caused a hole, resulting in the two adjoining seats behind our row being shorn away. The nose, the tail and the propellers were torn away.

What came to light in the subsequent Indian Airlines inquiry was that the flight had glided and had an almost perfect landing sideways. Had the plane hit a hard surface, it would have somersaulted with its wings hitting the ground, and the plane bursting into flames. The dry tank bed became soft because of the rain. As the plane glided on soft soil with the two engines taking the brunt of the impact the balance had not been lost. As it was raining, the fire in the engine caused by the friction had subsided. More significantly, the plane had stopped within 15-20 yards of high tension power lines. The side ways movement with a little backward tilt had pinned down passengers to their seats and helped them avoid injuries . They were all wearing seat belts.

The inquiry also revealed that only the two seats in the row behind Mr. Bhattam Srirama Murthy and me had strewn away as the sheared engine block hit the belly of the plane at that spot. Fortunately, there were no passengers in those two seats. Most of the other seats were occupied. Except for the pilot suffering a small concussion on his face and Mr. Bhattam's little fingers giving some pain, no one had been hurt. While the aircraft was totally damaged, the fragile seating area had remained intact. All the luggage could be retrieved without any damage.

"No movie could have depicted such a safe plane accident better", said the airlines inquiry report. "Had the plane hit the boulders in the tank, or touched the high tension power lines nearby or did somersaults, none would have survived". But it did not happen. Why? The airlines report added, "It appears as if some one by design had arranged the crash landing in the tank and averted a disaster when the 'Avro' could not withstand the adverse weather". Which Power did it? And why?

By the way, I received a call from the President. He spoke to me about the miraculous escape of all the passengers. He also quietly informed me that he did not feel like spending a fortnight atop the Hills. He might come for a day or two for *'darshan'*. I did not know why he changed his mind. Strange things happen. How do they happen? Why do they happen? They are beyond our comprehension.

4

A PREMONITION ON UGADI EVE!

I was to conduct the *'Ugadi'* (Telugu New Year) celebrations at Ravindra Bharati in Hyderabad in the presence of Chief Minister Dr. M. Channa Reddy that year. I was fully aware of Dr. Channa Reddy's respect for traditions and his unusual ire if something were to go wrong with the function. Although I was all set to leave for Hyderabad, I happened to remain at Tirupati without any valid reason. Sitting in my Tirupati camp office, I kept on asking the camp clerk whether the flight had landed and whether it was time for my departure. But I did not have the inclination to leave for the airport and board the flight. Finally, I did not. The result?

× × ×

'Ugadi' is the most significant of festivals in Telugu people's lives. It immediately reminds one of "*Panchanga sravanam*", "*Ugadi pachchadi*", (chutney prasadam) "*kavi sammelans*" and cultural programmes mirroring Telugu culture. The TTD had initiated celebration of the Telugu New Year as per tradition at Ravindra Bharati only the previous year. I had meticulously planned and conducted the function. *Vedic* chanting and recital, "*Panchanga sravanam*", "*kavi sammelans*" and felicitations to pundits formed part of the programme. Renowned scholar Malladi Chandrasekhara Sastri came forward to do the "*Panchanga sravanam*". As the 1979 celebration was a great success, Dr. Channa Reddy wanted that TTD conduct the 1980 programme on a grander scale.

The TTD did not have a full-fledged board those days. It had only three official Persons in Charge - Revenue Principal Secretary - Dr. Ramesan, Chairman - Endowments Commissioner Chandramouli Reddy - Member and me, the TTD

Executive Officer - Member Secretary. The TTD management rested with these three-member committee.

All arrangements had been made for the *'Ugadi'* celebrations at Ravindra Bharati. I myself drew up the programme after personally selecting the participant Vedic scholars, poets and musicians. The Chief Minister was to be the chief guest and honour some pundits and distinguished persons. We had invited Ministers, judges and prominent people from many walks of life for the function. We paid great attention to every minute detail since the Chief Minister wanted the celebrations to be magnificent. We were aware of the Chief Minister's mood swings if something went awry. As the Master of Ceremonies, I had planned to leave for Hyderabad a day in advance to supervise the arrangements.

A flight (arriving from Hyderabad) used to leave Tirupati for Hyderabad at 1100 a.m. every day. If I were to leave by that flight, I could land in Hyderabad in the afternoon itself and ensure that everything was going on as planned. The flight ticket had been booked. I had early lunch. And the suitcase had been packed and placed in the car. Asking the camp clerk to monitor the flight landing at Renigunta airport, I was looking into files.

It was past 10 a.m. The camp clerk came in to tell me that the flight from Hyderabad would land soon and that I should leave for the airport immediately. I looked at him and said, "Alert me when the flight lands". The camp clerk was surprised, as I was given to arriving at the airport or any function on time. But that day, for some strange reason, I was lethargic or disinterested or might have been depressed. A short while later the camp clerk dropped in to announce the landing of the flight. I remained silent and apathetic. The camp clerk would not leave. He was worried. "Sir, the Airport Manager wants to know whether you have left residence or not". I mumbled "yes" and was again lost in nothingness. Meanwhile, my wife Gopika came in. She thought I had already left for the airport. Surprised to see me, she asked, "How is it you are still here? It is already nearing 11 a.m. - the takeoff time". Indifferently, I said, "It is time I left. I have to leave. But, I do not know why,

I am in no mood to leave". She reminded me of the function and my role in it and suggested that I hurry to catch the flight. I mumbled something vaguely. Still, once she turned her back, I continued to remain seated, fiddling with the files. I was fully aware that I should get up and leave. But at the same time some inexplicable inertia gripped me. A short while later, the camp clerk turned up again. "Sir, the Airport Manager says the flight is ready for takeoff. If you have already started he says, he will detain the flight for some time". I said "okay" and got lost in my confused state. My mind would not permit me to give him a categorical reply. I was at my wit's end. Responsibility dictated that I leave. But the urge to leave was absent. The camp clerk was visibly anxious. He seemed to be indicating that he should not be blamed if I missed the flight. A few moments later, the camp clerk hesitantly came in to say the flight had taken off – without me – having a confirmed ticket and the baggage in the boot of the car. Why did I not leave?

It was then that I stepped into the world of reality. The serious repercussions of my not leaving seeped into my being. What would happen to the function. I was not only supposed to coordinate but also compere and act as the host. I had to resort to fire fighting and make alternative arrangements. Immediately, I called up the Endowments Commissioner, Mr. Chandramouli Reddy, at Hyderabad and requested him to conduct the *'Ugadi'* programme on my behalf. He was taken by surprise. Though he was polite in his response, there was a streak of annoyance and irritation in his tone. He asked me whether I had any specific personal problem. I explained in embarrassment as to what had happened.

Mr. Chandramouli Reddy commented, "Prasad, if the Chief Minister were to ask why Prasad had not turned up, how could I tell him that he did not have the mood to come?" He suggested that I leave Tirupati by road and reach Hyderabad the next morning. But a strange feeling deep within me stood in the way of my making it to Hyderabad. I, therefore, pleaded with him once again,

"Sir, manage somehow, I do not feel like leaving the place. I cannot explain why." He cautioned me, "Don't act on instincts and impulses. This is a very important function and you have a very major and crucial role to play in making the function a success. I may oblige you by substituting. Still, I suggest that you leave by road immediately and catch up with the function".

Despite the Endowments Commissioner's advice, I remained unfocussed. "Damn it; what is happening? Why am I not leaving for Hyderabad? Why am I behaving in such an irrational and irresponsible manner", I said to myself. Still, I would not budge. Time was running out. The camp clerk's anxiety had turned into disbelief and curiosity as he had never seen me like that transfixed to my chair. I remained in a state of perplexed inactivity.

The camp clerk jolted me out of my confused, wakeful slumber by saying "Sir, some one has telephoned to say that he has just seen a bus from Tirumala ramming through the ghat road parapet wall and hurtling down into the valley in between two turnings. The man says he is telephoning even as he is witnessing the accident". The news stunned me. But the next moment, I realised the implications and the enormous work that lay ahead of me. Praying to Lord Srinivasa, I plunged into action at lightning speed. As a reflex action, I rushed to the car to leave for the spot. But, some inner voice asked me to alert all the concerned about rescue and relief operations before I left. I rushed back to my telephone. It being a Sunday, offices remain closed. I personally called up over phone some important officials – Deputy Executive Officers and Officers of the concerned departments like transport, engineering, mechanical, administration, hospital, ambulance, security, police, and fire service. All the three telephones in the camp office were kept busy and in a few minutes I managed to alert all. I asked the police to bring in wireless sets for communicating urgent messages even as I started with two cars in tow. (There were no cell phones those days).

Never had I seen such a disaster. The old ghat road, used for buses and other vehicles coming down, has more than 40 turnings or curves. The difference in the altitude between the top and the bottom of some of the curves is up to 50 feet.

The scene at the ghat road curve, where the accident took place, was ghastly and heart rending. The bus rammed into the parapet wall, capsized, hurtled down and rested on a hill slope, with tree branches arresting its downward ride. The bus was smashed and its widows and doors were crushed and dented. Three or four pilgrims were struggling to extricate themselves through windows. To reach the bus, one had to walk down or climb up about 50 feet through bushes, trees and boulders. Already, passengers and drivers of few buses and cars behind the fateful bus were helping some of the injured. Five or six injured were lying on the road, surrounded by a group of passengers.

"Save us", shrieked some of the passengers still stuck in the bus. Some others loudly chanted "Govinda ... Govinda.... Venkata Ramana — Srinivasa" and prayed for relief. Some passengers of another bus formed into a human chain to rescue the pilgrims crawling out of the mangled bus.

As I was taking stock of the situation, TTD engineers and ambulances arrived. The engineers started sweating the moment they realised the arduous task of rescuing passengers . With its belly up, the bus was stuck on a hill slope. "Without wasting precious time, rescue the passengers first", I pleaded with the staff. The engineers went into action. They cut open that part of the bus body, which was readily accessible, and pulled out many passengers - some severely injured and some with minor injuries in 20 - 25 minutes. But some passengers had their hands and heads stuck in the windows. They could not be rescued unless the bus body was cut open from the other side. Anxiety streaked the faces of the trapped passengers. "Won't you save us before the bus rolls down further into the valley", they seemed to be pleading helplessly. They could be seen but not rescued. By then, two or three seriously injured passengers had lost their consciousness. Doctors, manning a first aid center improvised at the site administered painkiller shots to the injured passengers and removed them to hospital. I was anxious to save those who were still alive. All of them had undertaken the pilgrimage out of their deep faith in Srinivasa. I prayed to the Lord that He should vindicate their faith by saving them. I was not certain. Some persons remained trapped between the seats and the crushed bus body. We could hear shouts and some feeble voices from inside – but could not access them. The trapped could be rescued if the bus body was cut open with gas cutters. Even the bodies of a couple could not be pulled out through the small opening of the bus body. Barring six passengers, all the rest had been rescued.

After discussions among themselves, the engineers made it clear that unless the bus was lifted, it would not be possible to rescue the passengers by making an opening through the top of the bus which was lying upside down. It was a challenge to our capacity and intelligence and my leadership.

Using all the powers at my command, I managed to position two derricks and enthused the engineers to plunge into action. Reaching the equipment to the site and positioning it was itself a Herculean task. And all were determined to lift the bus and save the passengers. The working area was very steep, rugged and uneven. Incredibly, within half an hour, they fixed hooks to the bus on all its four sides and lifted it. With redoubled vigour, mechanics got under the bus and sliced the body portion with gas cutters. Within an hour, those stuck in the windows and inside could be brought out. By then, it was 4 p.m. All the passengers rescued from the bus had been rushed to Ruia Hospital and given treatment. Many had suffered fractures and serious injuries. In all, four persons were killed and two critically injured. Because I had alerted the hospital even before I left for the accident site, doctors' teams were ready to receive the injured and initiate treatment. The TTD got all the passengers treated at its expense.

Even as the rescue effort was on, I assembled the administrative staff and entrusted responsibilities to each of them. The relatives of the dead and the injured had to be notified. Those coming to visit them should be provided food and accommodation. The pilgrims' luggage salvaged from the bus should be handed over to them or their relatives. Ambulances should be readied to take the dead to their native places. Those who suffered minor injuries should be provided transport facilities as per their preference to return to their native places. Poor passengers should be attended to with greater care. The collapsed parapet wall should be rebuilt immediately.

I can't recall how many assignments I had given. It was the only occasion — barring temple festivals — when I requisitioned and activated so many officials in so short a time to run on so varied errands. Only after I had called on every accident victim either in hospital or at guesthouses and spotted the satisfaction on their faces did I return home. That was around midnight.

Early next morning, I rushed to Tirumala to have *'darshan'* of the Lord and do *'Angapradakshinam'* by way of thanksgiving. For what? The newspapers carried the story of the bus falling into the valley and narrated in graphic detail how the entire TTD machinery under the Executive Officer's leadership moved at lightning speed to rescue the passengers. Many well-wishers called up to praise the valiant effort. As per schedule, I was supposed to be in Hyderabad. As I attended the *'Ugadi Asthanam'* of Lord Srinivasa, all the happenings of the previous day flashed across my mind. Somebody present there commented "Sir, it is very thoughtful of you to have stayed on for the *'Ugadi Asthanam'* here without leaving for Hyderabad to attend the function there. Your crucial presence has saved TTD". Visualising the Lord, I asked myself: Was I responsible for my 'inaction'? or was I responsible for my 'action'? - Who was responsible?

By not going to Hyderabad as scheduled I seemed to have served a greater purpose. But what continues to be a mystery is as to who stood in the way of my departure to Hyderabad.

5

A FITTING LESSON TO THE FIRST SERVANT

Which is the more sacred of the two – the *'laddu'* atop the Tirumala hills or the salt at the feet of Tiruvallur Veeraraghava Swamy? Can a mere mortal sit in judgment on such an issue?

"Vidyavinaya sampanne brahmane gavihastini
Sunichaiva swapakecha panditha samadarsinah"

Many interpret this Lord Krishna's counsel to Arjuna, as expressed in the Bhagavadgita *'sloka'*, to mean that one should treat all life forms equally. In fact, *'sama'* here does not connote equality. *'Sama'* here implies "Lord Himself" as defined by Lord Krishna in an earlier *'sloka'*. *'Sama'* is one of the thousand names of the Lord in *'Vishnu Sahasranama'*. It means that one should be able to see the same God that is present in every being. The God in the common man, and the pundit, rich man and the poor man, in the rodent and the elephant is one and the same – there is absolutely no difference in the Lord.

Preaching is one thing but practising another. Is it easy to digest and assimilate this basic principle contained in our *'sastras'*?

Can a TTD Executive Officer, who works in the precincts of Lord Srinivasa of Tirumala — the *'Kaliyuga Vaikuntha'* which annually attracts millions of pilgrims and billions of rupees by way of offerings — cultivate such a mature *'samabhavana'*? Is it easy for the Executive Officer to practise *'samabhavana'* when every one repeatedly calls him "the first servant of the Lord", without succumbing to the illusion of it being true?

The *'sastras'* have clearly explained the rationale behind deity worship. "The statue is not God. We worship not the statue but the godliness in that". God pervades the entire universe. The power in a statue that manifests on its own (*'swayambhu'*) is said to be of the highest order. But there is power *(sannidhana of the Lord)* in every deity of every temple. The deity's intensity of power, however, depends on the sanctity with which it has been installed as per the tenets of the *'agamas'*, on the purity and the devotion of founders and the ardent faith of the pilgrims who visit the temple. God is one and the same all over; there is no difference in His various forms, His capacities and attributes. He is omnipresent, omnipotent and a personification of perfection. This is evident from the above *'sloka'*. The difference lies in the intensity of the faith and capacity of those who had sanctified a particular idol in a temple. The *'jnani'* – the wise - would therefore, perceive God everywhere as *'sama'* – the same.

The illusion of my being the "first servant of the Lord" as Executive Officer made me somehow believe subconsciously that the real God was to be found only at Tirumala, and deities in other temples not so rich and those not patronised by large numbers of pilgrims could not match Lord Srinivasa. I might not have openly articulated it, but deep inside this thought got rooted.

I was once invited to the *'Brahmotsavas'* at Veeraraghava Swamy Temple in Tiruvallur near Madras. *'Garuda seva'* at the Tiruvallur temple is performed at 5-00 a.m during *'Brahmostavams'*, unlike at Tirumala, where it is at 9.00 p.m. As it would be convenient to reach Tiruvallur from Madras, I proceeded to Madras the previous evening with my wife and children. Early next morning, we were scheduled to leave for Tiruvallur.

We had dinner with an uncle of my wife. One of the relatives casually remarked that pilgrims visiting Veeraraghava Swamy traditionally offer salt at the feet of the Lord and jaggery in the temple pond (*'pushkarini'*). Devotees believe that all their hardships melt away like jaggery in water, if they make the offering. I laughed and casually remarked, "Some smart temple Trust Board or executive officer would have hit upon the gimmick to boost the market for salt and jaggery ". All of us had a hearty laugh at the joke and retired for the night.

× × ×

My wife Gopika, daughter Madhavi (9), son Sanjeev (5) and I got up early and reached Tiruvallur by 5 a.m. The decorated '*Garuda vahana*', carrying the benevolent 'Veeraraghava' in all His glory radiating compassion, was ready for the procession. We were received with temple honours. The present '*parepattedar*' in Tirumala temple, Sri Seshadri and some other TTD staff were also there to take part in the festival. Temple officials suggested that we have '*darshan*' of the Lord and consort before we joined the procession.

The wonderfully decorated statue of Veeraraghava Swamy in reclining position in the sanctum sanctorum was a feast to the eyes. The priests began the '*archana*' after ascertaining our '*gotra namas*'. Our son Sanjeev, who had been active till then, complained of stomach pain all of a sudden. "It would abate, be patient", we told him. But within a few seconds, his pain intensified. Clutching his stomach, he fell on the floor and started writhing. Seshadri whisked away the boy outside, so that our worship was not disturbed.

The '*archana*' was over a few minutes later. We went into the Ammavari temple in the same premises. Meanwhile, Seshadri returned to report that Sanjeev was still lying in the car groaning. Our reliable driver Gopal had been put incharge of him and a doctor summoned. We felt we could go out and see him immediately after the '*archana*' in the Ammavari temple was over. The priests started '*archana*' there.

A few seconds after the '*archana*' began, it was the turn of our daughter Madhavi to develop stomach pain. As the pain worsened within seconds, she started writhing in agony. Mr. Seshadri once again managed to send the girl outside. We were midway through the '*archana*' when the children's mysterious ailments distracted our minds. Should we focus on the '*archana*' or attend to the children? The priests continued to recite the glory of the Goddess, but our minds were elsewhere. Gopika and I gazed at each other. Concerned over the children's agony, Gopika kept looking outside. But we were not inclined to walk out in the middle of the '*archana*'.

The chief priest, who observed our predicament, expressed his misgiving, "It is very uncommon for such a thing to happen here. There appears to be some shortcoming - something has gone wrong somewhere...!!". Gopika looked askance at me. As I traversed down the memory lane, the comment that I had made about the salt and jaggery tradition the previous night struck me. "Have I committed an indiscretion by passing such a derogatory comment? ", I questioned myself. "Was it not impertinent on my part?"

The very next moment, I got the answer. Guilt-stricken I gave money to Seshadri and urged him to fetch salt and jaggery urgently for offering them to the Lord as per tradition. Meanwhile, I prayed to Veeraraghava Swamy, "Oh Lord, pardon me for my indiscretion". But could prayers be the panacea for tummy ache? Somehow, we did not feel like leaving the temple to see the children without offering salt at the feet of the Lord.

Mr. P.V.R.K. Prasad with wife Gopika and Children Madhavi, Sanjeev and TTD Parepathedar Seshadri.

A few minutes later, Seshadri returned not merely with salt and jaggery but also with Madhavi and Sanjeev smiling and jumping. Gopika and I could not believe our eyes. The children, who had been writhing in pain and had to be carried out a short while ago, were seen sprinting back into the temple. The priests, other temple staff and devotees, who had all witnessed the scene, were pleasantly surprised. An unusual calm descended on us.

With redoubled devotion, we offered salt at the feet of Lord Veeraraghava Swamy and immersed jaggery in the '*pushakarini*'.

It was only then that I seemed to realise that God is omnipresent and one and the same whether at Tirumala or Tiruvallur – or in any other temple, small or big, rich or poor, popular or otherwise. It is only our narrow mentality and inability to perceive Lord everywhere and in everything that makes us attribute superiority to certain forms and temples.

Was I guilty of not practising '*samabhavana*' in the illusion of being "the first servant of the Lord"? Did the Lord subject me to this ordeal to enlighten me that all forms are His and all names are His and that wisdom lies in perceiving this truth.

× × ×

6

MANOEUVRING THROUGH MASTER PLAN MAZE

My wife Gopi and I were packing up to leave Tirupati for good when I noticed a big crowd outside our bungalow. (After a four-year stint as TTD Executive Officer, I had been transferred). Straightaway I recognised some faces in the crowd. I could not forget them because they had rained stones only a few months earlier to vent their anger against me. Even as their presence baffled me. My personal assistant Narayana rushed in to tell me why they had come. I was surprised.

× × ×

Within a few days of my taking charge as TTD Executive Officer in 1978, I decided to have first hand knowledge of the state of affairs from the pilgrim's viewpoint. So, I entered the queue sheds like any other ordinary devotee, reckoning that the TTD staff would not recognise me since I had landed in Tirumala only a few days earlier.

It was a bitter experience. Pilgrims had to wait an excruciating 12 to18 hours before they could have '*darshan*' of the Lord. They had to sit on benches without back rests and that too in sheds, with asbestos sheet roofs. As the sun beat down mercilessly on

Tirumala before the implementation of Master Plan

the roof, the pilgrims underneath bore the brunt of the radiating heat. The young and the old were shouting for water to quench their thirst. Each shed could accommodate 500 to 600 pilgrims. The TTD staff, who locked up the sheds, sauntered outside. After inordinate waiting in the sheds, the pilgrims moved finally into the *'darshan'* queue. That queue ran almost for a kilometre. The pilgrims had to go up and down climbing steps and crossing bridges over roads before they could enter the sanctum sanctorum. By then, they were all sweating and panting. Hardly did they stand and close their eyes in front of the Lord to pray when the staff shooed them away to make way for others. For me it was a revelation. Pilgrims, who had travelled hundreds or thousands of miles, had only a split second glimpse of the Lord after what seemed to be endless waiting.

After *'darshan'*, the devotees would step out of the temple through the *'maha dwaram'*. Climbing a few steps they could enter Sannidhi Street. It was not a street – just an overcrowded narrow passage. The 150 yard-long lane was barely six feet in width. It presented a picture of total chaos and confusion, thronged as it was always with people. There were shops on either side of the lane. Hawkers selling pictures, balloons, and trinkets moved from one end of the street to the other all the time. Brokers took pilgrims for a ride and pickpockets had a free run. After the devotees made their way through the crowd, they reached a half-finished temple tower *('mondi gopuram')* and a makeshift shelter for Bedi Anjaneya Swami, who shared the scanty accommodation with unauthorised barbers. To the right of Sannidhi Street, (where the *'asthana mantap'*, canteen and free dining hall are now located), there was a huge slum of 1100 unauthorised structures like huts and sheds with tin/ asbestos roofs. Next to the Sannidhi slum, there were a couple of other slums with 500 sheds and huts including the one at the site where the present queue complex is located. They resembled the notorious Bombay slums.

I quickly realised that the holy temple of Lord Srinivasa lay amidst narrow lanes filled with filth, cheats, brokers and vendors, asbestos sheet sheds and slums. Pilgrims had to play the modern version of the snakes and ladders game before they could have the split second *'darshan'* of the Lord. The situation distressed me immensely.

I asked senior TTD officials as to why such an appalling situation in Tirumala had not been remedied. They pointed out that several attempts had indeed been made to improve matters. Plans had been drawn up for a modern queue complex for the convenience of pilgrims. But nothing could be done unless all the unauthorised structures and slums around the temple were cleared. The authorised mutts with their many unauthorised tenants, private encroachments, and illegal occupation of TTD structures skirting the temple on all its four sides had to be shifted elsewhere. There was a need to regulate shops, which had sprouted and proliferated without any rule or rhyme. Whenever an attempt was made to clean up the mess, the affected parties rushed to courts and obtained stay orders. All of them pursued businesses or occupations that centered round the temple. As a result, to protect their own interest, a powerful lobby had emerged. Whoever was the Executive Officer and whatever was the change he sought to bring in, his hands were quickly tied down with cases in courts of law. In 1978, the TTD was facing innumerable stays and litigations connected with its efforts to clear encroachments and deal with the menace of illegal occupation. A number of cases had been filed in courts ranging from those at Tirupati to the Supreme Court in Delhi.

Instances of brokers cheating and thieves stealing from pilgrims were very common as they took advantage of the perpetual *'Jatra'* like atmosphere.

The appalling conditions disillusioned and depressed me. I agonised. Could we not do something? Should we abandon Tirumala to exploiters? I had only questions but no answers.

I went through all the old records religiously. I could see that all Executive Officers who had preceded me, were hardly indifferent to Tirumala's development. They too were seized with a burning desire to develop Tirumala. For instance, the TTD Board had cleared several development projects like the construction of a modern queue complex. Even the foundation stone had been laid. But, paradoxically, there was just enough room in the slum to accommodate the foundation stone. About 500 huts and sheds housing more than a thousand families had to be demolished for the queue complex to come up.

The slum was located towards the south of South Mada Street. Besides the structures in the slum, some two and three-storeyed buildings on South Mada Street too had to be demolished to connect the queue complex with the temple. Whether it was the construction of a modern *'kalyana katta'*, (to facilitate tonsure) or a canteen complex or the widening of Sannidhi Street, the problem was the same: Houses and huts, shelters and shops and other unauthorised structures.

Why had the situation become so complicated? After all, the total area within a radius of ten and half square miles of the temple including forests atop the Hills belongs to Lord Srinivasa. How did so many structures come up? I learnt that some structures had emerged chaotically over a century with or without TTD permission. The TTD could not touch even a single unauthorised structure as every inch of the land was under litigation.

To sum up, it was a story of three cases and six stays in courts ranging from the Munsif court at Tirupati to the Supreme Court in Delhi. Thanks to the cases, TTD legal officers, lawyers and Tirumala panchayat staff had enough work on their hands, although the TTD could not lay its hands on the land for development.

I concluded after a thorough review that the cases were unlikely to be resolved for another 25 to 30 years. TTD's huge chest of funds, with ever increasing revenues, vast administrative machinery, brilliant ideas, and political and moral clout meant nothing as long as the legal maze persisted.

The enthusiasm with which I had taken over the TTD assignment to render better service to pilgrims evaporated in no time. Given the haphazard structures, narrow lanes, brokers' raj, queue sheds without amenities and unhygienic surroundings there was no way pilgrims could have peace of mind, tranquil atmosphere and satisfactory *'darshan'* of the

Lord. The plight of the devotees left me in agony for weeks. I felt powerless despite the vast powers I enjoyed as Executive Officer.

As I walked towards the temple from Alwar Tank Cottages one day, I imagined how beautiful it would be if a modern, spacious queue complex were to replace the narrow lanes, overcrowded huts and sheds in the area south of the temple. I visualised a two or three storeyed queue complex having restrooms, bathrooms and cloakrooms and facilities for supply of hygienic food and clean drinking water. The reclining chairs would allow pilgrims to rest their backs and stretch their legs. The elderly among the devotees could lie down in well furnished dormitories. Pilgrims could forget their fatigue and boredom over the indefinite wait for *'darshan'* by listening to soothing devotional music or watching the temple rituals on closed circuit TVs.

My vision began to widen as I neared the temple. Sannidhi Street would be at least 100 feet in width enabling pilgrims to have a beautiful view of the temple. There would be a huge canteen complex to provide good hygienic food to pilgrims with a five star kitchen. The new *'kalyana katta'* would be neat, clean and hygienic resembling sophisticated hair cutting saloons. There would be a well equipped auditorium in Tirumala for the conduct of lectures/devotional programmes of music and dance and perhaps even to perform the Lord's *'kalyanam'* enabling thousands of people to take part, and witness.

I was on cloud nine visualising the tantalising scenes when a cow running amuck through the overcrowded narrow lane of the slums grounded me. Would my dream ever become a reality? Could I turn Tirumala into a heavenly abode for pilgrims coming from far off places to fulfil their vows and have a glimpse of the Lord? Could I help them cherish unforgettable memories of their Tirumala trip? Would I ever get such an opportunity? These thoughts led me inevitably to the legal maze, and with that all my enthusiasm and energy quickly died down... My three or four years in TTD would be sufficient to get a few stays vacated and moving some cases from the lower to higher courts.

As I stepped into the temple, with irrepressible emotion, I asked the Lord, " Why am I facing so many hurdles when I want to provide amenities to Your devotees? Why am I haunted by helplessness? When will the things get resolved? Is there any solution at all? If there is one, would I have it? Or do you want Your devotees to continue to undergo hardship and suffering? For how long?" After unleashing the barrage of questions at the Lord, I slided into a contemplative mood. I felt the prompting of some inner voice.

The inner voice told me: "All along you have been focussing on how you should demolish illegal structures and remove huts and sheds to provide better amenities to pilgrims. But what about those living there? Are they also not dependent on Lord Srinivasa for their livelihood? Because He happens to be here, pilgrims come and as pilgrims come, the local people make their living. Were He not to be here, would these people have ever stayed here? Are they also not serving the Lord by serving pilgrims? Where could they go? Why should all of them go? While there be some unscrupulous elements, most of these people are simple folk, depending on the Lord and His devotees for their livelihood. Why don't you approach the issue from another angle? Why can't you initiate reform and development with a human face?"

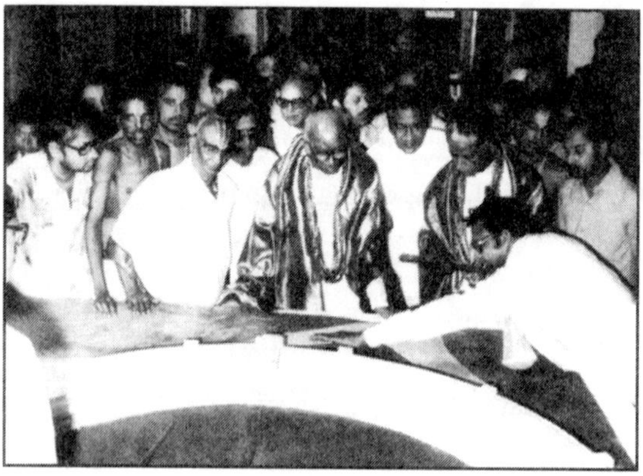

Mr. P.V.R.K. Prasad explaining about the Master Plan, Showing the model of the Vaikuntham Q Complex to Dr. Sanjeeva Reddy and Dr. M. Chenna Reddy.

Once the thought struck me, I felt suddenly at ease. I was engulfed by a new wave of enthusiasm and inspiration. The clouds of despair, which had enveloped me, began to lift. It became clear to me that I should draw up plans for Tirumala development, without ignoring the local people's viewpoint or hurting their genuine interests. Only then, something could be accomplished. I should, therefore, talk to community elders and leaders, take them into confidence and hammer out a solution that was acceptable to all.

Beginning the very next day I started discussing Tirumala development with persons like Lakshmipathi, Raghavan, Ramu, Krishna, Naidu, Chary, Ramachandra Reddy and a host of others, representing all sections like Mutt owners, authorised and unauthorised owners tenants, shop- keepers and hawkers.

The TTD Trust Board under Mr. Anna Rao's chairmanship had just been dissolved and a Persons-in-Charge Committee with the Revenue Secretary as Chairman, Endowments Commissioner as Member and I as Member-Secretary had come into existence. I put forth my views on Triumala's development before the committee and later discussed with the Minister for Endowments and the Chief Minister. "To develop Tirumala as an ideal pilgrim centre, we have to implement a Master Plan. For that, Sir, I need your blessings". With the Board and the Government giving me the green signal, I worked out a comprehensive strategy.

The strategy called for a survey of the entire Tirumala panchayat. All private structures like houses, huts and sheds around the temple were to be photographed. The survey should record the type of construction, area and the number of people living there and their status, that is whether they were owners, tenants or leaseholders. Once the survey was completed, the people being displaced would be paid compensation and shifted to a township to be constructed three km away from the temple. New accommodation would be given on lease. A committee was to be appointed to decide on the compensation so that the entire process would be transparent and not give scope for any allegations. All the affected people would be taken into confidence and persuaded to withdraw all their cases in courts and move to the new township

In a month, the names of people owning the structures and the number of people living in each of them were recorded as part of the survey. The TTD formed an empowered committee to discuss with local people the acquisition of their properties. The committee would also lay down the criteria for payment of compensation. Plans were also chalked out to shift '*mutts*' around the temple to a '*Mutt*' street away from the temple, that is beyond Mada Streets.

The committee, in another month, finalised the compensation to be paid for each variety of property to be acquired. Depending on the plinth area, type and location of the structure, each affected person could calculate the compensation he or she would get based on the standardised rates. As the compensation for owners, tenants and leaseholders had been spelt out and made transparent every one of the affected parties knew who would get what.

Initially, we took up the area meant for the modern queue complex to clear encroachments. We opted for a crescent shaped queue, to ensure that the entire load bearing structure came up on the tank bund. The TTD entered into agreements with property holders, resulting in a gradual and slow withdrawal of cases from the courts. As and when a property became free of litigation and an agreement was reached, action to demolish the structures was taken up.

As the demolitions progressed in the slum area, there was opposition from some pucca building owners in South Mada Street. Although most of the important people - owners, tenants and leaseholders - had magnanimously entered into agreements with the TTD and withdrew cases, a few, instigated by local leaders, went back on their commitment and stoutly opposed the demolition programme. Unless the pucca buildings on South Mada street were demolished, the queue complex and the temple could not be connected.

Around 11 am one day, Chief Security Officer Ramachandra Reddy briefed me on the furore over demolitions. He told me that some local leaders had collected a crowd and physically resisted the demolition under way. The demolition could not progress even for an inch. TTD engineering employees were engaged in a heated argument with the local people. "You can demolish the houses only after your bulldozers mow us down", one local leader had reportedly threatened. Unnerved by the cries and protests, Mr. Ramachandra Reddy, assisting the demolition programme, had come running to me. During the conversation, it came to light that the resistance was from the local leaders and the structures under demolition were not theirs.

I was stunned by the resistance. "After all, we have taken up the programme with their consent in writing. Why are they making an issue of it now after so many days?". A few leaders having their own personal agenda were behind this. I could only think of the Lord and concluded "If the Lord wills it, it happens. Who am I to worry about this. It is His place. If He does not want improvements, who am I to attempt and worry?". As I was lost in such thoughts, I happened to see the three letters 'IPS' on the shoulder badge of Mr. Ramachandra Reddy . He was an Indian Police Service officer of the rank of an Additional Superintendent of Police on deputation to the TTD. Involuntarily, I blurted out, addressing the policeman in him, "Why have you come to me? Being a police officer - that too belonging to the Indian Police Service - you are capable of controlling a small crowd". As if he got the message, Mr. Ramachandra Reddy mumbled something and left like a man possessed.

Mr. Ramachandra Reddy first targetted the leader who had threatened that bulldozers had to ride over their corpses for the demolition work to proceed. The leader was in no way concerned with the properties under demolition. He lifted him by the scruff of his collar and shook him in the air. "You are not the affected party. If you obstruct the staff on duty, I will beat you to pulp", roared Mr. Ramachandra Reddy like a lion provoked. The unanticipated development sent shivers down the spine of the leader and his followers, who took to their heels. The crowd, which appeared hostile a few minutes earlier, curiously watched the demolition. Thereafter, the demolition drive in South Mada Street went uninterrupted. Subsequently, some other house owners and tenants, who had till then hesitated, signed agreements with the TTD on parting with their properties.

Demolitions progressed at lightning speed. The enthusiasm and the effort put in by the TTD staff in carrying out the stupendous job is unforgettable. The project involved more than the demolition of 3000 structures including choultries and mutts. It called for transporting the affected people with their belongings to new places, provision of alternative accommodation and food during the transit, and the removal of debris. After one year of such non-stop effort, land could be acquired for the construction of the present *'asthana mantap'*, *'annadana'* complex, canteen, *'kalyana katta'*, market complex and of course the queue complex. In addition, many structures in the four Mada streets were removed - Still, the most important Sannidhi street remained untouched.

Sannidhi Street (Street opposite the main temple entrance) during 1960's

Sannidhi Street, in front of the main entrance to the temple, was hardly six feet in width, and shrinking further with the traders nibbling at the road. One had to wade through waves of moving humanity. Unless the shops and structures were moved 50 feet away on either side the street could not be widened to 100 feet. If the shopkeepers agreed to move, I promised to construct new permanent shops for them. We told the shopkeepers, "We are initiating the move in the interest of pilgrims. But we will ensure that your interests are not compromised. Every shop owner will get a similar shop exactly in the same location 50 ft back. Please co-operate with us". In response to our repeated pleas, many shopkeepers agreed to the proposal. But they expressed their misgivings. "If we vacate now, but some others get allotments later with political interference?". Apparently, they did not have confidence in TTD officials, including me.

"Where is the guarantee that we will get back our shops and that too in the same order", they questioned. A 5 feet by 6 feet shop or space had a potential to earn lakhs of rupees per month... Those with power—political, financial or physical—were willing to do anything to possess a shop...at any cost.

Meanwhile, we studied to what extent the thousand-pillar '*mantap*' to the south of Sannidhi Street had to be shifted for widening Sannidhi Street to 100 feet. We persuaded the owners of '*Mutt*' properties behind the shops on the northern side of Sannidhi Street to the widening proposal and obtained their signatures on agreements. As we progressed, the worst we feared - court stays – happened. Few people approached different courts and obtained multiple stay orders. This was the most precious space in Tirumala and every inch was contested.

Sannidhi Street after widening in the masterplan in 1982.

All my efforts at persuasion had proved futile. There was no meaning to the Master Plan if Sannidhi Street could not be widened. Our team and I felt dejected. The euphoria over successfully continuing the work so far vanished in thin air. Court stays would mean the end of this activity at least for the time being. My limited tenure in the TTD ticking away left me frustrated. Perhaps, I was not destined to do this work. If that were to be the will of the Lord, why should I bother. If I were destined to do it, He would show me a way out.

A very consoling thought. But, it could not convince me. "Should we not put in our efforts, although we ardently believe that a divine power orchestrates everything?" We tried in vain to open a dialogue with those who had obtained stays.

As a last resort, I spoke to the Advocate General and our legal advisors. We approached the High Court, got all the cases in different courts transferred to the High Court for a collective hearing and filed our response. We explained the Master Plan objectives - how it was being implemented and the importance of widening Sannidhi Street as part of the plan. Most of the affected people had agreed to vacate. We put it in black and white that new shops would be allocated to all those whose shops were to be demolished. The TTD would stand by its commitment without fear or favour and render justice to one and all. Accepting our arguments, the High Court at one stroke vacated all the stay orders on a Friday morning. Taking the order as Lord's endorsement of our efforts, we took up Sannidhi Street widening that day itself. Before the concerned could realise as to what was happening, we planned to complete demolitions by Monday preventing further litigation in higher courts. The operation, of course, was not without its share of hiccups.

On receipt of the High Court orders on telephone and fax, our engineering staff took up demolitions, as security staff provided cover. Standing in front of the temple, I was watching the work in progress. Suddenly, groups of people rushed into Sannidhi Street shouting and bawling and started raining stones on me. I was purplexed. The crowd included a few shopkeepers, many petty vendors and some outsiders. A security guard and the Vigilance Officer, Mr Dhilleswara Rao, standing by me were injured. As a reflex action one security guard opened fire into the air. Other security personnel rushed towards the crowd. As the stones were aimed at the main gate (*Mahadwaram*), where I was standing and the pilgrim line for darshan was moving, the temple doors had to be shut to protect the pilgrims. The situation was brought under control in a few minutes and the temple doors were re-opened. The demolition of shops resumed. Tears rolled down my cheeks over the unfortunate incident. I mulled repeatedly, "Am I responsible for all this?". The abrupt closure of the temple doors deeply disturbed me. I believed that I had the Lord's blessing for what all I was doing. Then why did this happen? Perhaps, the Lord willed it otherwise. Should I stop the work? I was confused...

Before I could gather my thoughts, Sannidhi Street had been cleared as planned - But, I was haunted by the vision of the few shouting shopkeepers.

Of course I permitted the shopkeepers to carry on their business in temporary shelters until the new shops came up.

I took over the total responsibility for the allocation of the newly constructed shops. I ensured that the new shops were allocated in the same order in which the owners had them earlier. The transparent policy we followed gave no scope for any irregularities. There were, of course, pressures from all quarters –political and administrative - for allotment of shops. The detailed pre-demolition exercise in building the status records, with detailed photographs which were made public, smoothened reallotment.

By the time I was transferred from the TTD in May-June 1982, I could see the effect of the Master Plan. A modern queue complex, a spacious *"kalyana katta"*, *'asthana mantap'*, a five-star kitchen, a huge canteen complex, a massive market complex, and an *'annadana'* complex were either completed or nearing completion. A dining hall that could accommodate 5000 people had been commissioned. Mr. L. V. Ramaiah, an oil merchant from Anantapur, became the first donor for the *'nityannadana'* (daily provision of meals) scheme by contributing Rs.16 lakh. (Subsequently, a number of donations were received making it one of the most popular schemes). Through this scheme, we wanted to ensure there would not be any sale of food in Tirumala in a few years. The TTD should provide free food to all pilgrims. A few guesthouses and a big canteen (the present Mayuri complex) were taking shape beside Venkateswara Guesthouse. Reconstruction of the Bedi Anjaneya Swami temple had been completed.

On the occasion of the consecration of this temple, Lord *'Malayappa Swamy'* (the processional deity of Lord Srinivasa) along with *'Sridevi'* and *'Bhoodevi'* were brought in a procession in Sannidhi Street. *'Oonjal'* (*swinging cradle*) service was arranged for the Lord in front of Lord Anjaneya. Thousands of pilgrims sitting in Sannidhi Street as well as the widened roads on all sides had an exciting experience. I bowed before the Lord and looked back. Right opposite was the Tirumala temple tower. In between the tower and the Anjaneya temple, the 100-foot-wide Sannidhi Street looked like a runway. The Lord seemed to be having His *'oonjal'* ceremony on a runway. No longer were the pilgrims shoving one another on the narrow lane. It was a dream come true. I felt supremely happy. What a great mission had been accomplished! By whom? (Was it me?)

× × ×

A few months later in June 1982, I was transferred. I had already handed over charge. As we were packing up, I saw the large crowd at my bunglow gate. My Secretary Narayana informed me that two groups of people from Tirumala had come to meet me. One group comprised the shopkeepers from Sannidhi Street and the other, the residents displaced from Mada streets and slums and resettled in a new township. Why would they want to meet me? I had already handed over charge. What could I do for them?

"When you planned the demolition of houses and shops, we doubted your sincerity and integrity. We were suspicious. We abused you; we resisted you and we attacked you. We did not believe that you would stand by your promises. But, you have implemented all assurances. We cannot point out a single case of injustice. In spite of our attacks and non-cooperation, you gave everyone of us our due. We are ashamed of our conduct. Our guilty conscience did not permit us to meet you earlier. Now that you are leaving...", their voices trailed off into silence, as tears welled up in their eyes. I was deeply touched.

'In fond remembrance of our relationship with you, please accept our gifts". The Sannidhi Street shopkeepers group presented me a *Panchaloha* (five metal alloy) statue of Bedi Anjaneya Swami. The other group from Mada Streets and slum dwellers presented me with three *Panchaloha* statues of Srinivasa, Sridevi & Bhudevi ... Wonderful idols, which are fit to adorn any great temple. Looking at those touching gifts, I recalled the happenings of the previous two years, including the haunting scenes of the stone throwing and the temple closure. I realised that the Power, which safeguarded their interests, was not mine. But which Power rendered them justice? Which Master had facilitated the Master Plan execution in so short a period?

× × ×

7

THE ARDENT WISH OF THE DEVOTEE AND THE LORD

The room was crowded; but the silence was eerie.

In front of us was an erudite scholar in his eighties, reclining against the wall on a cot. Rallapalli Anantakrishna Sarma's face was radiant. An ardent devotee of Lord Srinivasa, he was overwhelmed as he fondly looked at the Tirumala *'prasadam'* and the appointment order in his hands. Tears of devotion were streaming down his cheeks. With great difficulty, he whispered in a quivering voice, "Oh Lord, have you at last chosen to shower your blessings on me?"

Every one in the room was deeply touched by what seemed to be a dialogue between the noble soul and the Almighty. It took me 16 hours to understand why it had happened like that then.

× × ×

The enclosure in the temple (opposite the Hundi) where the Copper Plates containing the 32,000 Sankirthanas of Annamacharya were discovered.

The famous poet composer, Tallapaka Annamacharya, a great devotee of Lord Srinivasa, is a very familiar name to most of the Andhras, and to music lovers and devotees all over India. During his lifetime, Annamacharya worshipped the

Lord daily with garlands of devotional verses. He was said to have written more than 30000 devotional songs or *'keertanas'* about Lord Srinivasa. The rulers of those times, realising the need to propagate *'Bhakti'* and to preserve the great literary and spiritual treasure of the *'Keertanas'* for posterity, got them inscribed on copper plates. Specially trained missionaries (mendicants) popularised those *'keertanas'* in villages. That is why every Telugu-speaking mother even to this day lisps the lullaby, *"Jo Achyutananda, jo jo Mukunda"*, when she rocks her child to sleep. The fall of Hindu kingdoms and the ascent of the British led to a gradual decline in the popularity of the *'keertanas'*. Although a few songs remained popular, but the name of Annamacharya started to fade in people's memories.

The copper plates, deposited in a secret chamber in a wall of the Tirumala Srinivasa temple, were discovered in the early decades of the 20th century when *'mahants'* administered the temple. It is not known as to who put those up there and when. It is said that all the 30000 *'sankarteenas'* were found inscribed on copper plates. But callousness had resulted in most of the copper plates getting lost. It is alleged that the authorities concerned, without realising the value of the treasure, had melted some of the copper plates for the copper value – eternally losing the devout outpourings of the great saint-poet for ever. Only 11000 *'keertanas'* are available now. Sri Veturi Prabhakara Sastry and Sri Rallapalli Anantakrishna Sarma were said to have played a leading role in helping the TTD administration codify, compile and edit these *'sankeertanas'*. For some *'sankeertanas'* , they also prepared musical notations.

Mr. Rajagopala Raju, who preceded me as Executive Officer, and Mr. Chelikani Anna Rao, Chairman TTD, took up Annamayya *'keertanas'* publication. (Mr Anna Rao served the TTD in various capacities for about three decades including as Executive Officer). They entrusted the job of editing and printing to Mr. Rama Subba Sarma, a scholar and teacher in TTD oriental college. Mr. Rajagopala Raju extended financial assistance to TTD Music College students to practise and specalise in Annamayya *'keertanas'* under the guidance of the then Music College Principal, and a great Carnatic vocalist, Mr. Nedunuri Krishna Murty. The now famous musicians, Mrs.

Sobha Raju and Mr. Balakrishna Prasad, were among those trained by Mr. Nedunuri Krishna Murty. The credit for preserving and propagating Annamayya *'keertanas'* goes to all of them.

Two months after I took over as TTD Executive Officer in 1978, I sent for Mr. Rama Subba Sarma and inquired of his activities. He told me that the transcription of all the *'keertanas'* from the copper plates had been completed. The regular Telugu manuscripts were ready, but steps to preserve the copper plates and edit manuscripts and print them, were yet to be taken up. Also unfinished was the task of interpreting a large number of words in the *'keertanas'* warranted by the nuances the words had undergone over a few centuries. It was a gigantic task that could take decades of dedicated work.

Interspersed as they are with Sanskrit and Telugu, Annamayya's *'keertanas'* appeal to both scholars and lay people. The *'keertanas'* cover a broad range of classical Carnatic music to folk songs. They are sensual as well as devotional. They lend themselves to be sung as *'bhajans'* as also simple lullabies. The underlying values are progressive. Interestingly, centuries ago, Annamayya had underlined the equality of all human beings by singing that after death 'the place occupied by a revered Brahmin is the same as that of an untouchable". That is why his songs have an enduring quality and appeal to all sections of people. The objective of all the *'keertanas'* is to depict Lord's *'leelas'* and share with all of us the sweet thrill of divine worship and absolute surrender to the Lord. Research into Annamayya's works continues to this day and will continue for years to come because the *'bhakti'* philosophy he propounds is known for its depth and breadth.

Unlike Tyagaraja's *'keertanas'*, Annamayya's *'keertanas'* have not been passed on in the *'guru-sishya'* (from teacher to disciple) tradition. What came to light after the discovery of the copper plates was that they mentioned only the *'raga'* for each *'keertana'*. So, we know the *'raga'* in which Annamayya sang the *'keertanas'* but not their *'swaram'*. Every *'keertana'* dedicated to Lord Srinivasa highlights the Lord's name at the end.

Annamayya's life, works and message had roused my curiosity and whetted my interest. I felt that it was not enough if the *'keertanas'*, a treasure house of literary and spiritual values, were edited and published. Each home and every tongue should savour the *'keertanas"* sweetness. It was this realisation that made me launch the 'Annamacharya project'. We appointed Mr.Kamisetti Srinivasulu, a dedicated Telugu scholar working as lecturer in one of the TTD colleges, as Project Special Officer (Director later). Prof. Subbaraya Sarma was to look after the preservation of copper plates and the editing and printing of manuscripts. Mr.Kamisetti Srinivasulu was to oversee the composing of music, training of artists, involvement of other senior musicians and propagation of the *'keertanas'*.

The objectives of the project were identified as folllows:

- Preserving copper plates with the *'keertanas'*
- Publishing all the *'keertanas'*
- Composing tunes *('swarams')* to the *'keertanas'* according to their *'raga'* with the help of well-known musicians
- Getting them sung by famous musicians
- Forming musical troupes to propagate them from village to village
- Preparing audio and video cassettes
- Training of trainers in a wide range of *'bhajana'* forms and establishing *'bhajana'* troupes in villages.
- Inviting 'b*hajana*' troupes to Tirumala every year for participation in *'metlotsavam / Brahmostavams'*
- Organising competitions among students
- Adapting some *'keertanas'* to classical dance forms
- TTD adopting Tallapaka village
- Encouraging research into Annamayya *'sankeertanas'*.

We promoted research into Annamayya's works in universities. Among the first batch who earned Ph.Ds with TTD fellowships were Mr. Medasani Mohan and Mr. P. L. N. Prasad.

'Bharat Ratna' Mrs. M. S. Subbulakshmi rendered *'Balaji Pancharatnamala'* as part of this project.

A troupe, comprising musicians Kumari Sobha Raju and Balakrishna Prasad and instrumentalists like Mr.Vaidyanathan, started giving Annamayya music concerts, with Mr. Kamisetty Srinivasulu as commentator. Their concerts, based on tunes composed by eminent musicians, received tremendous response. Contrary to the general impression that classical devotional music had lost its appeal with the advent of film music and light music, large numbers of people - young and old - turned up to hear the devotional *'keertanas'*. I had to overcome a delicate problem before the programme could be launched. Carnatic musicians wanted the *'keertanas'* to be rendered in pure Carnatic tradition giving more importance to the music part. But I feared that the lay public might not relish it. As a way out, I suggested that the musicians stick to the *'keertanas'* - *'raga'* and *'swaram'* but cut short *'alapana'* and render them in a style that appealed to the lay public. The TTD's objective is to inculcate *'bhakti'* towards Lord Srinivasa. Music is only a means to communicate the *'bhava'* (the philosophical meaning) in an effective way. TTD's loyalty in this context is not to classical music styles. (The TTD audio cassettes, now in circulation, carry *'keertanas'* rendered in a blend of traditional and light music). We decided that the troupes should necessarily practise some new *'keertanas'* every month and they should be reviewed before they were rendered before audiences and later converted into audios/videos. I held review meetings with the musicians once a month.

It was at one such meeting that Mr. Kamisetti Srinivasulu broached a subject that triggered a great churning in my mind, leading to a chain of unusual events overnight.

As it would not be possible to get free time during the day, I used to hold such reviews after dinner around 10.30 PM. During such sessions, the artists sang all the new songs they had practised.

At the end of the review one night, I casually told Mr. Kamisetti Srinivasulu that I was leaving for Bangalore early next morning. Hesitatingly, Mr Srinivasulu said: "Sir, if you don't mind, may I suggest that you call on Sri Rallapalli Anantakrishna Sarma who is unwell? We owe the massive Annamacharya project to him. Sri Rallapalli is one of the few great scholars who toiled for years transcripting the *'keertanas'* from the copper plates, unravelling the language of Annamayya's time and bringing to light the values embedded in the *'keertanas'*. Other stalwarts like Sri Veturi Prabhakara Sastry and his assistants have received adequate recognition and honours but not Rallapalli". As he gave Sri Rallapalli's address on a piece of paper, I told him that I would see Sri Rallapalli, if time permitted.

Once Kamisetty Srinivasulu and the musicians left, I found myself in deep contemplation. I had never met Sri Rallapalli and, therefore, knew next to nothing of his erudition. Yet my mind would not rest. Sri Rallapalli, apparently was one of those who facilitated the massive Annamacharya project, by selflessly and tirelessly bringing to light the literature in praise of Lord Srinivasa and making it intelligible by giving it the right form. Yet, he remained unsung and unhonoured in contrast to his colleagues. Had some injustice been done to him?...

Perhaps, I should call on him and decide whether I should do something. Although I tried to sleep, I could not. Some restlessness overtook me. Even at 1 '0' clock in the night, I was seized by this problem. Meeting him the next day might not suffice. Why should I not do something to Sri Rallapalli and that too immediately? What could I do? ...

Like a man possessed, I called up the Deputy Executive Officer (DEO) over phone, woke him up, and told him, "Look, I am leaving for Bangalore at 6 a.m. tomorrow. By then, I want a certificate appointing Sri Rallapalli Anantakrishna Sarma as TTD *'asthana vidwan'* and materials presented to *'asthana vidwans'* at the investiture ceremony like the gold dollar (carrying the Lord's image), a shawl, *'laddu prasadam'*, *'akshintas'* etc - delivered at my bungalow. I would like to have all these before I leave".

From his reponse, I could make out that the Deputy Executive Officer (DEO) was flabbergasted. The DEO knew the procedure for the appointment of a TTD *'asthana vidwan'* – conferring a prestigious title. The TTD annually constitutes a committee of experts to decide on the appointments of *'asthana vidwans'*. The committee reviews the areas/fields in which *'asthana vidwans'* have so far not been appointed, consider eminent people in those fields and recommed a short panel. The TTD Board considers the recommendations and chooses the persons. Informal consultations with the Chief Minister and the Endowments Minister are held. Later the consent of the awardee is obtained before a formal announcement is made. During Lord's *'brahmotsavas'* at Tirumala the title is conferred on the artists in the presence of a gathering of devotees. This had been the well-established procedure. When the Deputy Executive Officer tried to explain the procedure, I cut him short by saying, "Leave it all aside. By early morning, before I leave, whatever I have said shall be done". The Deputy Executive Officer muttered something, communicating his disbelief.

Thanks to TTD staff's efficiency, all the materials requisitioned had landed at my home before I left for Bangalore. On arrival at Bangalore, I sent word to Sri Ralapalli's residence that I would be calling on him in the afternoon. At 3-00 p.m., my wife Gopika and I reached Sri Rallapalli's home. A number of people, with sadness writ large on their faces, had assembled there. On inquiry, I was told that Sri Rallapalli, ailing for some time, was seriously ill. We were conducted into a room.

There was uneasy silence in the crowded room. Sri Rallapalli had been unconscious for almost a week. It was, perhaps, his son who took me near him and tried to communicate something to his father. The old scholar in a coma, would not respond. Holding the *'prasadam'* and other things, I felt embarrassed. The son looked at me helplessly. Might be to satisfy me or overwhelmed by the developments, he loudly shouted into the ear of his father four or five times, "*'Prasadam'* and Lord's blessings have come from Tirumala for you". We noticed movement in the frail body lying still... With great effort, he opened his eyes. His half- open eyes stared at me. His son told him who I was. I did not know whether he made out anything.

Swayed by some inexplicable emotion, I adorned him with the dollar necklace, covered him with the shawl and placed in his hands the order appointing him TTD *'asthana vidwan'* (poet laureate) and the *'prasadam'*. His sons lifted his head, propped him up with pillows and made him lean against the wall. Then I noticed; he was looking not at me but at the *'Srivari prasadam'* and the appointment order in his hands... Tears streamed down his cheeks. His lips quivered. Slowly, he lisped a few words in a whisper. We could not make out what he was saying. His sons tried to listen to him with their ears close to him. He was not talking to us. He was talking to the Lord. Finally, we could comprehend him say, "Oh Lord, have you at last chosen to shower your blessings on me?". He cried as he seemed to have an intimate dialogue with the Lord.

We felt that we should not disturb him in his state of bliss. Gopika and I quietly left the place after a few minutes.

Sixteen hours later, (i.e.,) the next morning as Gopika and I were about to leave for Tirupati, our Bangalore Information Centre manager brought the daily newspaper carrying a big picture of Sri Rallapalli Anantakrishna Sarma, on the front page.

Sri. Rallapalli was no more. Soon after we left the house of Sri Rallapalli the previous day, he had breathed his last with the hand resting on his chest clutching the *'prasadam'*.

Why did this happen? Was it a mere coincidence?

Then only I realised what I had done. The anxiety in the Deputy Executive Officer's voice resounded in my ears. The well laid out procedure to appoint an 'a*sthan vidwan'* flashed across my mind. The Executive Officer does not have any discretionary powers in such sensitive issues, which have to be only decided by the board. If the Executive Officer acted unilaterally, the board could recommend his immediate recall and disciplinary action to the government. I was aware of the position. Why did I behave like that? What force had compelled me to decide in the middle of the night? What could I do now? But I could not undo the past. So, I was mentally reconciled to abiding by any resolution that the TTD Board might adopt.

The Board, under the chairmanship of Mr. B. Nagi Reddy, unanimously ratified my decision without any arguments after it heard me. The Board members felt honoured to be associated with such a decision, willed by the Lord.

Then quietly I asked Mr. Nagi Reddy, "What would have been the Board's reaction had Sri Rallapalli been alive?"

Mr. Nagi Reddy, who had woven tales into films under the Vijaya Films banner, was perplexed by my question. For a few moments, he remained silent. Then he looked at me thoughtfully and said, "Look, Prasad garu, whatever has happened was destined to happen that way. We should accept that. Therefore, you should neither raise such questions nor expect answers. Okay?"

"O.K" — I nodded. That was the only explanation I too could think of.

× × ×

8

THE GOD THAT (NEVER) FAILED?

"How unkind of you, Srinivasa? You strand me and my family, coming to see you, in the midst of the ghat road in the dead of night! I will never come for *'darshan'* again during my lifetime. This bitter experience will do". The elderly gentleman, who had been venting his anger against Tirumala Srinivasa, was shaken by the experience he underwent half an hour later. Crushed by contrition, he was seen repeatedly slapping his cheeks and muttering that his salvation lay only in *'Govinda nama'* recitation and the *'darshan'* of Srinivasa.

× × ×

When I was the TTD Executive Officer (1978-82), like all other Executive Officers, I was all the time consumed by a desire to improve the *'sevas'* in the temple and provide better amenities to pilgrims. That was one of the main reasons why I attended as many *'sevas'* as possible ranging from *'suprabhatam'* in the morning to *'ekanta seva'* in the night as many times as I could. One *'seva'* which I never liked to miss was Friday *'abhisheka seva'*.

The Friday *'abhisheka seva'* begins with participant devotees going in a procession at 4-30 a.m. Therefore, invariably, I made it a routine to leave Tirupati on Thursday afternoons, conduct inspections en route and reach Tirumala by 4 p.m. Atop the hill, I usually conducted joint inspections and reviews with other officials . Arriving at the temple later, by about 6 PM, I would stay on till 9-30 p.m. for the *'pulangi seva darshan'* before reaching the guesthouse. At 4-30 a.m on Friday, I would take part in the *'abhisheka seva'*.

One Thursday in 1980, my usual programme went haywire. Some unexpected work and an important visitor prevented me from leaving for Tirumala. In spite of my urge to leave, I had to stay on up to 8 p.m in the office itself. I thought I could leave by 9-30 p.m. after having dinner at home. That deadline too had passed. Though I finished my dinner and was ready to leave, I remained in the camp office (located in the Executive Officer's bungalow), attending to incoming phone calls. My personal assistant Narayana and the driver had been waiting since 3 p.m for my scheduled departure to Tirumala. It was past ten. My wife Gopika dropped in and enquired why I had not yet left. Generally, she used to accompany me for the Friday '*abhishekam*'. She was not to join me that day as we had some guests at home. Pointing out that I was already late, she suggested, "Why don't you stay here for the night and leave at 3-30 a.m.? I could also come with you" I shot down her suggestion. "I should have gone long ago. Right now, I am leaving". Still, I felt lethargic. For the next 20-30 minutes, I was once again lost in God knows what. Nothing particular prevented me from leaving. But, still I would not leave. Meanwhile, Gopika peeped in twice or thrice, saw me at work and returned pursing her lips, wondering as to what could have happened to me.

Perhaps, it was past 10-30 in the night. Suddenly, I folded the file I was looking into, leapt up from my seat as if prompted by some one and hopped into the car. I asked the driver to proceed to Tirumala. In a few minutes, we reached the Alipiri toll gate at the foothills. (For security reasons, the ghat road was closed to traffic those days for some hours in the night). The tollgate staff, who opened the gate for me, reported that the pilgrim traffic to Tirumala was heavy that day. Heavy rush meant a waiting of seven to eight hours for the '*darshan*'.

The cold breeze during the midnight car journey should have lulled me into a nap. But that night, I remained awake. Upset over the setback to the normal schedule, I was eager to reach Tirumala as early as possible – for what, I was not sure. In fact, it did not matter so long as I reached Tirumala before 4 a.m. Yet, for some inexplicable reason, I was keen on landing at Tirumala early. "Go faster", I instructed the driver. However experienced a driver is, he would not go fast on the *ghat* road during nights. The driver, however, plodded on.

Our car had negotiated all the curves in the *ghat* road. As we were within a kilometre of Tirumala, an elderly gentleman standing in pitch darkness at the end of the last curve was frantically waving his hands signalling us to stop. Our car headlights revealed an Ambassador car behind him. Our car screeched to a halt. What was he doing there in the dead of night? Even before I could raise the question, he came near my car and spoke in English, "Sir, like you, we have come on a pilgrimage. Our car has broken down. We have to go uphill urgently". In a tone tinged with anxiety, he pleaded, "Sir, won't you give us a lift?" Deferring all questions, I asked him how many passengers were there. There were in all five – the elderly gentleman, his wife, daughter and son-in-law and their driver. In my car, beside me there were the personal assistant and the driver. The thought as to how so many of them could be accommodated in my car never struck me. I invited all of them to board the car along with their luggage. Only then I noticed that his daughter and son-in-law were in *"madhuparkams"* (clothes dyed in turmeric) indicating that they had just been married. Surprisingly, all the worry and anxiety of mine vanished the moment the strangers boarded our car.

Even before we covered the one kilometre to reach Tirumala, he poured out his tale of woe. The gist of the story in his own words:

"I am a hotelier from Mysore. I know no God other than Tirumala Srinivasa. That was why I wanted to perform my daughter's marriage atop the Hill. However, at the insistence of the bridegroom's father I had to perform it in Mysore. I told the bridegroom's family that I would be taking the bride and the bridegroom immediately after marriage for a *'darshan'* of the Lord, the same day. They agreed. The marriage at Mysore took place at 10 a.m. today. We calculated that if we were to leave Mysore at 11 AM for Tirumala, we could manage the special *'darshan'* (Rs.50 fee then) at 7 p.m. and return to Mysore by next morning. All the relatives are still at Mysore to take part in the post-marriage rituals scheduled for tomorrow morning. But as ill luck would have it, railway level crossing closures and traffic jams threw the spanner in our works. It was past 10 p.m. by the time we reached the Alipiri gate. The gate was closed for the night.When we narrated our plight and the urgency of the *'darshan'* before midnight, the tollgate staff relented and opened the gate. You too must have entreated them similarly….."

He stopped his narration at that point. Responding "yes, yes", I did not disclose who I was. I could make out the rest of his story: The car broke down on the *ghat* road. His sole concern at that point of time was to ensure *'darshan'* of the Lord for his daughter and son-in-law before the temple closed for the day at 12 midnight. He lost his patience as his schedule was upset. The breakdown of the car compounded his misery. They could neither go to Tirumala, nor return to Mysore. He felt miserable as he could not contact anybody (no cell phones those days) or get the car repaired. There was no possibility of anyone coming to their rescue soon as the toll gate would not be opened until at 4 a.m. They were stranded on the ghat road, in the middle of the forest. Walking to Tirumala in pitch darkness was possible. But *'darshan'* was impossible because they could not make it before the temple was closed. He found himself in a mess. His faith in the Lord, which prompted him to bring his daughter and son-in-law to Tirumala had slowly evaporated – giving rise to frustration, anguish and anger.

"Oh Lord, I have reposed faith in you and I have prayed every moment of my life. I brought the couple straight from the wedding altar braving hardship en route just for your blessings. But you let me down. Are your fair? The newly-wed are not destined to have a glimpse of you. See, how they are spending their first night after marriage.… I cannot return to the wedding hall in time. You have not vindicated my faith in you. There is now no alternative to keeping awake in biting cold and pitch darkness on the ghat road. What sort of a God are you? Do you delight in subjecting your devotees to agony? Do you abandon them in the forest without any consideration? How blindly have I trusted you and come here much against the wishes of all my relatives and friends. I should have heeded to them and started leisurely after all the functions were over. But, I thought of fulfilling my vow to bring the bride and the groom for your blessings immediately after the marriage. What blessings you are giving... You have taught me a great lesson. I will not come to the hills any more". He was feeling humiliated over his helplessness in the presence of the newly wed when he sighted our car. He was very excited as he boarded the car, saying "You seem to be someone deputed by God".

Even as he spoke thus, our car reached the Tirumala guesthouse around 11-30 p.m. After profusely thanking me, he was in a great hurry to take the newly wed for the *'darshan'*. He was worried about *'darshan'* tickets and accommodation for the night. I told him, "Don't worry. Have a wash, we will go in the car". A room was opened for them. In a few minutes, I left them in the temple premises, leaving instructions with temple staff. Shortly before the *'darshan'* for the day ended, they had special *'darshan'*, *'aarti'* and *'prasadam'* to their hearts' content. They were treated as TTD guests for the night and provided accommodation and food.

Overnight, the TTD staff towed their car and repaired it. I had no occasion to meet them again. When I enquired about them after the Friday *'Abhisheka seva'*, I learnt they had already left for Mysore at 4 a.m.

× × ×

Two days later, he wrote me a letter. Apparently, he had found out who I was. The letter said: "Even if our car had not broken down in the *ghat* road and reached Tirumala at 11 p.m., we would still not have had *'darshan'* because of the heavy pilgrim rush. We would not have had accommodation. That was why our family Lord, Srinivasa, seemed to have engineered our car breakdown and sent you, his first servant, specially to look after us. The Lord fulfilled his devotee's wish. We had not had such a great satisfying *'darshan'* in our lives. Unable to comprehend the Lord's mysterious ways, I lost my discretion and patience and cursed Him?... Oh. Lord!! I am now dying of remorse. Thank you very much for your timely help"...

What did I do? Who scripted all this and timed it?

× × ×

9

WHEN A C.M.'S WRATH KNOWS NO BOUNDS

All of a sudden the Chief Minister flies into a rage at a meeting of Ministers and senior officials.

"What does this IAS officer think of himself? We post him as TTD Executive Officer thinking he will work wonders. Instead, he plays politics. If he is so enamoured and has the guts, let him quit the IAS and plunge into politics. How dare he carries on a political campaign against us? I will see how he can get away". So fumes the Chief Minister, swaying with emotion, against a Joint Secretary-level IAS official.

The Chief Minister is supreme in a Government elected by the people. When anger seizes a Chief Minister, who will have the urge, inclination and courage to stand up to him and rescue a junior official?

In the 1979 incident narrated above, Dr. Marri Channa Reddy, known for his short temper and sharp tongue happened to be the Chief Minister, and me, the unfortunate IAS official.

× × ×

From the day I was picked up for the post of Tirumala Tirupati Devasthanams' (TTD) Executive Officer, I faced problems. Our daughter Madhavi developed inflammation of the knee and pain when I wanted to avoid the assignment. Wondering whether I was spurning Lord Srinivasa's call to go over to Him, I finally agreed to take up the assignment. When I took charge from the Additional Commissioner of Endowments, Mr. Anandarao Mudaliar, who was holding the charge, at an auspicious moment and was ready to leave for Tirupati, I had a brush with the Chief Minister. About a year later, I had to face Chief Minister Channa Reddy's wrath again...

I was crestfallen when I learnt from the Chief Secretary, Mr. S. R. Ramamurthy, that the Chief Minister had poured out his anger against me in the presence of ten Ministers and Secretaries. I had no inkling as to what crime I had committed. In fact, not even Mr. Ramamurthy had any clue to the Chief Minister's indignation. At my request he ascertained the reason from the Chief Minister himself. It was "TTD's release of advertisements to newspapers which are critical of his Government and policies".

The TTD had released advertisements to a magazine launched by Mr. Ratnasabhapati, a disciple of former Chief Minister Vengal Rao and Cuddapah Congress leader opposed to Dr. Channa Reddy, and "Eenadu", Telugu daily critical of the Chief Minister. On the very day the advertisements appeared, the media also carried reports criticising Dr. Channa Reddy's policy decisions. The Chief Minister apparently suspected that I was helping his critics by releasing advertisements.

In fact, I formulated a clear-cut advertisement policy right at the beginning of my TTD tenure. Circulation was to be the sole criterion for the release of advertisements to dailies. Thirty-eight TTD departments regularly undertake spiritual and welfare activities, warranting frequent release of advertisements. But so far as magazines were concerned, I instructed the TTD to release ads for all inaugural issues as most of the publishers believed that a TTD advertisement in the very first issue was a blessing from the Lord. The TTD Public Relations Officer discharges these tasks. Once a policy decision is taken, concerned officials implement it and the Executive Officer would not interfere. On enquiry I found that the PRO had adhered to the policy decisions while releasing the ads. It was sheer coincidence that news reports critical of the Chief Minister appeared on the day the ads were published. As it happens all over, here too some of the Chief Minister's sycophants showed him the newspapers/magazines and apparently dinned into his ears: "See, how atrocious this is: an Executive Officer, who works under you, gives ads to newspapers which write against you". Tale-carriers, who try to demonstrate their loyalty, or cover up their inefficiency or just vent their jealousy, are to be found in any system. They betray their mindset depending upon the occasion. Obviously, I might have been the target of some of them.

My conscience was clear and my hands were clean. I had no role in the release of the ads. Even the ads released by the PRO were in tune with the policy. Yet, the Chief Minister suspected or was made to suspect me. To be fair, the Chief Minister had not said anything to me directly... That the Chief Minister suspected me was only a piece of information from the Chief Secretary. Okay, but what should I do now?

I faced two alternatives: the first was to offer an explanation by meeting the Chief Minister and the second was to leave the matter at that stage and reply when the Chief Minister questioned me ... After pondering deep and long, I chose the first alternative.

An employee has to have credibility wherever he happens to work. I felt it was foolish to serve silently when the Chief Minister himself doubted my loyalty and integrity for no reason or rhyme. I, therefore, decided to meet the Chief Minister and clear his misgivings.

Immediately, I collected copies of the ads and newspapers and relevant circulars on TTD's advertisement policies, went to Hyderabad and called on the Chief Secretary. He called in Mr. S. Santanam, Secretary and Mr. V. Govindarajan, Joint Secretary, to the Chief Minister. When I showed them the clippings and explained the advertisement policy, they agreed that I committed no wrong. But I was anxious to convince the Chief Minister.

Every one hesitated to approach the Chief Minister. Those were the days when even top officials shuddered to face an angry Dr. Channa Reddy. I myself had a taste of it - I recollected my earlier experience.

× × ×

In fact, even on the day I took over as TTD Executive Officer (i.e.,) a year earlier, the Chief Minister took me to task as some people had carried tales against me. That too, within an hour of my taking over charge from Mr. Anandarao Mudaliar, in-charge Executive Officer.

The Chief Minister summoned me and pointedly asked, "Do you want to work as Vengal Rao's agent against us?". I was nonplussed for a moment. Restraining myself from muttering a reply, I reasoned to myself: "My place of work is Lord Srinivasa's precincts in Tirumala. If I am destined to serve him, He will script whatever is to happen".

Once Dr. Channa Reddy cooled down, I tried to explain: "Sir, I am not able to make out what you are saying. I worked as Secretary to Chief Minister when Mr. P. V. Narasimha Rao was Chief Minister. Then, everybody dubbed me a PV's man. When Mr. Vengal Rao was Chief Minister, I served as Collector of his home district Khammam. For that reason, you are stamping me as a Vengal Rao man. Sir, we are loyal to our jobs and not to individuals. You are unnecessarily suspecting my bona fides". His grievance was that a day earlier I had called on Vengal Rao's close associate and TTD Chairman Chelikani Anna Rao and reportedly assured him of his continuance as TTD Chairman. I smiled to myself as I realised how the facts had been distorted and communicated to the Chief Minister.

Mr. Anna Rao, who had returned from the U. S. a day earlier, dropped in at my home to congratulate me (on my appointment as TTD Executive Officer). I explained this to the Chief Minister. When the TTD was constructing a *'kalyana mantapam'* at Khammam, Mr. Anna Rao used to visit Khammam. Beyond meeting him on such occasions as Khammam Collector, I had no close relationship with him. "When I know that the TTD Chairman's appointment is the Chief Minister's prerogative, why would I poke my nose? Anyway, I have never imagined that I would lose your confidence within an hour of taking charge. I am still here physically, although my luggage had left for Tirupati. Please appoint anyone whom you trust as TTD Executive Officer and permit me to go on leave", I told the Chief Minister.

Despite my intense desire to work as TTD Executive Officer, I had no alternative to talking in that vein because I could not allow even an innuendo to besmirch my reputation. As I was about to get up and depart, leaving the matter to Lord Srinivasa, there was a metamorphosis in the tone and tenor of

Dr. Channa Reddy. Pleasantness returned to his angry countenance. The seriousness in his voice gave way to gentleness. In his characteristic style, he said: "Look Prasad; we have respect for Vengal Rao. But he is working against us. You know how important Anna Rao is to Vengal Rao.... ". He was certain that Mr. Vengal Rao himself had sent Mr. Anna Rao to my home.

"Prasad, we have total confidence in you. We don't want to shift you so soon from the TTD post. Go and work well". So saying, he patted me on the shoulder affectionately. It was against such a backdrop that I went to take up the TTD assignment. Now, the ad calamity had descended on me.

× × ×

I was determined to meet him. Finally, the Chief Secretary and the Secretary to Chief Minister took me to the Chief Minister's residence in Tarnaka. The joint Secretary to the Chief Minister, Mr. Govindarajan, was also present. The Chief Secretary briefed the Chief Minister on the purpose of my visit.

Listening to the Chief Secretary, the Chief Minister pounced on me. I could hardly open my mouth. But who could stop a Chief Minister? "Prasad, we never thought you would act like this .... that you could be so disloyal and indiscreet. Do you encourage our opponents by releasing advertisements? Is this the way you should be behaving towards a Chief Minister?". Non-stop, Dr. Channa Reddy spat fire and brimstone on me. Mr. Santanam tried to intervene, but the Chief Minister was in no mood to pause.

When he cooled down a bit after a few minutes, I started speaking. I tried to tell the Chief Minister that the release of ads was done at the PRO level; it was in accordance with the laid down policy and that anybody's preferences and prejudices had no role in the entire issue. He listened rather reluctantly; but would not change his views. He told me point blank that I was privy to the whole matter.

"You had served as Secretary to Chief Minister P. V. Narasimha Rao. You were Collector of Khammam during Vengal Rao's regime. Are you not aware of the adverse political repercussions of your actions? Do you want us to trust you if you feign innocence? Enough is enough", he said pointing an accusing finger at me.

The Chief Secretary, the Secretary and the Joint Secretary to the Chief Minister tried unsuccessfully to butt in. When the virtual monologue came to an end, silence reigned supreme in the room. Benumbed by the turn of events, all of us quietly exited the room.

Indira Gandhi was due to arrive at Tirupati in about a week. Chief Minister Channa Reddy was to accompany her. In case, the Chief Minister's flames of anger were to leap up again and that too in front of all at Tirupati? I could not entertain the very thought. After having lost the Chief Minister's confidence, serving at Tirupati, by mortgaging self-respect was against the very grain of my character. So, the minute I came out of the Chief Minister's residence I scribbled a letter to the Chief Secretary requesting him that I be transferred out of Tirupati. "If you need time to locate a substitute, permit me to hand over charge to the senior most official and proceed on leave."

I was scheduled to visit Puttaparthi on my way back to Tirupati to take part in the release of M. S. Subbulakshmi's "Balaji Pancharatnamala", - an LP record and audio cassettes brought out by the TTD - by Sri Satya Sai Baba. I went there rather reluctantly. After the release of the cassette, Sai Baba invited us into his room. Mrs. Subbulakshmi, her spouse Sadasivam, my wife Gopika and I went in. A personification of simplicity and tenderness, Sai Baba spoke to us very affectionately. Praising TTD services in general, Baba all of a sudden seemed to address my shattered mind. "Look, Bangaru (his affectionate way of addressing a person). Your being posted as TTD Executive Officer is God's will. Your appointment is not in the hands of either the Chief Minister or the Chief Secretary. Had not God willed it, no one could have appointed you. And without His will, no one can remove you. You have been doing good work. Carry on the good work in the name of God". The way he read my mind like an open book surprised me.

Baba's remarks set off a fresh round of churning in my mind. I asked myself as to why was I so much upset when I had not committed any sin or crime? True, my actions had sowed suspicion and triggered anger in the Chief Minister's mind. So what? If Lord Srinivasa had beckoned me to the TTD, as Baba put it, it was for the Lord to decide whether I should continue there or not. What was the point in agonising over an issue over which I had no control? Should I not leave the matter to the Lord?

Yet, unable to repress myself, I called up the Chief Secretary after landing in Tirupati to ask, "What has happened to my relief request? ". The Chief Secretary noncommittedly replied, "I have shown your letter to the Chief Minister. He is yet to okay it". I wondered why the Chief Minister had not decided on the matter. In the course of the tele-talk, the Chief Secretary revealed a Chief Minister's remark: "Does Prasad think he is indispensable and that no substitute can be found?". The information merely whetted my anxiety, instead of assuaging it.

Mrs. Indira Gandhi was arriving at Tirupati in the next couple of days amid rumours of her relations with Dr. Channa Reddy having soured. After deeply thinking over the recent developments and the immense immediate tasks on hand, I had '*darshan*' of Lord Srinivasa and poured out my agony and left it at that.

Mrs. Indira Gandhi did arrive as scheduled. The Chief Minister was also there. He was normal. The tour was a great success. Shortly before Mrs. Gandhi left, our public relations officer Ravula Suryanarayana Murty had handed me a photo album

Sri P.V.R.K. Prasad with the Prime Minister Smt. Indira Gandhi and the Chief Minister Dr. M. Chenna Reddy.

of Mrs. Gandhi's Tirumala visit. I took it to the Chief Minister and requested him to present it to Mrs. Indira Gandhi.

Surprisingly, he would not. He took me to Mrs. Indira Gandhi and made me present the album to her. Introducing me, Dr. Channa Reddy told her: "Here is a highly competent IAS officer. I handpicked him for the assignment here. He is efficiently and vigorously carrying out a number of developmental schemes". He hailed a photographer to take a snap of mine along with him and Mrs. Gandhi. I thought, it was unusual. The VIPs departed.

The next day, the Chief Secretary wanted to know how Indira Gandhi's visit went. "Anyway, what transpired there?" asked the Chief Secretary rather curiously stating that it was the Chief Minister who was enquiring about my reaction.

In the next day's mail, I received a special parcel from the Chief Minister's office. I was overtaken by pleasant surprise when I opened it.

It contained the photograph of mine taken with Mrs. Indira Gandhi and Chief Minister Channa Reddy. The Chief Minister autographed the photograph and wrote, "With best wishes.... Keep up the good work". May be that was the way he wanted me to understand that he had nothing personal against me.

Much later, addressing meetings during the Godavari and the Krishna '*Pushkarams*', the Chief Minister praised me to the skies. I still wonder why things happened that way!!

10

DEATH DOES NOT DETER A DIVINE MISSION

Srimannarayana Ramanuja Jeeyar was lying in a critical condition at Mahaveer Hospital in Hyderabad. I quietly sat next to him, and clasped his hand. The sensation of touch made him open his eyes slowly. His eyes held me in an affectionate gaze. With great difficulty, he lisped a few words.

"... I may not be able to conduct this extraordinary, *'maha yagna'*. My successor in the *'peetham'* will act as the *'yagna karta'*. Whether I am alive or not, you have to ensure the success of the *'Sri Lakshminarayana Sahasrakunda Maha Yagna'*. You should make all the arrangements".

With a quivering voice and in a sonorous tone, he spoke haltingly as he stroked my hand affectionately. He once again shut his eyes. I was greatly disturbed by this development.

A few hours later, I heard the tragic news of his passing away. In despair, I felt I had been thrown into pathless wilderness. I felt like the *'Gajendra'* in *'Gajendra Moksha'* who cried out for rescue. But I was not *'Gajendra'*. Who would bail me out?

× × ×

A few months after I took over as Executive Officer of the Tirumala Tirupati Devasthanams, the Government abolished the Trust Board headed by Sri Anna Rao as Chairman. Pending the constitution of a new board, the Government appointed a Persons-in-Charge Committee of three officials in its place. They were Principal Secretary, Revenue, Dr. Ramesan (Chairman), Endowments Commissioner and former TTD Executive Officer Chandramouli Reddy (Member) and me, the Executive Officer (Member-Secretary).

The committee was all powerful. The Government entrusted to the committee the responsibility of overhauling the entire TTD administrative set-up and drafting a new law to confer autonomy on the TTD. Since the other two officials in the committee, holding busy positions, had other responsibilities, the task of initiating changes and drafting preliminary reports devolved on me as Member Secretary. As a result, I had to draft Laws and concept papers, besides discharging day-to-day responsibilities as TTD Executive Officer. It was during this busy time that Jeeyar Swami came to Tirupati to meet me.

Tridandi Srimannarayana Jeeyar had already been known as a *'swami'* with a great following. He had established a *'peetham'* after taking to *'sanyasa'* and initiated many programmes to spread spirituality among tens of thousands of homes. He was highly renowned for his captivating oratory, extraordinary erudition, scriptural knowledge and organisational skills. He had made millions of devout people write *'Ramakoti'* through a *'Rama nama japa'* campaign. He got 108 *'Ramakoti stupas'* erected at as many places all over the country including one at Tirumala. A few years before I joined the TTD, he had also conducted a large *'yagna'* at Tirumala.

I took the initiative and made suitable arrangements for his stay at Tirumala when I learnt that he was coming to see me. I called on him when he arrived. He commended some of the programmes I had taken up at Tirumala. As he talked, his spiritual insights reflected the depth of his scholarship. After a while, he paused and cast a penetrating look at me. Why had he paused? What was he planning to communicate? I was all ears. I saw his eyes lighting up as he said, "Prasad, to promote peace and harmony among people, we have been thinking for long of conducting a *'Sri Lakshminarayana Sahasrakunda Maha Yagna'*. I feel the appropriate time has come. We have to carry out this major programme only atop Tirumala Hills".

He was keen that the proposed *'yagna'* should be much bigger than the one he had conducted earlier. In this, 1000 *'homa kundas'* had to remain lit until the *'yagna'* was complete. *'Rithviks'* had to make offerings into the *'homa kundas'* continuously. A variety of materials had to be procured on a large scale for the *'maha yagna'*. Pandals had to be erected at the *'yagna'* site for the huge congregation. Facilities had to be provided to pilgrims visiting the *'yagna'*. Accommodation had to be provided to about 5000 *Vedic* scholars taking part in it. It also called for making several other arrangements such as lighting, transport, board and of course *'darshan'* facilities on a large scale.

Jeeyar Swami had estimated that the *'yagna'* would cost not less than Rs. 30 lakh. But he added, "The TTD has to cooperate by providing a substantial part of the expenditure as advance. The TTD has also to meet the travel costs and honoraria of all *Vedic* scholars"

I was still absorbing all the information and working out the implications in my mind when he asked me, "So, Prasad, what do you think?" I did not know how to respond. So, I sought some clarification. "What is the funds position now for the *'yagna'*?" He replied with a smile, "We will go round the State and collect donations from householders. All the donors will take part in the events and each couple will be accommodated at one *'yagna kunda'*. Since the collections will exceed Rs.30 lakh, the TTD can retain the excess and use it for *'dharmic'* activities".

Then I clearly grasped the situation. Jeeyar Swami did not have any corpus on hand for the *'yagna'*. The TTD had to advance a part of the Rs.30 lakh expenditure.

I could not commit myself either way then and there. Many doubts haunted me. Was it proper for the TTD to tie up with a *'Swamiji'* in the *'yagna'* he planned atop Tirumala Hills? Could the TTD act as the co-sponsor of such an event? Jeeyar Swami believed that as donations would pour in, he could repay the TTD advance. Donations might come when the TTD's name was also invoked. What would happen if the anticipated donations did not materialise? When we found it difficult to attend to the thousands of pilgrims visiting Tirumala every day, could we provide minimal facilities to people thronging the *'yagna'*? Could the TTD administrative machinery withstand the stress and strain? Amidst such doubts, I told Jeeyar Swami, "I would get back to you after discussing the matter in the Persons-in-Charge Committee". But, I realised that it was I who was filled with self-doubt. Jeeyar Swami exuded enormous self-confidence. He declared, "This is God's will. This is bound to happen"

I placed the matter before the committee. Endowments Commissioner Chandramouli Reddy, who had worked as TTD Executive Officer earlier, had great regard for Jeeyar Swami. He felt that when any such spiritual activity took place atop Tirumala Hills, the TTD had to ensure Lord's *'darshan'* and amenities to devotees taking part in it. He pointed out that any such programme conducted anywhere drew devotees in large numbers. In Tirumala, the numbers would be larger. So, the TTD administration had to work very hard. He said "As Executive Officer, you will not have even breathing time for two months. During my tenure as Executive Officer, I faced a similar situation when a *'homam'* was conducted by the same Swami though on a smaller scale". He briefly shared his experience, and finally concluded, "You alone have to decide what is to be done now. If you feel confident that you can manage, please go ahead". Chairman Ramesan remained neutral. But, he posed the critical question, "If some other *'swamiji'* comes tomorrow and wants to perform another *'yagna'*, what will you do?". A very valid question, which had been nagging me also. We could not resolve the issue. I suggested that the entire committee meet Jeeyar Swami and take a collective decision.

Though the committee had been granted considerable autonomy, I thought I should consult those who wielded the real powers. I conveyed the information to the then Endowments Minister Veeramachaneni Venkata Narayana and Chief Minister Dr. M. Channa Reddy. They did not raise any objections. They merely said, "Do whatever you think is right". Thus the ball was back in my court.

Finally, the Persons-in-Charge Committee met Jeeyar Swami. He explained at length as to why such a great *'yagna'* had to be performed at only a sacred place like Tirumala and what benefits would flow from it. He quoted from the *'sastras'* extensively. We were touched more by his burning passion to undertake such a mammoth task and his immense faith in the social purpose it would serve than by his erudition and oratorial skills. The committee agreed to cooperate with him in the conduct of the event at Tirumala. This decision was taken mostly on the strength of his personality, credibility, organisational abilities and following. (Of course, I was aware that the actual execution would finally devolve on the TTD).

As per the understanding with Jeeyar Swami, the TTD would advance the funds for the *'yagna'*. In addition, it would donate all the materials required. Jeeyar Swami would transfer all the surplus (amount left after all the expenditure was met and advance repaid) for TTD's *'dharmic'* activities. Jeeyar Swami finalised the auspicious moment for the start of the *'yagna'*. It was to take place two months later. All the preparatory works were grounded.

A massive campaign was launched throughout the southern States about the great *'yagna'*. A month rolled by. Brisk arrangements were under way for the *'Sri Lakshminarayana Sahasrakunda Yagna'* atop Tirumala Hills. The TTD had to shoulder multifarious responsibilities like the levelling and the cleaning of the *'yagna'* site, erection of pandals, procurement of materials like fuelwood and ghee, transporting them to the top of the Hills, planning for the accommodation and provision of food to pundits according to their customs and traditions, provision of drinking water facilities at the yagna site, catering to the additional rush of pilgrims, deputation of TTD staff to coordinate with the organising committee formed by the Swamiji and ensuring that the pilgrims visiting Tirumala for *'darshan'* were not inconvenienced because of the *'yagna'* . A separate accounts cell was formed to maintain proper accounts. It had become a full time job. Yet, I did not deem it a burden as I had the satisfaction of taking part in a massive spiritual programme for the welfare of the humanity. I mobilised the required staff and resources. Sri Gopalacharya Swami was the coordinator on behalf of Jeeyar Swami to look after the ritual and spiritual side. Sri Venkateswarlu, Chairman of Kakatiya

Cements (who subsequently became the TTD Chairman for a term), not only donated money and substantial quantities of materials required for the *'yagna'* but also worked round the clock to coordinate activities, going on at a feverish pitch. We also learnt that Jeeyar Swami had completed three-fourths of his tour schedule and that householders had been responding well to his call for donations. There were just three weeks left for the start of the *'yagna'*.

All of a sudden, one day, I had a telephonic message to the effect that Jeeyar Swami had suddenly fallen ill at Warangal. Concerned over his health, I left for Hyderabad en route to Warangal. On arrival at Hyderabad the next morning, I learnt that Jeeyar Swami's condition had worsened, and he had been brought to Hyderabad and admitted in Mahaveer Hospital. I rushed to the hospital.

On reaching the hospital, I met Sri Gopalacharya Swamy, Sri Sribhashyam Applacharyulu, Jeeyar Swamiji's favourite disciple (the present China Jeeyar), and other followers, of the Swamiji outside the Swamiji's room. I was feeling quite anxious as I stepped into his room. Jeeyar Swami was lying on the bed, almost unconscious. I sat beside him and waited. A little later, I gently took his hand into mine. The tactile sensation made him open his eyes slowly. As he saw me, his eyes lit up with some inexplicable pleasure pulsating his entire being. Affectionately, he squeezed my hand. He signalled me to come nearer. I moved. In a quivering tone, he inquired, "How are the arrangements going on?". I explained. He shut his eyes again. Silence reigned for a while. With some effort, he slowly opened his eyes again. Looking affectionately at me, he whispered, "By the time the *'yagna'* takes place, we may not be there. Our successor will be the *'yagna karta'*. He is young and enthusiastic. But you have to shoulder the burden of supervising all the arrangements. This is God's will. It should take place with your total involvment". He seemed to slip again into unconsciousness. I sat speechless and confused, holding his hand for a while.

As I had some urgent work, I returned to Tirupati straight. The news awaiting me on my arrival at Tirupati was that "Jeeyar Swami has reached the lotus feet of God".

The Swamiji's passing away made me rudderless. The '*yagna*' was to begin in the next few days. It was a rare mega event planned by him. The TTD had committed its resources and personnel on the strength of his forceful personality. His absence had left a great void and called into question the justification for conducting the '*yagna*' committing TTD's resources further. Should we go ahead or call it off? Lakhs of rupees had already been spent, in addition to the time and effort of hundreds of workers during the previous two months. Would such a massive event not take off? I had taken the initiative to involve many TTD employees and devotees in this task. If the '*yagna*' did not take place, all our efforts would have been in vain. What would happen to the money advanced by the TTD? What purpose would the devotees' donations serve? What could be my explanation to all the concerned sections of people? How could I wriggle myself out of such a situation?

I was feeling agitated and dejected. I went into the Tirumala temple, with a number of thoughts crowding my mind. I poured out before the Lord, "We have initiated the programme in the hope that you, the omnipotent, would shower your blessings on the entire humanity. I do not know what to do? Should the '*yagna*' go on or not? ". I sat for a while. As I came out, there was a message saying China Jeeyar had been selected as the successor of Jeeyar Swami.

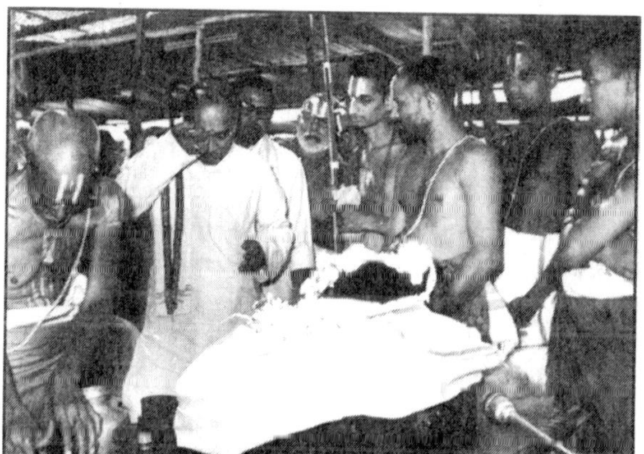

Sri P.V. Narasimha Rao, Union Minister participating in the Yagnam.

I held prolonged discussions with my officials. Many questions cropped up. Should we go ahead with the *'yagna' when Jeeyar Swami was no more?* He was the architect and catalyst. What would happen if we abandoned the programme? If we were not to abandon, how should we proceed? Would we emerge unscathed if we went ahead? Could the junior Jeeyar step into the shoes of his Guru? How would the devotees respond? Only questions — no answers.

Two days later, the incoming Jeeyar Swami went to Srivalliputtur, got initiated into *'sanyas'*, assumed charge as *'peethadhipati'* and arrived at Tirumala as Tridandi China Sreemannarayana Jeeyar. Still in his teens, China Jeeyar impressed every one with his boundless enthusiasm, shimmering spirituality, a disarming smile, pleasant communication skills and maturity of thinking. He gave the impression that he could handle any complex issue with equanimity. That settled the issue. No more thoughts of abandoning the *'yagna'*.

Briskly walking around and guiding others through his magnetic eyes, he emerged in the next few days as a leader acceptable to every one there. He took over as the *'yagna karta'* of the *'Sri Lakshminarayana Sahasrakunda Yagna'* and plunged into action as if Peda Jiyyar Swami had taken possession of him.

There was no looking back. As the Tirumala Hills reverberated to the Vedic chantings of *'rithviks'*, as the rings of smoke spiralling from the *'homa kundas'* enveloped the skies as blessings from *'yagna purusha'*, as the continuous chant of the divine by thousands of householders whipped up a wave of devotion among pilgrims, the great *'yagna'*, succeeded beyond expectations, and dispelled all misgivings. The *'yagna'* came to a magnificent end with the blessings of China Jeeyar on *'purnahuti'* day. I had tears of joy. Who could say how we got over a crisis, how everything went beyond our expectations and which power facilitated the conduct of the *'yagna'* unhindered. The TTD received much more than what it had advanced and spent towards the *'yagna'*.

Visit of His Holliness Sri Tridandi Srimannarayana Chinna Jeer to the Temple during the Yagnam.

Anybody can now vouchsafe that our assessment of China Jeeyar was not wrong. In the past 25 years, he has grown from a *'Vamana'* to a *'Trivikrama'* by inspiring lakhs of followers through spiritual activities like community *'Vishnushasranama parayan' 'Geetha Jyothi'* and educational and social activities through the Jeeyar Educational Trust. He has eclipsed his own guru, Peda Jeeyar.

I am a Madhwa. All Madhwas believe that *'Hara (Lord Siva)* is the greatest disciple of *'Hari'*. A person who hates *'Hara'*, an ardent devotee of *'Hari'*, cannot be a true *'Vaishnavite'*. But, this line of thinking is not acceptable to most *'Sri Vaishnavites'* at Tirumala. Although heading a *'Sri Vaishanava peetham'*, China Jeeyar went on a pilgrimage to Manasa Sarovar in 2002 and did a *'pradakshina'* of Mount Kailas, underlining the relationship between *'Hari'* and *'Hara'*. His courage of conviction and strength of character have resulted in providing a new direction to his ever increasing following. It was not for nothing that Lord Srinivasa blessed him to perform a *'yagna'* of that magnitude at such a young age, within days of taking over as *'Peethadhipati'*.

11

THE DEMANDING LORD AND THE SATISFIED DEVOTEE

As I was immersed in an important meeting on a Thursday in October 1980, the temple *'Peshkar'* phoned me seeking advice on a pressing problem. A 20-member group of devotees from Karnataka had been insisting on presenting a necklace of 108 gold coins and having *'darshan'* of the Lord adorned with their necklace after the *'abhisheka seva'* the next morning. Engraved on each of the coins were images and the names of the Lord and His consort.

According to the procedures in vogue perhaps for centuries, devotees had to drop their offerings to the Lord in the *'hundi'*. Or they could have the satisfaction of handing over the offerings to the temple staff and obtaining a receipt. The offerings were then sent to the TTD treasury. If the devotees wanted to see the Lord adorned with their offerings, they had to pay a fee - *'vartana'* as it was called - which was equivalent to the cost of the offering. (This rule perhaps had been introduced to meet the pressure from kings, *'zamindars'* and the affluent for getting the Lord decorated with their offerings).

The *'Peshkar'* had already explained the procedure to the devotee group. But the members of the group were in no mood to comply with the procedure. They repeatedly told the *'Peshkar'* that they had got the necklace prepared as directed by Lord Srinivasa and that the Lord had also instructed them to proceed to Tirumala to offer it to Him and get His blessings after he was decorated with the necklace. They also mentioned that the Lord had told them that His servant would sort out incidental problems, if any. Unable to decide on their pleas, the

'Peshkar' called me. Very interesting!!! I told him, "I will be atop the Hills in an hour" and accordingly reached Tirumala.

× × ×

Mr. D.N. Nagaraja Rao was the head of the family of devotees that came from Lakkapalli village in Chickmagalur district of Karnataka. This was what Mr. Nagaraja Rao narrated:

Some 15-16 years previously, Lord Srinivasa, appearing in a dream, asked Mr. Nagaraja Rao, "Will you offer me a necklace of 108 gold coins?" Mr. Nagaraja Rao did not bother about the dream. The next day, some devotees happened to visit him and offer the Tirupati *'laddu prasadam'*. Immediately, the previous night's dream flashed across his mind. Mr. Nagaraja Rao told the family members about his dream. Every one in the family was an ardent devotee of the Lord. Yet they did not have the economic resources to present a 108-gold-coin necklace to the Lord. In fact, they were not in a position to get one gold coin, leave alone 108. A primary school teacher, Mr Nagaraja Rao had to look after his parents, brothers and sisters and his own family even at a young age. Although the family owned some land, it remained barren and yielded little.

So, the Lord's unreasonable request was not taken seriously.

That very night, the Lord appeared in dream to Mr. Nagaraja Rao again and reminded him of His desire. Mr. Nagaraja Rao was perplexed, excited and confused. He took the matter to heart. He called up all the family members the next morning and narrated the dream. As they could not afford gold coins, they decided to get a copper coin necklace interspersed with a few silver coins and gift it to the Lord. That night, the Lord appeared in dream to Mr. Nagaraja Rao again and pointedly told him that He wanted a gold necklace and not a copper one. Mr. Nagaraja Rao could not sleep for the night and went on pondering the strange, persistent demands from the Lord. He waited for the dawn to break to take his family members into confidence and find a solution. Early in the morning, the entire family discussed the Lord's wish. "Even if we collect all the *'mangala sutras'* of the women in the family, we cannot get one or two coins prepared. How could we produce a 108-gold-coin necklace?" Finally, they felt that the Lord who expressed the desire would Himself show a way out. However, on their part, they decided to make some genuine efforts.

From that day onwards, the family members decided to forgo one meal a day and allocate the money thus saved towards the gold coin necklace. All the family members, including the children and the elderly, strictly followed the unanimous decision. The money thus saved for six months enabled them to get two coins made. That left a deficit of 106 gold coins. Leaving the matter to the Lord, the family continued its prayers and savings through fasting.

Gradually, there was improvement in the economic condition of tho family. One of the brothers of Mr. Nagaraja Rao got a good job. The next year, an irrigation scheme enabled the family to take up cultivation in the lands hitherto left fallow. The family began reaping good harvests. As months and years rolled by, others in the family got jobs. The gold coin mission gained momentum thereafter. Sixteen years later, they could get a thick gold chain with 108 gold coins made, as desired by the Lord. Once the necklace was ready, the Lord appeared in dream and told Mr. Nagaraja Rao, "You have got the necklace ready with your collective effort. I am pleased. Won't all of you come to my Hills and present the offering and have my '*darshan*' with the necklace". Noticing his anxiety and hesitation, the Lord showed him a person, and said, "If you face any problems at Tirumala, he will help you". (Why didn't he appear in between?!)

As I listened, I could discern their deep and pure faith and dctermination to abide by the Lord's instructions. It had taken 16 long years for them to bridge the gap between poverty and commitment and come to the Hills to make the offering to the Lord. They had just enough money to go back to their Lakkapalli village. Suddenly, something struck Mr. Nagaraja Rao. Overwhelmed with piety and pleasure, he uttered, "It is you — yes — it is you whom the Lord showed me in the dream. Yes ...Yes ...You only. He wanted me to meet you only". As he swayed with emotion and clutched my hand, my eyes became wet.

I could understand their plight. They did not have the money to pay the fee for adorning the Lord with their gift; they did not have money even to buy tickets for the *'abhishekham'* or even *'darshan'* after the *'abhisheka'*. All that they had was boundless faith in the Lord. "We abided by the Lord's directive and He will ensure that our work is done — not our work — His work".

I was deeply touched. Tears rolled down my cheeks. I realised that as a servant of the Lord, I vindicate and uphold their faith in the Lord. If they had to pay the fee to adorn the Lord with the necklace, they should have at least Rs. 2 lakh, a very conservative estimate of the cost of the necklace. And as Executive Officer, I did not have the discretion to waive the stipulated fee which is called *'vartana'*. It was a conflict between my responsibilities and their faith in the Lord. As I watched their anxiety to see the Lord adorned with the necklace after 16 years of relentless effort, I could not turn down their request. The *'Peshkar'* was certain that no exemptions had been given earlier and wondered whether even the Board had powers to take such a decision. Such matters which ran contrary to tradition and caused revenue loss, had to be taken to the Government.

I strongly felt I should somehow justify their faith in the Lord. "Who am I to come in the way between them and the Lord? Or stand in between them and frustrate their desire? After all, my job is to render service to the Lord and provide satisfaction to His devotees"... Once such thoughts overtook me, I instructed the *'Peshkar'*, "Exempt them from the payment of fee and fulfil their wish". They need not pay for *'abhishekham'* tickets. Treat them as VIP guests. Though the *'Peshkar'* was surprised, he was happy as he could appreciate the situation.

The Lord was adorned with the gold coin necklace after the Friday *'abhisheka'* the next morning. All the members of the family, chanting "Govinda, Govinda", had *'darshan'* of the Lord to their hearts' content. How could I describe the emotions of joy and happiness that enveloped them on realising their 16-year-old dream?

A few days later, in the next TTD Board meeting I brought up the subject and explained my 'transgression of rules'. Although I had no idea of the consequences, I was prepared for the worst. But since all the Board members happened to be deeply religious-minded, Mr. Nagaraja Rao's story of devotion moved them too. The Board ratified my decision to waive '*vartana*' fee on the necklace. It also resolved that "exemption from payment of fees should be given in deserving cases where the poor go out of their way to make any offering to the Lord in future".

Even to this day, the necklace story remains a mystery to me. Which Power prompted Mr. Nagaraja Rao to get the necklace made? And Who prompted me to oblige him?

12

RENAISSANCE OF DAASA SAHITYA

The hall near the *'pushkarini'* in Vyasaraja Matha in Tirumala was reverberating to the *'Govinda...Jaya Govinda...Bhaja Govinda,' 'bhajan'*, being rendered with rapture by a large group of Srinivasa *'daasas'*.

The devotional tidal wave whipped up by the *'daasas'* with their *'nama smarana'* and rhythmic dance lashed me. A dip in that ocean of devotion elevated me to ethereal heights. As my happiness brimmed over, I said, "Your devotion as Srinivasa *'daasas'* is boundless and extraordinary. Tell me what I can do for you as Tirumala Tirupati Devasthanam Executive Officer".

"Arrange a nice and satisfying *'darshan'* of Lord Srinivasa", they said in one voice. I was amazed. The *'daasas'* had only Srinivasa at the tip of their tongues all the time; they had the image of only Srinivasa engraved in their hearts. So they were content in seeking just a good *'darshan'*. Who would not? Lord Narayana himself is standing there in Tirumala in *'archavatara'*.

"Is that all? No one can arrange good *'darshan'* or satisfactory *'darshan'*. If Lord wills it, it happens, Otherwise, even if the Executive Officer or the entire Trust Board arranges a VVIP *'darshan'*, the VVIP may not have good and satisfactory *'darshan'*. As Executive Officer, I shall do my best to arrange *'darshan'* as I try to do for other VIPs". However, is there nothing else I can do for these *'daasas'?* , I said to myself and shut my eyes.

In that moment, a picture of all human beings becoming Srinivasa *'daasas'*, every one striving for liberation through *'Harinama'* recital and the benign rays of the Lord bathing every home flashed across my mind. I visualised the *'bhakti'* movement gaining momentum with the renaissance of *'Daasa Sahitya'* and *'Daasa Pandha'*. (Who could have been the painter?). Inspired thus, I became unmindful of my powers and made an announcement on the spur of the moment. That marked the beginning of a massive movement in 1980. Here is a peep into that past.

× × ×

During January-February 1979, a *'daasa'* devotee, Sri Parigi Vasantha Kumar, dropped in to request that I be the chief guest on the last day of the Purandaradaasa *'aradhanotsavas'*. He informed me that Guru Govinda Vithaldaas was conducting the festivities at Vyasaraya *'mantap'* near the *'pushkarini'*.

"Let me see", I told him casually. But he was not inclined to take a 'no' for an answer. He persisted in urging me to take part in the programme.

So, I asked him, "After all *'aradhantsavas'* are routine. Why are you so insistent?"

Taking the query as an opportunity, Sri Parigi explained in detail the *'daasa'* philosophy and the *'daasa'* form of worship.

In the past, common people had no access to sacred books like the *'Vedas'*, the *'Sastras'*, the *'Upanishads'*, the *'Mahabharatam'*, the *'Bhagavatam'* and *'Itihasa Puranasas'* because they were all in Sanskrit. Some great scholars in Karnataka felt the need to spread the spiritual knowledge among the lay public without any bias or prejudice based on caste or religion, creed or sex. They accomplished their objective by bringing out *'Harikathas' 'keertanas'*, *'devaranamas'* and *'bhajans'* in simple Kannada, the language of the common man. The *'Vyasa'* literature thus became the *'daasa'* literature.

Eminent scholars and Madhwa *'sanyasis'* (ascetics) like Sri Narahari Tirtha, Sri Vadiraja and Sri Sripada Raja pioneered the movement. They were followed by Sri Vyasaraya and his disciples, Sri Purandaradaasa and Sri Kanakadaasa and later by Vijayadaasa, Gopaldaasa and Jagannadhadaasa. As a result of their efforts, the essence of the *'Vedas'* and the *'Upanishads'* could be taken to every nook and corner of Karnataka in simple intelligible language. But after the fall of the Vijayanagar Empire and the advent of Muslim rule the movement gradually lost momentum. There were, of course some famous *'daasas'* appearing on the scene once in a while to revive the movement here and there. But the mass base had eroded and the movement was confined to a few *'daasas'* and their followers. The potential of the movement had not been realised. The movement could not go deep and wide into public consciousness for want of an institutional framework and encouragement.

The devotion of those who take the *'daasa deeksha'* is boundless and unflagging. He who takes the vow leads the *'daasa'* way till the end of his life. Even as he remains a householder, he totally surrenders to Lord Hari as a *'Daasa'*. Depending on his spiritual attainment, he can compose *'devaranamas'* singing the glories of the Lord. As he grows in stature, he can initiate *'sishyas'* and as a *'guru'*, he can invoke the blessings of the Lord and confer *'ankita nama'* (a spiritual name) on the disciple who takes a vow and follows the *'daasa'* way of life. For one to become the disciple of a *'guru'* in this *'guru-shishya'* tradition, no qualification other than a resolution to remain a true devotee of the Lord, following the tenets and teachings of the *'guru'*, is required.

The Purandaradaasa *'aradhanotsavas'* that year were taking place under the auspices of Guru Govinda Vithaldaasa, a *'daasa'* guru in this *'guru-sishya'* tradition, concluded Sri Parigi.

Before he became a *'daasa'*, Guru Govinda Vithaldaasa was a sub-overseer in the Karnataka Government's Public Works Department. After joining the *'daasa'* movement he rose to become a *'guru'*. He composed 800 *'devaranamas'* and moulded 250 disciples by giving them *'deeksha'* and *'ankitanamas'*. At no point of time did he raise any questions about the caste of the disciples. For example, he gave a Muslim devotee, Hussain Saheb, who had evinced interest in *'Haridaasa deeksha'*, an *'ankitanamam'*.

What Sri Parigi told me roused my curiosity in the *'daasa'* institution. Its catholicity and aspects like a householder leading the *'daasa'* way of life, and practising and propagating the essence of sacred books to promote spirituality among the semi-literate and illiterate and granting of *'deeksha'* based on one's spiritual quest without reference to caste or creed or sex appealed to me.

As Sri Parigi concluded his exposition, I was convinced that I should attend the Purandaradaasa *'aradhanotsavas'* at Vyasaraya *'mantap'* near the *'pushkarini'*. "I will definitely attend your programme", I assured him. Once I went there, I had the opportunity to learn many new things. One who takes the *'deeksha'* should strive not merely to improve one's own spiritual knowledge and put it into practice, but also propagate the essence of the *'Ramayana'*, the *'Mahabharata'*, the *'Bhagavata'* and *'Itihasas'* containing Vedic knowledge among common people through simple *'bhajans'*, *'keertanas'* and discourses. Of course, one is expected to do these even as one leads the life as a *'grihasta'* (Householder)

Sri Parigi introduced one such *'daasa'* to me. His *'ankitanama'*, given by his *'guru'* was *'Khagavara Dwhaja Vithaldaasa'*. He was one of the principal disciples of Guru Govindadaasa. On that day, Khagavara Dwaja Vithaldaasa also delivered a discourse. What a splendid communication it was!

What flowed from him was akin to a spiritual Ganges. Laced with *'slokas'* and verses from the *'Gita'*, the *'Upanishads'*, *'Devaranamas'* and *'Harikathamritasara'*, his talk electrified the audience and put them in the divine orbit. I was simply floored. Sri Parigi, sitting beside me, said, "Many devotee groups in Karnataka, Andhra Pradesh and Tamil Nadu want Khagavara Dwhaja Vithaldaasa to address them". After having heard him, I was not surprised. A walking encyclopaedia of spiritual knowledge, he held forth on subjects ranging from the importance of devotion to the ways of liberation in a simple and sweet language and cast a spell on the audience. We yearned for more from him.

Incidentally, I asked Sri Parigi. "What is he by profession? A teacher?...". I was dumbfounded by what Parigi said with a smile. Khagavara Dwhaja Vithaldaasa was Nagaraju before he became a *'daasa'*. He was not even a high school graduate. He was not very proficient even in reading or writing Kannada, his mother tongue. A postman in the Postal Department, he happened to take part in Guru Govinda Vithaldaasa's *'Hari aradhana'* and *'Harinama parayana'* programmes. The participation brought about a sea change in his thinking. He requested Guru Govinda Vithaldaasa to give him *'deeksha'*. Only after testing Nagarju for a year and being satisfied with his spiritual potential, Sri Vithaldaasa gave him *'deekhsa'* and renamed him Khagavara Dwhaja Vithaldaasa. I could hardly believe the transformation he had undergone within seven or eight years of his initiation.

How could a semi-literate postman metamorphose into a great scholar? Who gave him the capabilities? And who provided the inspiration? To all my questions, Khagavara Dwhaja Vithaldaasa's reply was, "Lord Srinivasa through my *'guru'*".

Guru Govindadaasa keenly studied the *lives of various earlier daasas* and wrote about 200 *'daasas'* not much known to the world and published eight volumes titled *'Haribhakta Vijayam'*. My interest grew as I heard more and more about the depth and feeling of devotion *'bhakti'* in *'daasa'* literature, its objectives and the dedication with which *'daasas'* had been carrying on their mission. The talk on *'Harikathamritasaram'* by Sri Appanacharya, who was invited to deliver the 'key-note address', mirrored the depth of his knowledge and understanding of *'daasa'* literature and philosophy. On enquiry, I learnt that such a learned scholar was working as a lecturer in the TTD Oriental College and that he also came from a family of *'daasas'*.

Having had a lot of fascinating insights into the *'daasa'* tradition, I went into an introspective mood. 'Daasas' had relentlessly been striving for generations to liberate, *'Vedic'* knowledge from the confines of a few select scholars and spread it among common people through simple, intelligible literature and absorbing music. Should such a movement be allowed to decline for want of support? Could I not do something as a servant of *'Hari'* (as TTD Executive Officer) to the *'daasas'* who believed that *'Harinama'* recital would lead to liberation?

Electrified by the experience, I asked them involuntarily, "Tell me what I can do for you as TTD Executive Officer?" The congregation mostly consisted of sishyas of Sri Guru Govinda Vithaladaasa from all the southern states – drawn from various walks of life – working and retired government officials, bank employees, businessmen – petty employees working in private companies – a number of ladies in various stages of spiritual growth – mostly householders – rich and poor – old and young.

All that they wanted was a good *'darshan'* of Srinivasa to their heart's content. However, "is there nothing else I can do for these *'daasas'*", I asked myself. Deep inside, I felt it was an opportune moment to do something. But I had no clear notion as to what I should do.

When I reflected on the question "Could I not do anything more?" I was transported into the scenario of a society full of *'daasas'* and *'bhaktas'*, every village, town and city being influenced by the *'daasa'* movement and being affiliated to the TTD. I visualised the whole population savouring the devotional music and leading contented lives. In my mental picture, I saw the TTD paving the way for the renaissance of the *'bhakti'* movement through these *'daasas'*. As if in a trance, I announced offhand: "The TTD will launch a *'Daasa* Sahitya Project' to collect and publish information about all the past *'daasas'* and their compositions *'devaranamas'*. This project will create *'daasa'* cells in every village to spread *'daasa'* literature among the lay public on a continuing basis. We will soon appoint a Project Officer to take up this massive project." As my eyes fell on Sri Appanacharya at that moment, I added, "Where is the need for a search?. We will have Sri Appanacharya as our Project Officer to organise and lead this movement". *'Daasas'* applauded the announcement by raising *'Govinda'* slogans.

After the programme, when I got back to my senses, the reality hit me. How did I make an announcement? Was I authorised? Had I acted like a politician? I had to make a proposal and get it approved by the TTD Board before I could launch any project costing several lakhs of rupees and that too on a permanent basis. Why had I named even a Project Officer".

I realised that I was not under my control when I made the announcement. It was unusual of me to have acted like that. But I soon rationalised. "As a servant of the Lord, I did what seemed right to me. It is for Him to decide whether the proposed project should materialise or not".

Fortunately, the Board members took upon themselves the responsibility of getting my announcement ratified when it met next. The Board wholeheartedly approved the '*Daasa*' Sahitya Project and the appointment of Sri Appanacharya, an eminent scholar both in Telugu and Kannada, as Project Officer.

The '*daasa*' movement spearheaded by the '*Daasa Sahitya Project*' of the TTD has spread to all corners in the Southern States and Maharashtra in the last two decades, promoting the '*bhakti*' movement. The number of '*bhajan*' troupes promoted by the project has swelled from a few hundered in the beginning to a few thousands now. Women in '*sindhoor*' and turmeric coloured sarees and men in dhotis and saffron colour headgear dancing and singing 'H*ari sankeertana*' can be seen during religious festivities – particularly in Tirumala during '*Brahmostavams*' and '*Metlotsavams*'. Seeing thousands of these devotees singing the glory of the Lord and dancing with abandon is a rare sight and great experience.

Whenever two '*daasa*' devotees meet, they greet each other with '*Hare Srinivasa*'. They begin and end all conversations including those over telephone with '*Hare Srinivasa*'. Spiritual camps, '*daasa aradhanotsavas*', get-togethers, seminars, competitions in '*sankeertanas*' and '*bhajans*' have all gradually become part of the project. Many research works on '*daasa*' literature in Telugu, Kannada and English languages, many books in simple style and 24 audio cassettes have been released. Many exhibitions on the '*daasa*' set-up have been held. Oil paintings scientifically depicting complex subjects to be studied by a '*daasa*' practitioner have been brought out. They include subjects like creation, universe, path of spiritual progress etc on '*srushthi – sadhana*', '*srushthi-prakarana*', '*kesavadi rupas*' '*papa purusha visarjana*', '*Omkara swaroopam*', the significance of the 'lotuses' in human body, the divine forms in human body - the deities in charge of various functions in a human body and the way they inspire the human being. The project has collected the paintings of many *'daasas'*, their compositions, articles used by them and the idols they worshipped. Conduct of exhibitions during *'daasa aradhanotsavas'* and other fairs is an important activity. Singing and dancing in abandon has spread so strongly and deeply that in the recent times, annual *'metlotsavams'* are being organised in places like Adoni, Kolar, Chitradurga, Karighatta and Devarayani Durga on the lines of those in Tirupati/ Tirumala. When I attended the *'Srikrishna vajrakavacha samarpana'* festivities at Udipi, *'bhajan'* troupes from far off places in Andhra Pradesh like Srikakulam, Vizianagaram, Rajahmundry, Nallajarla, Tadepalligudem, Vijayawada, Anantapur, Adoni, Kurnool, and a number of troupes from Tamil Nadu took part in the celebration singing *'Bhajans'* in Kannada. Swamijis showered praises on Telugu *'bhajan'* troupes rendering Kannada *'bhajans'* with great devotion. The *Daasa* Sahitya Project has been influencing many families in the entire South India. My wife Gopika is one of those influenced by the *'daasa'* literature in the last 20 years.

Dasas in Metlosshavam

Like me, for the first time, she was exposed to the *'daasas'* when we were in Tirumala. She took part in the 1979 three-day Purandaradaasa *'aradhanotsavas'*. While I attended only the concluding session, she took part in all the sessions and heard all the discourses on the three days. She did not know Kannada. Attracted by the richness of the devotional literature in the original, she learnt Kannada language and mastered reading, writing and speaking. She translated eight books of *'daasa'* literature into Telugu and got them published by the Guru Govind Vithaldaasa Seva Samithi. She formed the Seva Samithi in Hyderabad along with Mrs. Sunanda, Usha Venkobarao, Rakumabai, Vedamma, Lakshana, Vaijayanti, Usha and Rukminamma to undertake *'bhakti'* and *'gnana'* activities. They meet periodically, perform *'Bhajans'*, and discuss *'daasa'* philosophy.

It is my wife Gopika who brought to my knowledge that many of the *'daasas'* who devoted their lives to Srihari were from Andhra Pradesh. Gopala Daasa belonged to Uttanoor of Mahaboobnagar district. Vijayadaasa spent a considerable time in Chippagiri near Guntakal and Seshagiridas from Modalukal near Gadwal.

The core philosophy of the *'daasa'* movement that "Lord Hari is the only Master and I am his servant" might appear simple. But it calls for seeing the Lord in every thought and deed and in every being. Generally, *'bhakti'* tends to be sidelined in any serious argument, as it is characterised as *'moodha bhakti'* (blind belief) devoid of knowledge. However, the *'daasa'* Sahitya project does not promote blind belief or faith. Knowledge or *'jnana'* as propounded in *'Vedic'* literature is to be acquired and all the prescriptions of the *'sastras'* have to be observed. Real *'bhakti'* can be sustained only by acquiring correct knowledge of the *'sastras'*. Lack of familiarity with Sanskrit is no handicap as great *'daasas'* who were well versed in *'Vedic'* (Vyasa) knowledge have ensured that the same is available in simple Kannada.

In a nutshell, Daasa philosophy propounds:

Lord Hari is supreme.

The world is real and not an illusion as propounded by some schools of thought.

There are three different entities (1) God (2) *'Jivas'* (living entities), (3) *'Jada'* (non-living) and each is different from the other.

Lord alone is independent and all living beings are not independent but subservient to the Lord – as 'daasas'

Each being is different from the other and there is a gradation of souls

Realisation of the Lord is liberation

Realisation can be had by having total and unflagging faith in the Lord borne out of true knowledge (as propounded in '*sastras*') which leads to absolute surrender to the Lord.

Sri P.V.R.K. Prasad at the Head of the procession near Govinda Raja Swamy Temple Tirupati in connection with "Metlotsavam"

There are three standards – ('*pramanas*') to draw conclusions - direct, indirect and inference. The Lord can be realised through *'Vedic'* knowledge by applying these standards.

Even today, I wonder how an announcement made by me in a fit of emotion almost a quarter of century ago on the *'Daasa'* Sahitya Project without any proposal or report or recommendation or evaluation or the approval of the Board has led to a strong and powerful movement. I feel embarrassed whenever some one tries to give credit to me for the project. How can we dismiss the developments as a mere coincidence: - the celebrations being organised at Tirumala in 1979 in Vyasaraya Muth founded by a great pioneer of the *'Daasa'* movement, the presence of Guru Govinda Vithala Daasa, a great *'daasa'* , Sri Apannacharya, himself a great *'daasa'* and coming from a great *'daasa'* traditional family being present there as a guest lecturer. There are just too many coincidences. I am aware that the power and spirit that made me an instrument to impulsively announce the project is not mine. The Lord willed it that way.

'Hare Srinivasa!

13

ENDLESS WAITING FOR THE FLEETING MOMENT

It had already been 12 hours since the pilgrims entered the queue sheds. Yet they had no idea as to how long they had to wait patiently for the *'darshan'* of Lord Srinivasa of Tirumala.

The queue sheds were reverberating to the devotees' chantings, "Oh, the Lord of Seven Hills, Venkata Ramana, Govinda, Govinda". Silence punctuated the bouts of shouting. Some devotees were stretching to get over the strain of prolonged sitting on wooden benches. Hungry and tired, small kids were either crying for food or resting in their mothers' laps. The elderly were letting out sighs out of sheer fatigue. Fed up with the wait, grown up children wanted to know, "How long would it take to enter the temple?". Meanwhile, some one raised the "Govinda, Govinda" slogan. Involuntarily, most in the queue sheds responded with "Govinda, Govinda".

A teenaged boy was complaining to his father. "What is the point in calling the Lord so many times and for so long. We will only be straining our throats and collapsing in sheer exhaustion. We then manage to get into the queue to have *'darshan'* that perhaps lasts a second. A 12 -14 hour wait for a fleeting *'darshan'?* Why should we encounter so many difficulties to see our own God! " ... What a pathetic way to manage affairs ... The TTD administration is very insensitive to the needs of the piligrims...

It was not the first time that I heard devotees waiting in the queue cursing the TTD management. When I took over as Executive Officer, I entered the queue sheds anonymously and waited for 12 to 16 hours a couple of times to have first - hand experience of the devotees' plight. The reactions and the comments of the frustrated and exhausted pilgrims waiting for hours in not so comfortable surroundings had been as anticipated. In the few months I had been Executive Officer, I heard similar remarks many times. Whenever I heard such comments, I was consumed by a sense of shame. Something had to be done – done quickly. But what!

Driven by a passion to worship their family deity Lord Srinivasa and to seek His blessings, tens of thousands of ardent devotees would journey miles and miles braving many hardships and wait for hours on end in queue sheds only to have a glimpse of their resplendent deity just for a second.

A majority of the letters I received daily as Executive Officer concerned only about '*darshan*'.

"What sort of a '*darshan*' do we get when we come to Tirumala with offerings to fulfil our vows, after trudging the footpath and waiting in the queue sheds for hours? Have you ever stood in the queue and had '*darshan*'? Are you bothered only about VIPs? Don't you appreciate the common devotees' misery ...? ". Receiving such pointed and insulting letters was routine for an Executive Officer. I was no exception. Devotees, disenchanted with the '*darshan*', viewed Tirumala Hills as a topsy-turvy world in which all TTD employees acted as heartless brokers. Their discontent often led to wordy wars with TTD employees. The patience of devotees, who had waited for hours, was put to test further on their entry into the temple when the staff continuously directed them to move on and on.

Their anger against the staff on such occasions often reached a flash-point. The skirmishes robbed the devotees of a quiet and serene '*darshan*'. They returned disappointed. I studied the problem from all angles for a few months. I asked myself whether I could not at least minimise the inconveniences in the queue, if not facilitate better '*darshan*'? For the devotees in the queue, 'going to toilet' posed a problem. Once one entered the queue after leaving the queue sheds (toilets were available in the sheds only) one could not go to a toilet until one had '*darshan*' and come out after a couple of hours. I saw some elderly people abandoning even *'darshan'* and walking out of the temple queue in their uncontrollable urge to go to the toilet.

As I stood at the flag mast in the temple one day and saw an elderly devotee rushing out cursing his fate and the TTD management, I prayed to the Lord whether I could not do anything to help such people. The Lord would not respond. But a TTD senior employee, who seemed to have read my mind, suggested, "Sir, if mobile toilet boxes were stationed beside the queue outside the temple, devotees could enter the temple after relieving themselves". Great idea! I implemented the suggestion within a few days and also provided a tap for washing legs and hands. I received a number of letters appreciating for this seemingly simple facility.

One day I was upset when I saw a woman hitting a door threshold and falling as she lifted her child to have a glimpse of the Lord near *'padi kavili'* (where the offerings to the Lord are counted). Her husband expressed his annoyance with the Lord, "Can't you do away the door thresholds?".

I too wondered why the hurdles like door thresholds stood in the way of devotees having a fleeting glimpse of Him. Glimpsing the magnificent Lord from a distance the devotees would not pay attention to anything else including these doorsteps. Their irritation was understandable. Just as the question, the answer too popped up immediately. (Who gave me the answer?). In a couple of weeks, I gave shape to the Idea. Pilgrims would no longer experience the thresholds because ramps were provided at the doors near the *'padi kavili'* and upto the sanctum sanctorum. We also got a long wooden platform matching the doorstep height installed between the doors of the sanctum sanctorum and the *'padi kavili'*.

The devotees' response to these two seemingly simple measures was tremendous. As they get on to the ramp at the *'padi kavili'* door threshold, the pilgrims walk on the wooden platform and have *'darshan'* of the Lord till they reach the sanctum sanctorum. As they sight the Lord's bewitching form, they go into a devotional trance, shed tears of joy and shout

"Govinda, Govinda" right from the *'padi kavili'* door, forgetting all the fatigue caused by prolonged, restless waiting in the queue sheds. We could thus provide the devotees an opportunity to view the Lord for a longer period.

But that was small consolation. The main problem of reducing the devotees' waiting in the queue defied any solution. In another initiative, we arranged for the circulation of cool fresh air on the way from *'Ramulavari Meda'* (beyond *'padi kavili'*) to the sanctum sanctorum. As a result, the pilgrims and staff were spared suffocation for want of fresh air which aggravated their irritation and restlessness. We also introduced the system of shifting the staff near the sanctum sanctorum, every two or three hours, it is these employees who literally pull and push pilgrims. Consequently, instances of the staff venting their fatigue on pilgrims came down. But the core problem of reducing the waiting time in the queue was yet to be resolved.

I spent sleepless nights over the problem. Occasionally, I thought, "Why should I worry about it? After all, whether a pilgrim has satisfactory *'darshan'* or not depends on his destiny and God's grace".... If that was the way the Lord willed it let it be. However, in the next breath, I felt, "Whatever be the dictates of the destiny, what is my role as TTD Executive Officer? Is not looking after devotee's comforts my primary responsibility?

Determined to sort out the *'darshan'* issue for good, I used to stand before the Lord in the sanctum sanctorum and pray, spend several hours observing the moving pilgrim queues, and seek their suggestion from temple staff. The time spent there was worthwhile in that it revealed several things, which I would not have known otherwise. The several hours I spent in the sanctum sanctorum provided me an insight into the movement of the queue line, problems faced by the pilgrims, satisfaction levels etc.

The scenarioa used to be like this. The queue line from *'padi kavali'* enters *'bangaru vakili'* on the right side, covers the hall and enters the narrow *'Ramuluvarimeda'* and finally the

'Kulasekarapadi' adjoining the sanctum. When the pilgrims reach the sanctum they move two or three feet to the left, corresponding to the width of the sanctum's opening. From there, the queue turns back. In the short span of their covering two or three feet to the left, they come nearest to the Lord to have *'darshan'*. Because of the pressure to faciliatate *'darshan'* to a large number of pilgrims every hour, the TTD deploys a number of employees to keep the line moving. Standing on either side of the queue line they use all techniques - goading, pleading, shouting, pushing and pulling to make pilgrims move faster. Every pilgrim wants a peaceful, undisturbed *'darshan'*, which has to be managed during these three or four seconds covering the four-foot wide opening.

These three or four seconds the pilgrim spends nearest to the Lord ultimately decide whether he/she has satisfactory *'darshan'* or not. *'Darshan'* is the ultimate dream a pilgrim seeks to realise.

To my horror, I noticed that the pilgrim was disturbed, shouted at, or forced to take a number of small, small decisions– all distracting his attention. In one's entire trip starting from one's home, till one's return, these three seconds are the busiest. But the pilgrim does everything other than having *'darshan'*. Naturally, the pilgrim, feels so cheated and frustrated that he or she takes it out on the nearest temple employee.

It is interesting to make an analysis of what the pilgrim is subjected to during those crucial three or four seconds. The pilgrim finds himself in a packed queue line which has three persons abreast. For every four or five feet there is a temple volunteer to make sure the line moves fast. At the crucial place, near the triangle where the pilgrim moves from the right to the left covering three or four steps in front of the sanctum, volunteers/temple officials are deployed. However, these temple staff do not stand between the God and pilgrims. That privilege is taken by the temple priests. Three priests are placed on the other side of the queue, that is the Lord's side. They literally and figuratively stand between the Lord and the devotee - one on either side and one in the middle covering those four feet. On one side, a priest holds the *'theertham'* offering it to devotees, and on the other side, a priest holds the *'satari'*, placing it on the head of the devotees. The middle one asks the devotees to move fast. Of course he helps the administration in ensuring that the line moves fast. The devotee is disinclined to move away as he/she stands before the Lord. Moving the queue quickly, however, is necessary. Giving *'theertham'* is a must. *'Satari'* signifies the blessing of the Lord, as it carries the symbolic feet of the Lord. However, the pilgrim's attention is on good, undisturbed, peaceful *'darshan'*.

"Are we helping the pilgrim to have satisfactory *'darshan'* and realise his/her dream or creating a nightmare?".

Thus I learnt that the *'teertham'* and *'satari'* rituals disrupted the devotees' concentration and prevented them from seeing the Lord even for a second to their heart's content. In the absence of senior officials on occasions, I was told, the priests stretched their hands for *'dakshina'* from devotees even as they offered *'teertham'* and *'satari'*. Thus the pilgrims concentration was all the more disturbed not only by *'teertham'* and *'satari'* but also by the need to pull out their purses and offer change to the priests and clean their hands before and after taking *'teertham'*. After travelling for days and waiting in the queue for hours, a devotee would like to stand before Lord Srinivasa and say his prayers. But one was deprived of the pleasure because one was kept otherwise busy with *'teertham'* and *'satari'* rituals, offering *'dakshinas'* to the priests, feeding the *'teertham'* to children and cleaning and wiping one's hands.

Between the *'tertham'* and *'satari'*, the pilgrims, had one clear uninterrupted 'second' to have communion with the Lord. Generally, the third archaka in the middle would interfere with the pilgrim only after a second or two. I noticed that a majority of the pilgrims, during that undisturbed moment with the Lord, would bow down with folded hands closed their eyes, to offer prayers.

Prayer in our culture is identified with *'dhyana'* i.e., communicating with the Lord with mind's eye. Therefore, closing one's eyes in prayer is an involuntary reflex. Of course, during this indulgence, the third priest does his duty asking the pilgrim to move to be serviced by his colleague with the *'satari'*.

I promptly withdrew the middle priest, as there were volunteers posted behind the queue line, to do the job.

I wondered if the *'teertham'* and *'satari'* rituals could not be shifted outside the sanctum sanctorum so that the devotee's concentration was not distracted. It should be easy to implement the idea because neither the priests nor the TTD had anything to lose. The pilgrim without being disturbed, could get three to four seconds of quiet *'darshan'*. "What a great idea!" Feeling so< I decided to implement it straightway, but I could not. The priests resisted, saying, "For centuries we have been giving *'teertham'* and *'satari'* here only. Do you want to breach the tradition? Nothing doing". The talks I held with *'archaka mirasidars'*, scholars and temple laureates did not provide any solution. They wanted the tradition to be respected. They argued that 'the pilgrim' would feel bad if *'theertham'* and *'satari'* were not offered in the presence of the Lord. They were in no mood to appreciate the rationale behind my proposal. Tired of arguing with them, as usual I turned to the Lord and prayed, "Oh Lord, this is beyond me. I wanted this to be done in the interest of the devotees. If you deem it right, you will have to get it done in your own way".

Torn between a great idea and my inability to execute it, I spent a night. Whenever I woke up, I prayed to the Lord seeking a solution. But the Lord would not speak.

The next day, a VIP – perhaps the Endowments Minister or a central minister - came to visit the temple. Some politicians and officials followed the VIP for *'darshan'*. After the *'darshan'*, they stood in line on either side from the sanctum sanctorum up to *'Ramulavari Meda'*. I stood beside the VIP. The *'aarthi'* was over. The priests went on offering *'teertham'*, and *'satari'* after *'aarti'* to all. I stood distracted as I had not been able to implement a good idea.

This thought process of mine was interrupted, as I heard Some one saying "Sir, you have forgotten to offer me *'teertham'* and *'satari'*. I turned that side. The priests, who had gone to the end of the line offering *'teertham'* and *'satari'* left him out and began offering them to the people on the other side. In response to his call, the priests offered him also *'teertham'*, *'satari'* and *'aarti'*. The moment I saw what was happening, I found the solution to the problem. I proceeded there briskly and directed the priests, "Stand here only and offer *'teertham'* and *'satari'* to all pilgrims returning after *'darshan'*". That would be about 20 feet from the entrance to the sanctum sanctorum.

My sudden directive stunned the priests. They tried to peddle their old arguments. I did not give them any scope. "If you have not breached the tradition by coming up to the *'Ramulavari Meda'* entrance today to offer *'teertham'* and *'satari'*, what would happen if you do it ever day like this? It shall be done this way from this moment......"

They would not keep quiet. "According to the age-old tradition, *'teertham'* and *'satari'*......"

"It doesn't matter. Whenever VIPs come, you are anyway coming up to this point to offer *'teertham'* and *'satari'*. Hereafter, you are providing them for every pilgrim only at *'Ramulavari Meda'* entrance."

They raised another point. "For long, the devotees have been accustomed to taking *'teertham'* and *'satari'* standing in front of the Lord and having *'darshan'*. If we change the practice, we may be hurting their feelings..."

"No problem. If any one questions you, blame the change on me. I will take care of myself". They had no alternative. How did the idea flash across my mind that day? Every day, there were VIPs in the temple and I observed almost every day the priests, moving up and down with the *'teertham'* and *'satari'*. Why had the idea not struck me earlier? Why??

In course of time, the TTD persuaded the priests to offer *'teertham'* and *'satari'* outside *'padi kavili'* in the prakaram.

Thus, we enabled a devotee to have uninterrupted and undisturbed *'darshan'* of the Lord for two or three seconds more. The measure was so greatly appreciated that I received more than a thousand letters.

However, the problem of indefinite wait in the queue sheds remained. In a day, only 17 to 18 hours could be allocated for *'darshan'* as the rest of the time was needed for *'sevas'* to the Lord. After all, even in Tirumala, a day has only 24 hours.

We were fairly certain about the number of people who could be provided *'darshan'* on a particular day in the week, depending upon the type of *'sevas'* performed on that day. However, we were not very clear about the number of persons who could have *'darshan'* in one hour. Installation of an electronic recording machine gave us an idea about the number of persons cleared in each hour. But, the figures varied drastically between one hour and another. Hence, we wanted to conduct a time and motion study.

The results were interesting. If the volunteers did not ask the devotees to "move on, move on", only 400 to 500 could have *'darshan'* per hour. If the volunteers asked the devotees to move on, the queue moved faster and enabled 800 to 900 people to have *'darshan'*. If the volunteers pressured them shouting to 'move on', 1000 to 1200 people could have *'darshan'*. If they touched and nudged the devotees, the number could go up to 1400-1500 and if they pushed, the number could shoot up to 1800 to 2000. If they dragged and pulled them, 2200 to 2300 could have *'darshan'*. All this happened when the *'darshan'* was not interrupted. But in those days, the *'darshan'* timings were not convenient. *'Dharma darshan'* started after the early morning *'suprabhatam'*. It was halted for an hour for cleaning *'Suddhi'* and *'tomala seva'* and resumed later. After an hour, it was stopped for *'archana'*. The *'dharma darshan'* resumed after *'archana'* had to be stopped again for *'naivedyam'*. Thereafter, depending on the day of the week, some special *'arjita seva'* like *'tiruppavada,' 'sahasrakalasabhishekam'* etc were performed. The *'dharma darshan'* would be resumed only after those *'sevas'* and *'naivedyam'*. By and large, the *'dharma darshan'* continued uninterrupted only after 10 a.m.

The first *'dharma (free) darshan'* would begin after *'suprabhatam'* only at 3-30 a.m. For that, the queue sheds would be opened at 12 midnight. To enter the queue sheds at 12 midnight, the devotees would wait three to four hours outside the queue sheds. Thus the first batch to have *'darshan'* had to wait six hours for the *'darshan'*. As several *'sevas'* followed , the queue line could not be continued. Generally, the devotees in one queue shed would be allowed to have *'darshan'*. It meant that 500 people could go in for *'darshan'* during that period. After *'tomala seva'*, another 500 devotees in the second shed would be allowed. Then the *'archana seva'* intervened. The *'darshan'* after *'archana'* would begin at 6 a.m. In between there were other *'sevas'* like *'suddhi'*, *'koluvu'*, and *'alankarana'*. Thus, between 3-30 a.m. and 7-30 a.m., at best only 1500 devotees could have *'dharmadarshan'*. Thereafter, two or three days in a week, there were *sevas* like *'tiruppavada' 'sahasrakalishabhisekham' and 'abhisekham'*. Uninterrupted *'darshan'* before 10 a.m. was thus impossible. Therefore, if one went near the queue sheds around 9-10 p.m and if one was not in the first 1500, one could have *'darshan'* only after 10-12 hours. That was the minimum waiting period. But the average was between 18 and 20 hours. Some had the misfortune of waiting for more than 30 hours. You could only imagine as to what they did waiting endlessly: *'Archana'* for the TTD Administration, particularly to the Executive Officer.

My intensive study revealed that frequent interruption of *'dharma darshan'*, spawned most of the problems. If the *'dharma darshan'* could be organised without any interruption, larger numbers of people (1800 to 2000) per hour depending on the rush for the day could be sent into the sanctum sanctorum, reducing the waiting time. The problem was simple. But where was the solution. I had to turn to the Lord and pray, "You alone have to bale me out".

Against such a backdrop, I used to receive a large number of letters of anger, anguish and frustration. One such strong worded letter disturbed me. "I went to the queue sheds at 9-00 p.m. and was sent into the fourth shed at 12 midnight. I was told that the people in the first queue shed would have *'darshan'* at 3-00 a.m. We could not have *'darshan'* until 10-00 a.m. Why? Did the people in the first three sheds have *'darshan'* for seven hours? Or did you make us scapegoats for the sake of VIPs? Why don't you allocate a separate time slot for VIP *'darshan'*? Why do you harass us by sending us inside the temple in instalments?" Many people had written similar letters in the past. But this letter landed at a different time. The author intriguingly happened to be one Mr. Srinivasa!

Within minutes, I stumbled on a solution to the problem. The VIP *'darshans'* referred to by the letter writer meant (for me) the *'sevas'*, which interrupted the *'dharma darshan'*. If all the *'sevas'* could be performed one after the other early in the morning and *'dharma darshan'* provided. Thereafter without any interruption, up to 2000 people could be cleared per hour. If *'suprabhatam'*, *'tomala seva'*, *'archana'* and some specified *'sevas'* were to be completed between 3-00 a.m. and 6-00 a.m, *'dharma darshan'* could begin at 6 a.m and continue until 7 00 p.m without interruption. The queue would move faster because of uninterrupted *'darshan'* for 13 hours. As *'dharma darshan'* would begin only after 6 a.m the early enthusiasts could start from 3 a.m. More number of people could have *'darshan'* with less waiting period. Between 3 a.m and 6 a.m all paid *'seva darshans'* and all VIPs could be covered.

Immediately, I consulted Peshkars Vasu, Krishnaswamy and *'pare pattedar'* Seshadri, Santanam and others. I also discussed the matter with temple priests, laureates and scholars and asked them to consider the proposal for the reorganisation of temple *'seva'* timings. There were some murmurs about the lack of time between first *'naivedyam'* and the second and feeble protests over *'seva'* systems going on for centuries being tampered with.

Miraculously, we could finalise everything in a few weeks. But for some mild protests from priests over interference with age-old traditions and *'potu mirasidars'* (grievance over preparing most of the *'prasadams'* early in the morning), everything went off smoothly. The TTD Board too approved the proposal. The result.

The devotees would reach the queue sheds from 3-00 a.m. At 6-00 a.m., the queue sheds would be opened enabling devotees to straightway go for *'darshan'*. The first batch in the queue sheds would generally wait for three hours. The waiting period for the second batch would go down because the *'darshan'* would go on uninterrupted. The waiting for the third batch would still be less and for the fourth batch lesser.

The transformation was so significant that the wait, which used to be 12 hours going up to 30 hours sometimes in 1978, got reduced to three hours. With the running of uninterrupted *'darshan'*, there used to be no waiting in the queue sheds for the pilgrims joining the moving queue. Within one hour, they could have *'darshan'*.

When the waiting time in the queue sheds went down, the number of days the devotees stayed in TTD *'choultries'* and cottages also came down. Consequently, the number of pilgrims using *'choultries'* and cottages went up. Devotees sleeping on roads for want of accommodation was a thing of the past.

To reduce the queues at the bus stand for buses to Tirumala and to stagger the inflow of pilgrims into Tirumala, we spoke to the Railway authorities and ensured that trains arrived between 5-00 a.m. and 10 a.m., instead of all of them arriving between 5-00 a.m. and 7-00 a.m. As a result, the wait in the bus stand for buses to go to Tirumala also was reduced, resulting in a staggered entry into the *'darshan'* lines.

A great devotee of the Lord and senior journalist Mr. Tirumalai working with The Illustrated Weekly of India who had written a caustic article about the TTD and the plight of the pilgrims a year earlier, met me to express his appreciation and happiness. "What a number of changes have you ushered in respect of *'darshan'*. What great ideas!" he said in wonder. I also wondered. Did I do? I knew that all these ideas were known and very simple – and definitely not mine. They got implemented .... How? By Whose grace?

14

'MIRASIDARS' BOW TO THE WILL OF THE GOD

"Akasatpatitam toyam yadhagachchati sagaram
Sarvadeva namaskarah Kesavam pratigachchati"

Prayers offered to all Gods ultimately reach only Srihari, just as all the water that rains from the skies falling at different places and flowing in different directions eventually reaches the ocean.

As I had *'darshan'* of Tirumala Srinivasa one day, this verse struck me and paved the way for solving a complex problem. The next few days witnessed a metamorphosis in the Tirumala Srinivasa's *'Kalyanotsavam'* ritual.

× × ×

The most popular among *'arjita sevas'* to Tirumala Srinivasa is *'kalyanotsavam'*. Hundreds of devotees take part in *'kalyanotsavam'* these days. Forty or fifty years ago, devotees and their families planning to perform the *'kalyanotsavam'* received temple honours, going by what my grandfather had told me. The devotee and his family were provided accommodation at the devasthanam *'Divanam' (official Guest House)* atop the hills and taken to the temple in a procession to the accompaniment of *'Mangala Vadya'* music. Those days, the *'kalyanotsavam'* was not a daily affair. Therefore, there was no limit on the number of participants. As it was an *'arjita seva'* whenever a devotee paid for the *'seva'* it would be performed. On an average, five or six *'kalyanostavams'* per month were being performed. The *'prasadam'* supplied to the devotee *'grihasta'* would be sufficient to feed 25-30 family members. As *'kalyanotsavams'* increased over time, the number of participants per family was restricted to five and the total

'Kalyanotsavams' per day to 20 as the venue could accommodate about 100 people. That was the situation in 1978 when I took over as the Tirumala Tirupati Devasthanam Executive Officer.

× × ×

The *'kalyanotsavams'* were performed in *'ranga mantapam'*, to the left of the*'maha dwaram'* (main entrance) in the main temple complex. The number of householders paying Rs.1250 each and taking part in the *'kalyanotsavam'* began to rise gradually. Because the *'ranga mantapam'* had limited space, the number of householders that could take part in the ritual was restricted to 20 and increased to 25 at the discretion of the Executive Officer. It had become routine for temple officials to warn that unless the householders booked in advance, they might not be able to take part in the *'kalyanotsavam'*. Many people visited Tirupati hoping to perform *'kalyanotsavam'* the same day. For want of room, they could not be entertained. Even if place were to be available, it was not always possible to accommodate the devotees because a fixed quantity of *'prasadams'* had to be prepared for each *'kalyanotsavam'* warranting advance notice. The devotees used to represent, "Sir, don't disappoint us. We have come from far to fulfil our *'kalyanotsavam'* vow". When their pleas were turned down, they berated temple officials as inconsiderate and insensitive. The Executive Officer had to go through the predicament of pretending to be not hearing such comments, which could neither be swallowed nor rebutted.

I asked myself, "Why can't we entertain devotees' requests for performing *'kalyanotsavam?"* Since devotee satisfaction should be the prime consideration, I began to study all aspects. But for every one step that I took, I had to retrace two steps. In no time, I realised that the problem was not so simple as it appeared to be on the surface and that a solution was highly difficult.

There were two major problems: First, the *'ranga mantapam'* was small in area, and could accommodate only a limited number of householders and their families. Secondly, the *'mirasidars'*, a powerful lobby in temple affairs, resisted even a minor change in the *'kalyanotsavam'* - a major source of their income. In many matters, the *'mirasidars'* had gone to courts ranging from the Tirupati magistrate court to the Supreme Court challenging proposed changes.

In this context, one should know a little about the *'mirasi'* set-up at Tirumala. *'Mirasi'* refers to the inherited right to take part in temple rituals. Those who perform worship rituals are called *'archaka mirasidars'* and those who prepare *'prasadams'* in the kitchen, *'potu mirasidars'*. *'Jiyyangars'* have inherited right to evaluate the quality and the quantity of materials supplied for temple rituals and to ensure that they are actually utilised. *'Golla mirasidars'* wake up *'archakas'* and *'jiyyangars'* early in the morning and accompany them to the temple with a lighted torch. The descendants of Annamayya, who recite devotional songs during the Lord's *'ekanta seva'*, are part of the *'mirasi'* institution. Subsequently, all these mirasis were abolished following a judgement of the Supreme Court.

According to the age-old tradition, the *'mirasidars'* are not paid in cash for their services. Instead, they get a specified share in the *'prasadams'* offered to Lord Srinivasa as *'naivedyam'*. For instance, for the *'kalyanotsavam'*, the *'mirasidars'* get 25 in each *'padi'* of 51 large *'laddus'* prepared as *'prasadam'*. Whether it is *'vadas'*, *'jilebi'*, *'pulihora'*, *'chakra pongali' or 'dadhyodanam'*, *'archaka mirasidars'* and *'potu mirasidars'* and others get a share. The *'mirasidars'* run a separate counter in the temple premises itself and sell their share of *'prasadams'* to devotees.

At the conclusion of the ritual around 4-00 p.m., *'potu'* Brahmins carry the *'prasadams'* in big baskets and deliver them to *'kalyanotsavam'* participants at their cottages. Many pilgrims used to complain that the *'prasadams'* were so large in quantity that they did not know what to do with them. In the olden days, when the *'prasadam'* itself was taken as food and the number of family members was large, it posed no problem. Sometime, finding *'takers'* was difficult. More so when the *'grihastas'* were in a hurry to return to their homes. We arranged for the free distribution such *'prasadams'* to devotees when some of the *'kalyanotsavam'* participants felt the *'prasadam'* was too much for them. The entire share of the temple's *'Anna prasadam'* was anyway distributed free to the pilgrims. But, as the number of pilgrims were many, only a few pilgrims got the *'prasadam'*. Hence, we also introduced the system of distributing small *'laddus'* to ensure that each pilgrim got some *'prasadam'* free of least. The *'mirasidars'* turned down the TTD administration request to sell their share of the 'Anna *prasadam'* to the temple so that the same could be distributed free to pilgrims in the queue line.

If 25 *'kalyanotsavams'* were performed every day, each *'archaka mirasidar'* get 150 large-sized *'laddus'* at the rate of six *'laddus'* on each *'kalyanotsavam'* ticket. *'Potu mirasidars'* too get a similar share. They also got large quantities of *'anna prasadam'* which they sold to pilgrims. They were not in favour of selling the *'prasadam'* to the temple itself as the resultant income was liable for income tax.

Besides the distribution of *'prasadams'*, the issue of materials used in the performance of *'homam'* as part of the *'kalyanotsavam'* haunted me. In *'kalyanotsavam'*, *'homam'* is performed. Only one *'homam'* is performed irrespective of the number of householders taking part in the *'kalyanotsavam'*. Temple authorities, however, had to supply materials as if a number of *'homams'*, are perform based on the number of participant householders. As the number increased, the quantity of materials like *'ghee'* supplied for the *'homam'* too went up, as per the scale laid down for each *'kalyanostavam'*. Once the *'seva* ' was over, *'mirasidars'* were entitled to the *'homa sesham'* that is the left over unused items.

"Why should the supply of *'homa'* materials be increased in proportion to the number of participants when the *'archakas'* performed only one *'homam'*?" Thinking on these lines, temple officials decided to supply materials only for one *'homam'*. The *'archaka mirasidars'* went to court and got the decision stayed.

The prices of *'ghee'* and other materials were going up. As the number of *'kalyanotsavams'* went up, the costs too escalated. The rate for the *'seva* ' could not be raised as the pilgrims had already been raising a hue and cry. My predecessor Executive Officers got entangled in litigation when they tried to control cost by reducing the quantum of *'homa'* materials supplied. To summarise, the TTD was helpless in bringing about any changes in the ritual (barring the raising of rates) and consequently had to subsidise the cost of conducting *'kalyanotsavams'*.

To satisfy the devotees, I arranged for the performance of 35 *'kalyanotsavams'* in the same *'ranga mantapam'* by improvising changes like re-arranging *'vahanas'* seats. Yet, every day the requests for the *'seva'* from a number of householders had to be turned down. I suffered silently as it had become a major daily irritant. Far from enabling the devotees coming from hundreds of miles to worship the Lord by performing *'kalyanotsavam'*, we disappointed them by spurning their requests. Who had given us such powers? For whose sake had the post of the Executive Officer been created? If facilities could not be provided to the devotees, why should I hold the post?

Unable to restrain myself, I bluntly asked the *'mirasidars'* one day, "Why do you refuse to cooperate with the TTD in serving the devotees? Which God has directed you to behave this way?"

Some of the *'mirasidars'*, who appreciated my agony, said in a hushed tone: "Sir, we don't have any objection. But all others should agree. They are concerned about forgoing their centuries old rights" But I did not lose hope. I remembered freedom fighter Surendranath Banerjee's statement that "Optimism and determination would ultimately triumph". But, why did the Lord tolerate all this? Should I keep quiet? It was the same Lord who gave me these thoughts and tormented me. I did not give up. I had a detailed discussion with TTD Trust Board members. For days on end, I talked to legal experts. I repeatedly consulted the *'asthana vidwans'* or temple laureates. Even as I continued the discussions, I proposed the shifting of the *'kalyanotsavam'* venue. I had to drop the idea of shifting *'kalyanostavam'* to outside the temple premises as there was great resistance. I had to content with shifting it from *'ranga mantapam'* to another place inside the temple to enable more number of devotees to participate. Towards that end, I got the stores and other materials on the southern side of the temple *'prakraram'* shifted elsewhere.

I could provide a *'mantapam'* in the *'prakaram'* enabling up to 200 householders to take part in *'kalyanotsavam'* along with their family members. Yet, I could not get the *'kalyanotsavam'* conducted there, despite there being demand for the *'seva'*. It was because six varieties of *'prasadams'* like *'laddus'* needed for 200 *'kalyanotsavams'* had to be prepared at the rate of 51 pieces of each *'prasadam'* (One *'Padi'*) for each *'kalayanam'*. Time for preparation and a place for preparing all this were major constraints. As the storing of materials and cooking had to be done inside the temple premises only, the magnitude of the problem increased directly in proportion to the number of *'kalyanotsavams'*. Whatever one attempted to do without taking the *'archaka mirasidars'* into confidence would end up only in litigation. The talks I held with elders had failed and none could offer me a solution. Mine turned out to be a cry in the wilderness.

× × ×

One Thursday evening, I stood before the Lord in the temple and poured out my agony and anguish in the fond hope that the Lord who is above all emotions like pleasure and pain, desire and hatred, would show me a way out. Were I to tightly clasp the Lord's feet and tell Him that I would not move until He provided me a solution? What a crazy idea! The Executive Officer's reign extended only up to the *'kula sekharapadi'* outside the sanctum sanctorum. He could not even step into the sanctum sanctorum, leave alone touch the statue. That was the priests' or *'mirasidars'* sole prerogative.

What was the situation before the advent of the Executive Officers long ago? Although I stood before the Lord's statue, my mind raced back to bygone decades and centuries. There were priests even when hardly a few devotees visited the Hills. And they were there when no *'kalyanam'* was performed on a day and even when just one or two *'kalyanotsavams'* were performed during a month. When people did not live atop the Hills a century ago, priests used to go up the Hills daily from Tirupati through forests, perform *'puja'* and return. When once the pilgrims started coming in large numbers, the priests began to live atop the Hills for pilgrims' convenience. Thus, for generations these priests had been serving the Lord by performing all the rituals from *'suprabhatham'* to *'ekanta seva'*, even when people did not visit Tirumala or deposit their offerings in the *'hundi'*. In course of time, the pilgrim traffic and the income increased. Some paid *'sevas'* were introduced *'arjita'*. Sevas as the families of *'archaka mirasidars'* too proliferated with their sons and grandsons coming into the picture. It would take on an average 16 years for an *'archaka mirasidar'* family to get its turn to perform the rituals for one year. Similar was the case with the other *'mirasidars'*. What motivated them to serve the Lord when the temple income was not high in good old days? Their share in the *'seva'* income had now gone up because of the increase in pilgrim traffic. Their higher share of income now attracted everybody's attention.

Enveloped in such thoughts, I stood before the Lord when some temple official disturbed me saying, "You have an urgent phone call". But that was the beginning of a deep introspection. I ceased to be emotional and began to think more rationally. The urge to do something for the devotees, however, did not die down.

How could I serve the devotees without rendering injustice to the *'archaka mirasidars'*? How should I bring down the subsidy burden on the TTD? I should enable as many people as possible to take part in the *'kalyanotsavam'*, without causing injustice to the priests. At the same time, neither the rate for the *'arjita seva'* nor the burden on the TTD should go up. How were these mutually conflicting goals to be realised?

× × ×

The next day happened to be Friday, when Venkateswara *'abhishekam'* takes place to Lord Srinivasa. As ordained by duty, I took part in the *'abhisheka seva'*. The milk the priests poured from above on the resplendent Lord Srinivasa finally flowed down to the feet whatever the intial point it fell upon. Involuntarily, I remembered the verse *"Akasatpatitam toyam yadhagachchati sagaram..."*. (The rain water that pours from the skies at different places finally reaches the ocean whatever route it may take in between.) Like lightning, an idea struck me. (Why at that spot only?). "What if we introduce a new type of *'kalyanotsava seva'* in the *'kalyanotsavam'* ritual? Whatever be the *'seva;* it is the worship of the Lord that matters. So long as there is no change in the ritual procedure, whoever performs whatever *'kalyanam',* the prayers go only to the Lord." In fact, the TTD management's powers were limited, for effecting any changes in the existing *'sevas'*, as it would amount to tampering with the existing practice and affects *'mirasidars'* share of income. There was no bar on introducing any new *'seva'*.

Thereafter, I did not waste a single moment. Emerging from the temple, I sent for *'Peshkars'* Krishnaswamy and Vasudevan, who looked after *'arjita sevas'*. I wanted them to consider the feasibility of introducing a special *'kalyanotsavam'*. I also consulted temple *'Asthana Vidwan'* laureate Appikatla Jagannadhacharyulu. "The idea is good but if the *'mirasidars'* go to court?" was the refrain of everybody.

My idea began to take shape. We could not make any changes in *'kalyanotsavam'* in its present form. In the new *'kalyanotsavam'* we proposed, there would not be any changes in the *'mantra'* or rituals. But the pomp and fanfare would be cut down. For each *'kalyanotsavam'* only two persons – husband and wife – and not five — would be allowed. Only two *'kalyanam laddus'* and two *'vadas'*, instead of basketfuls of *'prasadams'*, would be distributed. The householder would be presented an upper cloth and his wife, a blouse piece. Whatever be the number of such *'kalyanotsavams'*, materials for the conduct of only one *'homam'* would be supplied to the priests. There was no question of handing over the left over materials to the priests. Such special *'kalyanotsavams'* would be combined with the regular *'kalyanotsavams'*. Both *'kalyanotsavams'* would have one procedure and one *'mantram'* and performed simultaneously. The difference lay only in the *'seva'* ticket charge, the number of participants per ticket and in the quantum of *'prasadams'* distributed.

Since *'archakas'* had to perform the new *'kalyanotsava seva'* also and do the *'sankalpam'* for each participant, the devasthanam would pay them a specified amount for each *'kalyanotsavam'*. If the *'archaka mirasidars'* refused to perform the new *'kalyanotsavam'*. Along with the regular *'kalyanotsavam'*, they would have to perform this special *'kalyanastovam'* separately after the regular *'kalyanotsavam'* was over. The TTD had powers to make alternative arrangements if the *'archaka mirasidars'* did not come forward to perform any *'seva'* of the devasthanam.

We finalised the special *'kalyanotsavam'* proposal. The ticket for the special *'kalyanotsavam'* was fixed at Rs. 500 against the Rs.1250 for the regular, large *'kalyanotsavam'* (The current charges are Rs.750 and Rs.2500 for the special and large *'kalyanotsavam'* respectively.) Since *'anna prasadam'* distribution was not on the agenda in the special *'kalyanotsavam'*, the devotees need not make reservations weeks or days in advance. The demand on the temple kitchen *'potu'* could be managed. They could join the *'seva'* on any day of their choice. The devasthanam would pay Rs. 22 (of the Rs. 500 collected from householders) for each special *'kalyanotsavam'* to the *'mirasidars'* for their services.

The news of the special *'kalyanotsavam'* spread like wild fire and became the topic of discussion everywhere in temple circles. The *'mirasidars'* opposed the proposal. Even some TTD officials doubted the practicability of the proposal. The TTD Trust Board, however, welcomed it as a "revolutionary initiative, provided we can execute it" and gave its green signal. I had a face-to-face discussion with the *'mirasidars'*. To persuade the *'mirasidars'* I told them: "You are not going to lose anything by the special *'kalyanotsavam'* proposal. You do not get any share as no *'prasadams'* are involved. However, for each *'kalyanotsavam'* you will be paid Rs. 22. The new *'mantap'* facilitates the conduct of more than 200 *'kalyanotsavams'* a day. As the number of *'kalyanotsavams'* goes up your income too will go up proportionately". But they would not commit themselves. Two of the *'mirasidars'* who used to get the lion's share in *'prasadams'* (Dr. Ramana Deekhsitulu and Sri Narayana Deekshitulu) met me and said, "Although your argument is rational, we are not in a position to support you openly". Their moral support, however, boosted my confidence.

Finally, I discussed the proposal with legal experts and steeled myself for all eventualities, if the *'mirasidars'* went to court. I learnt that the *'mirasidars'* too had consulted lawyers and firmed up their line of action. Both sides were overwrought. Reviewing all the developments, I plunged into action in the firm belief that "there is no alternative if I have to render service to devotees and justice to the devasthanam". Accordingly, I sent notices to the *'mirasidars'*. I made it clear that the "devasthanam would utilise their services for this *'arjita seva'* also if they cooperate, subject to TTD Trust Board conditions". Quietly, one day I booked the first Rs.500 ticket for special *'kalyanostavam'* for my wife Gopika and me. I did not want to take any chances with any devotees as I had my own misgivings. Were the *'mirasidars'* not to cooperate? As a matter of abundant precaution, I directed 'P*eshkars*' Mr. Krishnaswamy and Mr. Vasudevan to make alternative arrangements too. They were directed to keep in readiness separate priests, and a separate *'homakundam'* and the required *'homa'* materials for a special *'kalyanotsavam'* for us. The arrangements were in place and nobody except three or four of us knew about them.

× × ×

The moment of reckoning finally arrived. My wife and I, who had paid Rs.500 for the special *'kalyanotsavam'*, sat with the householders who had paid Rs.1250 for the regular *'kalyanotsavam'* and asked the priests to begin the *'sankalpam'*. I was there as a householder and not as TTD Executive Officer. I showed them my Rs.500 ticket.

The *'archaka mirasidars'*, who had not anticipated the sudden introduction of the *'seva'* and participation by the Executive Officer himself as a householder, were thrown into utter confusion. The priests, who had been hoping for discussions and consultations for many days to come, were stunned. They had come to perform the regular *'kalyanotsavam'*. They looked at each other in bewilderment and all the *'mirasidars'* went into a huddle whispering to each other. Then, I chose to shout at the temple *'Peshkar'*, "Why are you delaying the matter? Are you performing the special *'kalyanostavam'* or not? Please arrange *'sankalpam'*.

Sri P.V.R.K. Prasad and Gopika Prasad performing the first "Special Kalyanotsovam" to the Lord.

The *'archaka mirasidars'* confabulated among themselves and as expected decided not to proceed further. At that point of time temple officers Krishnaswamy, Vasudevan, Seshadri and Santanam entered the scene with (government) priests and *'homa'* materials as planned earlier. The *'archaka mirasidars'* were flabbergasted. They could not approach the courts and get relief at such short notice. They had to decide one way or the other then and there. All the other *'grihastas'* who had been waiting for the regular *'kalyanostavam'* watched all this with curiosity, not knowing what was happening.

Finally, I told the *'archaka mirasidars'*: "You had better conduct the special *'kalyanotsavam'* for us along with others. Barring the *'prasadams'* aspect, the ritual for all of us is the same. If you cannot conduct the special *'kalyanotsavam'* for us, we will get the *'kalyanotsavam'* for ourselves conducted here itself, in front of this very *'homakundam'* and for this very Lord (processional idols), once the regular *'kalyanotsavam'* is over".

Although I uttered the words with bravado, I wondered whether I was committing any indiscretion as I watched the idols of Sridevi, Bhudevi and Srinivasa on the wedding platform. After all, I was responsible for all the tumult in the midst of so many householders. God should be observing me.

Meanwhile, the *'archaka mirasidars'* came to me. "Sir, please do not embarrass us. It does not befit an Executive Officer to sit like a householder and preempt an issue like this".

As I would not give up my demand, they climbed down.

For the first time in the Tirumala temple history, the *'archaka mirasidars'* though reluctantly, compromised on their rights and came forward to conduct the new *'arjita seva'* (special *'kalyanotsavam'*) as sought by the devasthanam.

I directed that from the next day onwards the special (mini) *'kalyanotsavam'* tickets should be sold to all who sought them. "No householder shall return disappointed on the ground the TTD did not permit him to perform *'kalyanotsavam'*," I said in a plain talk. The *'kalyanotsavams'* were shifted from the *'ranga mantapam'* to the newly constructed *'kalyana mantapam'* on the southern side of the temple. What a miracle! The number of special *'kalyanotsavams'* touched 100 a day in two weeks and spurted to 200 a day in a month. Gradually, we limited the number of large *'kalyanotsavams'* and increased the number of special (mini) *'kalyanotsavams'*. Isn't it a very simple idea? Why had it not been thought of earlier-by me-and others?

From where did the inspiration come? Which Power was behind it? The Lord willed it and timed it.

"Unjala Seva" being performed at the Samprokshana of the newly constructed 'Bedi Anjaneya' Temple in Tirumala.

In fact, I felt that it would have been ideal if a large *'kalyana mantapam'* were to be constructed in the midst of the present queue complex and the *'kalyanostavams'* performed there. All the pilgrims waiting for *'darshan'* can witness *'kalyanostavam'*. It was not possible, because the queue complex area was once a tank. I also thought of an alternative. Traditionally, all *'arjita sevas'* are conducted within the temple premises. But I was eager that as many devotees as possible should see the Lord during *'arjita sevas'*. That was why as a first step, we arranged an *'arjita seva'* in the name of *'sahasra deepalankarana'* (thousand lights 'seva') in the East temple street outside the temple. In a way, it was *'unjal seva'*. Since the processional idols were brought out of the temple for *'arjita seva'* once, we took them up to the renovated new Bedi Anjaneya Swamy temple on the occasion of sanctification of the temple and performed *'unjal'* in the Sannidhi Street. I felt that the future *'kalyanostavams'* too could be conducted outside the temples as the idols had been brought up to the end of Sanndhi Street once. In fact, we constructetd the *'asthana mantapam'* where 1000 *'kalyonstavams'* could be performed simultaneously. My sole objective was that as many devotees as possible (including those who did not buy the tickets) should see and enjoy the *'kalyanostavams'*.

But during my sojourn there, the *'kalyanotsavams'* did not take place outside the temple. Why could I not accomplish it?

Did it reflect my inability and helplessness? Or was it willed that way by the Power, beyond me?

15

DESTINY DECIDES EVEN 'DARSHAN'

The Chief Secretary and family who had set out from Madras by road were to reach Tirupati that evening. But there was no sign of them at 5 p.m., 6 p.m., 7 p.m., or even at 10 p.m. A call to their relatives in Chennai revealed that they had no information on their whereabouts after they had left. An ardent devotee of the Lord, the Chief Secretary, Mr. S. R. Ramamurthy, had been keen on taking part in Friday's *'abhisheka darshan'* of Lord Srinivasa at Tirumala.

Anxiety and concern about the safety of the Chief Secretary and his family mounted in me as they did not arrive as scheduled. My blood pressure shot up and I spent a sleepless night. Although I was TTD executive Officer, my post was a junior post of that of a Joint Secretary rank, four rungs below that of the Chief Secretary. All IAS and IPS officers ranging from a sub-collector to a principal secretary come under his jurisdiction. Those were the days when all officials were afraid of the Chief Secretary whether they were afraid of the Chief Minister or not. A Chief Secretary could, if he desired, bring about far-reaching changes in the administrative set-up. Even the Chief Minister would treat the Chief Secretary with a lot of respect and generally takes his advice.

Mr. Ramamurthy, who occupied such an exalted position, had expressed his desire to have *'abhisheka darshan'* of Lord Venkateswara twice or thrice to me.

"Prasad, I would like to have *'abhisheka darshan'*. However much I try, I have not been able to make it because of some impediment or the other. At least when you are Executive Officer, you should facilitate *'abhishka darshan'*, he told me very eagerly. I was surprised that he pleaded instead of ordering me. Should a Chief Secretary ask for such a small favour of an official who was way below him? I told him as much: "Sir, why do you speak in that vein? You can have any '*darshan*' you want. It will be arranged in a trice".

"We think so. But do you believe that '*darshan*' depends on our wishes? After I took over as Chief Secretary, I have planned to have '*abhisheka darshan*' many times but without success. Finally, I may retire without having the fortune of '*abhisheka darshan*', said the Chief Secretary in sadness.

It had been two years since I took over as TTD Executive Officer. Right at the beginning of my tenure, I had laid down clear-cut guidelines for taking care of VIPs on a visit to Tirumala. When once the Executive Officer laid down a policy, it would be strictly adhered to from the top to the bottom. It was neither difficult nor impossible to fulfil the '*darshan*' desire of a Chief Secretary.

That was why, I reassured the Chief Secretary, "Sir, it would be enough if you call me a day in advance whichever Friday you want to have '*abhisheka darshan*'. I will take care of everything. Just a phone call will do".

Still, he was diffident. As some doubt continued to haunt him. "We thought so even in the case of my brother-in-law Padmanabham. What happened?," Mr. Ramamurthy aired his apprehensions.

"Oh, that one!" I said and recollected what transpired.

× × ×

Some time earlier, I had called on the Chief Secretary by prior appointment to discuss TTD matters. A personification of purity and simplicity, Mr. Ramamurthy was a man of few words. Known as a very efficient administrator, he was an ardent devotee of Lord Srinivasa.

The moment I met him, Mr. Ramamurthy said, " Only this morning you figured in our discussion". I thought that something must have gone wrong when a Chief Secretary thought of a junior official. "Have I committed any indiscretion?" I asked him anxiously.

He laughed. "There is nothing of that sort. My brother-in-law works for Britannia. His long-standing desire has been to climb the hills and have Balaji *'darshan'*. Every time he plans the trip, he meets with some setback or the other and is forced to cancel his programme altogether. This time I told him that I would speak to you".

"Is that all?" I exclaimed.

"Don't dismiss it casually. Do you believe that Lord's *'darshan'* can be had as per our wishes? Anyway, I want Padmanabham to have the most satisfactory *'darshan'* with your help. Unless you take it up seriously, I am afraid history may repeat itself", Mr. Ramamurthy expressed his fear.

I assured Mr. Ramamurthy, "Leave the Padmanabham matter to me". I was confident of fulfilling the Chief Secretary's wish.

When I reached Begumpet airport to return to Tirupati the next morning, Mr Ramamurthy was there along with his brother-in-law. He had come merely to introduce Mr. Padmanabham to me. Mr. Ramamurthy reminded me, "Somehow you should ensure an unforgettable *'darshan'* experience to Padmanabham".

I smiled to myself and wondered what appeared to be his antediluvian concerns. Why should he be worried when I gave him the assurance as Executive Officer? "Leave it to me, Sir. I will take care of everything." So saying, I boarded the flight along with Mr. Padmanabham.

As per the details given by Mr Padmanabham, a few of his friends from Madras were to join him in Tirupati that day. All of them would be setting out to Tiruumala by walk around 3-30 p.m. They were to have *'darshan'* in the evening, stay overnight and have *'suprabhata darshan'* and *'archanaantara darshan'* the next morning.

As Mr. Padmanabham happened to be a close relative of the Chief Secretary, who repeatedly voiced his concern over *'darshan'*, I took special interest in making all the arrangements. The Reception Officer at Tirupati would attend to him and his friends until they left for Tirumala. A security guard would accompany them on their uphill climb. Once they reached Tirumala, the Tirumala Reception Officer would attend to all of their needs including *'darshan'* and be with them until they left Tirumala. Once everything was in place, I got lost in my work again.

When the phone rang at 3-30 p.m., I lifted the receiver thinking that the Tirupati Reception Officer perhaps wanted to inform me of the departure of Mr. Padmanabham and party to Tirumala. It was from the Tirupati Reception Office only. But what I heard was different.

"Sir, we have loaded the luggage of Mr. Padmanabham and party into the car. We have also arranged for their being dropped at Alipiri for the walk up the hill. But shortly before getting into the car, Mr. Padmanabham all of a sudden started writhing with unbearable stomach ache. We have had no opportunity to ascertain exactly what he was suffering from. Even now, he is still in great pain. We are unable to stand the sight...." I cut him short and directed him to take Mr.Padmanabham straightway to Ruia Hospital. I told him that I would be coming there and immediately hopped into the car. The doctors, who examined Mr. Padmanabham had given him palliatives. "Kidney stones have caused the pain. There is no danger. But he needs total rest for a few days", the doctors made it very clear.

Mr. Padmanabham's friends went up the hill and had satisfactory *'darshan'*. But Mr. Padmanabham spent the evening in bed, depressed. "How is it that although you have made all the arrangements as Executive Officer, I could not have *'darshan*", he asked me in despair. I had no answers.

He was then not in a position to move. I called up the Chief Secretary and narrated all that had happened. "Sorry, Sir. I could not facilitate *'darshan'* for Mr. Padmanabham". He sighed. 'Oh... once again? .... Very unfortunate ... Leave it, you can't be blamed He was simply not destined to have *'darshan'*. It was the Lord's wish".... He said understandingly. As per doctors' advice, we sent Mr Padmanabham by flight to Chennai, the next morning

× × ×

Against such a backdrop, Mr. Ramamurthy telephoned me to inform that he was planning to have *'abhisheka darshan'* that coming Friday. I told him reassuringly, "Sir, simply because something happened to your brother-in-law, why should you think it would recur in your case too? Don't worry; come down and I will look after everything. (In whose hands is looking after?). Just call me before you start", I told him.

As he feared, a few hours before he was to leave Hyderabad by flight, the Chief Minister sent for him to attend an urgent meeting. It resulted in the cancellation of the Chief Secretary's programme for that week. Since he was very keen on *'abhiskha darshan'*, he sought and obtained the Chief Minister's clearance to visit Tirupati the following Thursday and Friday.

The new week rolled in and Thursday dawned. As planned, Mr. Ramamurthy was to leave with his family from Mr. Padmanabham's residence in Madras at 3-30 p.m. and arrive at Tirumala by 6-30 - 7-30 p.m. He was to have *'darshan'* during *'pulangi seva'* that night and *'abhisheka seva'* the next morning.

Having fine-tuned all the arrangements, I called up the Chief Secretary at Madras at 3 p.m. The Chief Secretary said, "We are delayed a bit. We will be starting in an hour". That was the last time I spoke to him on that day.

When I phoned Chennai at 8-30 p.m., I was told that the party had left at 6-30 p.m. and they might reach Tirupati around 10 p.m. But they had not arrived at Tirupati by 10 p.m. Beyond 11 p.m., the Alipiri gate at the entrance to the *'ghat'* road remained shut those days. I, therefore, entrusted an officer with the job of ensuring that the Chief Secretary's car reached Tirumala safely whatever be the hour in the night. Sitting in my camp office atop the hill, I instructed my staff to inform me the moment the Chief Secretary's car entered the *'ghat'* road. I once again reviewed the arrangements for the *'abhisehka darshan'* of the Chief Secretary and his family in the morning. The *'pulangi seva'* for that night was over. But Mr. Ramamurthy and his family had not turned up. I called up Madras at 11-30 p.m. again. The news that Mr. Ramamurthy and his family had not reached Tirumala unnerved their relatives. "How come, they had not reached?".... What could I say?

I feared that some untoward incident might have happened en route. I called up Nagari and Puttur police stations in Chittoor district on the Madras-Tirupati road and told the police that the Chief Secretary was coming in a private car and that they should alert me if they located his car.

Minutes and hours punctuated by repeated calls to police stations enroute and Chennai, rolled by. We informed the Chief Secretary and the police of Tamil Nadu about the AP Chief Secretary who left Madras, not arriving at Tirupati. Wracked by anxiety and tension, I kept awake all through the night.

Friday morning broke with the temple priests chanting suprabhatham at 3 AM

"Kousalya Suprajarama poorva sandhya pravartate
Utthistha nara sardula kartavyam daivamahnikam"

Weighed down by sadness, anxiety and confusion, I was gazing at the *'mahadwaram'* (main gate to the temple) from the sanctum sanctorum. I had directed the staff, "Escort the Chief Secretary and his family straight into the temple whenever they arrive". I was optimistic of the family landing any moment. In case they did not turn up? Fear and worry returned to me. No news. The *'abhisheka seva'* started.

The *'abhishekam'* too was over. It was 7-30 in the morning. Unable to restrain myself, I turned to the Lord wondering as to what could have happened. Except for the bewitching smile on his face, and mischievous glint in his eyes (that day being Friday and we could have *'netradarshanam'* of the Lord), I got no response from the Lord. I was still in the temple and was about to leave when there was a phone call: "Prasad, this is Ramamurthy calling". I felt relieved.

"Sir, How are you? Where are you? Are all safe?", I asked him agitatedly.

"All are safe. I am calling from Madras". I was immensely relieved after I heard those few words from the Chief Secretary. "But what...? Even before I completed the sentence, he unfolded the midnight mystery.

Mr. Ramamurthy along with his family members and brother-in-law Padmanabham left Madras at 6-30 p.m. in a car. As a matter of precaution, they arranged a spare car to follow them. The car by which Mr. Ramamurthy's family was travelling broke down before it crossed the Tamil Nadu-Andhra Pradesh border. It was 8 p.m. The driver tried to repair it. Even if it could not be repaired for any reasons, they thought, they could reach Tirumala in the spare vehicle following them. And so they did not try to board Tirupati-bound buses. Time was ticking away and it was already 10 p.m. The car that should have followed them was to be seen nowhere and the snag in the car by which they travelled could not be fixed. Stranded at a place where there was no habitation within sight, they could not seek anybody's help either in person or over phone (no cell phone facility those days). After 10 p.m. even buses would not ply on that route. Although one or two lorries passed that way, they would not halt. The Chief Secretary and his family had to spend the entire night awake in pitch darkness in a no-man's land. By 5 in the morning, the driver managed to repair and start the car. Even if they were to start at that hour, they concluded, there was no prospect of their reaching Tirumala and attending *"abhishka seva"*. So they decided to return to Madras, deeply disappointed. The moment they reached Madras, they had a call from the spare vehicle driver from Tirupati. "Sir, by which route did you travel? I reached Tirupati via. ... Looking for your vehicle."

When we met a week later in Hyderabad, Mr. Ramamurthy and I reviewed where things had gone wrong. We concluded that we failed despite meticulous planning.

Finally, Mr. Ramamurthy said, "Prasad, do you still believe that *'darshan'* of the Lord is in our hands? Although one has power and position and a huge retinue of staff, can one have *'darshan'* without Lord's grace? I will come to Tirumala whenever the Lord beckons me. It is not my wish and effort that matter. The Lord shall will it... I shall await His call...."

The call from the Lord came very soon. He and his family along with Mr. Padmanabham had *'abhiseka darshan'* of the Lord to their hearts' content. After the *'darshan'* Mr.

Ramamurthy affectionately patted me on my shoulder, and said, "One day you might become the Chief Secretary. But there is no greater post than that of the Executive Officer. As Chief Secretary, I had to struggle a lot for the call from the Lord to have one *'darshan'*. But you have been blessed by the Lord to have His *'darshan'* so many times and to attend to his devotees daily.

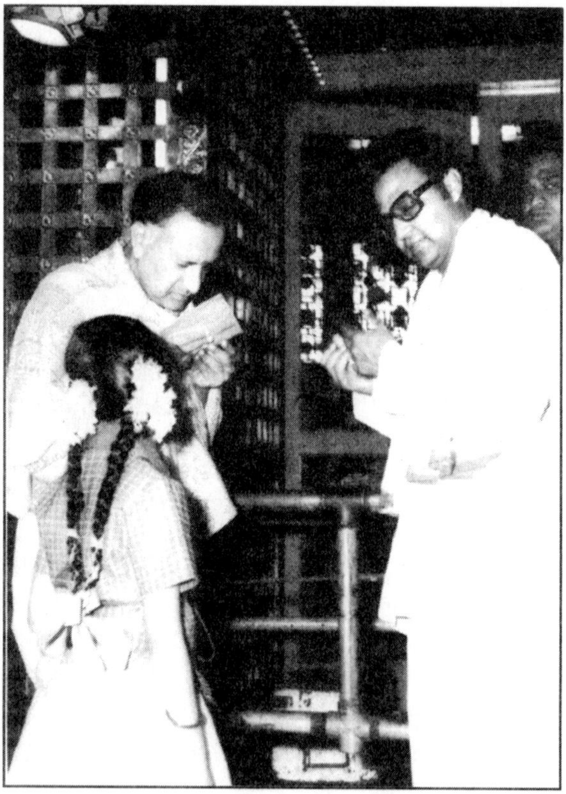

Mr. S.R. Ram Murthy, Chief Secretary receiving prasad from Mr. P.V.R.K. Prasad.

Innumerable have been the instances of people coming with high-level recommendations not having satisfactory *'darshan'*, and the nameless without any recommendation having the satisfaction of a great *'darshan'*. Why does it happen?

16

CONTROVERSIAL PADMAVATI GUEST HOUSE

Endowments Minister Veeramachaneni Venkatanarayana was fuming at me over the phone...

"What Prasad, you make us hang our heads? What is the point in constructing VIP guesthouses costing lakhs of rupees, ignoring facilities to lakhs of common pilgrims? Who has given you the clearance? As Endowments Minister, even I am in the dark. The Chief Minister too has no knowledge. But Opposition parties, fully armed with the details, are raising the issue in the Assembly. How are we to answer the Opposition? Chief Minister (Dr. Channa Reddy) is spewing fire at me. What should I tell him? What an embarrassment....."

I was dumbstruck. For a few moments, I could not utter a word. Collecting my wits, I could only mumble, "I would like to brief you in detail". But he was in no mood to listen.

"You need not offer me any explanation. First, send a written reply to the question being raised in the Assembly. Later, if necessary, you can talk to the Chief Minister himself and clarify", he said cutting me short and hanging up the phone.

I could not give him a firm reply because there was an element of truth in his charge. It was a fact that I was getting an ultra modern VIP guesthouse constructed at a cost of Rs.15 lakh at Tirumala. (The Rs.15 lakh of Rs.1979-80 would be equivalent to a few crores of rupees now). It was also a fact that the TTD had taken up the construction of a guesthouse at such a huge cost for the first time on its own. Since I happened to be the Executive Officer when the construction was on, I was answerable. If I failed to give a convincing explanation, the Opposition parties would certainly lambaste the Government, and the Chief Minister, would direct his wrath against me once again.

I was weighed down by the prospect. Construction of the guesthouse was a fact. Its costing Rs.15 lakh was a fact. And that the TTD meeting the entire expenditure was a fact. What was there in that for me to refute?

× × ×

In the 1970s, Tirumala had only limited, good accommodation facilities like NGC cottages, TB cottages, TB Guesthouse and Sri Venkateswara Guesthouse - all constructed with donations from philanthropists. The donors had a right to stay in their guesthouses free of cost for a specified number of days (30 at that time) in a year. And it was the donor cottages, the best among the available lot, which were earmarked for VIPs. VIPs were provided accommodation mostly in the NGC and TB Guesthouse area. When a VIP like a Chief Minister or a Prime Minister or Union Ministers visited Tirumala, a cottage with just two rooms would not suffice. Occasionally, we had to allot 10-15 cottages to accommodate officials, security and intelligence staff and political followers accompanying a VIP.

The TTD staff quite often faced acute embarrassment when donors on a pilgrimage sought their own cottages when VIPs happened to be occupying them. When I took over as Executive Officer in 1978, donors frequently complained that the TTD was riding roughshod over their rights by "temporarily misappropriating" their cottages in the name of VIPs. Even when donors had reserved their cottages two to three months in advance, the cottages at times were allotted to VIPs turning up at the last minute. Denied their own cottages, the donors had to be cajoled into accepting alternative accommodation.

The issue was getting more and more complex when there was a heavy inflow of VIPs. Even when more donor cottages were constructed, the unabated VIP rush eluded a solution. In fact, some VIPs insisted on the allocation of certain cottages, much to the inconvenience and embarrassment of their donors.

Mr. Rajagopala Raju, who had preceded me as Executive Officer, had been fed up with the VIPs versus donors controversy over cottages allotment. When a VIP party occupied 10-15 cottages, the TTD staff faced innumerable hassles in receiving them, providing breakfast, lunch and dinner, organising *'darshan'* and distributing *'prasadam'*. When the President or the Chief Minister or a Prime Minister visited Tirumala, the problems get compounded. More than 50 cottages would be occupied by the VIP, security personnel and other accompanying staff. The entire area would be cordoned off into a security zone and visiting pilgrims were virtually shooed away from the area.

As a permanent solution to the problem, Mr. Rajagopala Raju proposed the construction of Padmavathi Guesthouse, exclusively for VIPs. The guesthouse, lying almost on the summit of a hillock, is in one corner and away from donor cottages. Pilgrims would not be subjected to harassment in the name of security when a VIP stayed there. The guesthouse planned would be spacious enough to accommodate any VIP including the President of India. The personal and security staff of a President and the Chief Minister, who might accompany him, could all easily be accommodated. It was to have its own kitchen and dining hall. Since all of them would stay at one place, provision of food, planning of *'darshan'* and distribution of *'prasadam'* would become easier. It would be taken up with TTD funds and not come under the donor scheme. Once this VIP guesthouse came up, there would be no occasion to deny donors their cottages. Security arrangements for the VIP would become easier as the guesthouse was located atop a hill. Mr. Rajagopala Raju thought over all these aspects, convinced the TTD Board of the need to build a VIP guesthouse at its own cost and initiated construction. The construction had just begun when I took over as Executive Officer.

The project, launched by far-sighted Rajagopala Raju, immensely impressed me. From Padamavthi Guesthouse atop the hill, one could have a glimpse of "Ananda Nilayam", the spire over the sanctum sanctorum of Lord Srinivasa, on the northern side. A lush green valley unfolds itself on the southern

(Chandragiri) side. What appealed to me the most was the fact that common pilgrims' movements in Tirumala would not be disrupted even if the Prime Minister and the Chief Minister were to stay there simultaneously. That was why I was determined to get the guesthouse completed as early as possible. By 1980, the construction was almost over. The TTD had incurred an expenditure of Rs.15 lakh by then. Significantly, the construction kicked up dust as fast as I tried to complete it.

I had already antagonised certain sections of Tirumala by implementing the Master Plan. We demolished houses around the temple, and took up construction of a township to accommodate the displaced. We took up the queue complex construction and were planning to increase the number of donor cottages. The Board had approved the construction of an additional floor on all existing TB/ATC cottages. Plans had been drawn up for the construction of Narayanadri and Garudadri Guesthouses on the lines of S. V. Guesthouse under the donor scheme. We had also finalised the construction of a 100-room free choultry for poor pilgrims under the donor scheme. All this entailed cleaning of authorized/unauthorized occupants and also affected a number of traders and petty shopkeepers, who were likely to be displaced.

Padmavathi Guest house became the subject of animated discussion among certain sections as the Master Plan was being implemented in full swing. It was the costliest accommodation, involving TTD money. Those, who feared loss of their domination in Tirumala because of the master plan, and local leaders who were cut up with the removal of slums, began accusing me of squandering away TTD money. A section of the disgruntled TTD unions too added fuel to the fire. The thrust of the campaign was that I was building a luxurious palace, costing Rs.40 lakh to Rs.50 lakh, to curry favour with the Chief Minister and other Ministers, ignoring common pilgrims' interests. I was convinced that sooner the guesthouse was completed, the better it was for all pilgrims including cottage donors. That was why the criticism did not upset me. But how could I ignore a question being raised by the Opposition in the Assembly?

I was embarrassed when the Endowments Minister blamed me for his inability to defend himself before the Chief Minister. Although construction of a guesthouse at a cost of Rs.15 lakh was a fact, I could not explain the rationale behind it in one sentence over the phone to the perturbed Endowments Minister. Again, I could not have communicated my suspicion that local leaders' dissatisfaction over the Master Plan execution triggered the question in the Assembly. How would the Chief Minister and the Endowments Minister respond if the Opposition parties were to point out that instead of one costly VIP guesthouse many choultries could have been constructed?

The Endowments Minister had already made his point, "Why should we construct the guesthouse? It too could have been taken up under the donor cottage scheme. We need not hang our heads in shame before the Opposition".

In fact, no cottage constructed under the donor scheme till then had exceeded a cost of Rs.3 lakh. Which donor would come forward to part with Rs.15 lakh for a guesthouse? Assuming that some donor agreed to foot the guesthouse construction, would not history repeat itself if the donor turned up on the day a VIP happened to be there? Moreover, an additional Rs.6 lakh had to be spent on furnishing, lighting etc. in the guesthouse. Who would pay for it? But if the Chief Minister were to ask, whether the TTD was justified in spending so many lakhs of rupees on a single guesthouse, what could be our explanation?

A myriad questions, doubts and suspicions assailed me. The focus of both the Chief Minister and the Endowments Minister was on saving themselves from embarrassment and not on whether the project was warranted or not. The Endowments Minister had already made it clear that the Chief Minister would not appreciate even if I logically justified the guesthouse construction. What all they wanted was Government's face saving in the Assembly.

For the Government to convincingly explain how the absence of a VIP guesthouse spawned many problems, first, the

Chief Minister and the Endowments Minister should appreciate the fact and approve it wholeheartedly. Then only, they could attempt to convince the Opposition. Even if they conceded that the construction was justified, I did not believe that they would be allowed to make the point because the Opposition would not forgo an opportunity to attack the Government. Why would the Chief Minister, in such circumstances, take the risk of defending the TTD? Even if he took the risk, the Opposition would charge the Government with pursuing anti-people policies and cite the construction of luxurious palaces for leaders at the cost of ordinary pilgrims. Would the Chief Minister keep quiet, if he knew I was responsible for all the embarrassment to him?

The longer I thought, the more my brain heated up. If I were to put the facts in black and white, it would result in embarrassment to the Government and show-cause notices to me. And I had neither the inclination nor the expertise to whitewash the whole thing by presenting a distorted version that would inveigle the Opposition. Even if I had such skills and the Opposition learnt the reply was misleading and contrary to facts, the Government could not escape censure and I, my exit.

In fact, I was not the author of the guesthouse construction. But, after thinking over it from many angles, I too felt that it was essential. But I could neither bring round the Government to my viewpoint nor act against its interests. What was to be done? I had to send the reply to the Assembly question in two or three days. The next morning, the TTD Trust Board was to meet. Originally, I planned to get the approval of the Board, to provide an additional Rupees Six Lakh for furnishing the guesthouse. In view of the developments, I hesitated to introduce the subject in the agenda. It had a long agenda and I was yet to prepare for it. Finding myself deeply mired, I could not sleep for a long time in the night. Past midnight, I concluded that there was little I could do and thought of the Lord as a last resort. "Lord, I believe that I am not committing any indiscretion and that the project is in the larger interests of the public. I depend on you to resolve it". Within minutes of saying the prayer, I fell asleep.

× × ×

Early in the morning, I looked up the Board agenda. Tension started building up in me over the Assembly question, although I hoped Lord Srinivasa would somehow heed my prayer. The time was up for the Board meeting but a solution to my problem was still elusive. The only alternative left for me then was to place the matter before the Board members and ascertain their opinion and act accordingly. (I was aware that the members, appointed by Dr. Channa Reddy would not do anything that would besmirch his reputation.)

As a last attempt, I stepped into the temple before attending the Board meeting. I prayed, "Lord, seeking refuge in you, I will pause thinking further. I place the matter in your hands". I offered '*pranam*' to the Lord and drove straight to Sri Venkateswara Guesthouse where the meeting was taking place. The moment I got down the car, I ran into the "saviour".

He was Mr. R. P. Goenka, TTD Trust Board member, Chairman of the RPG Group and a big industrialist. At the previous Board meeting, he had sought a good site for the construction of a donor cottage costing about Rs.5 lakh. I was reminded of his request the moment he spoke to me. As if some one was pursuing me, I dashed to him. I straightway broached the subject. "You wanted a site for a donor cottage. Instead of constructing a small cottage, why don't you donate for Padmavathi Guesthouse complex and accept it under the donor scheme?"

The pace at which I made the offer startled him. Recovering, he asked how much the guesthouse would cost.

In my characteristic way, I held forth: "Goenkaji, this is a wonderful guesthouse meant exclusively for VVIPs. It has many distinctions. We have so far not thought of associating donors with this project. But the moment I have seen you, I felt like offering. If you are interested, I will show you round the guesthouse right now..."

"Definitely. But how much is it going to cost?" My tantalising details of the guesthouse whetted his appetite. But he wanted all the details before he committed himself.

"I don't think it will be a big burden for you. We have so far spent Rs.15 lakh. Including furnishing, lighting etc, the cost will be within Rs.20 lakh. I suggest that you first take a look at the way the guesthouse is shaping up. We can discuss other things later". As he listened, his interest grew. (How did it happen?)

"Let us go", I told Mr. Goenka. There were still 15-20 minutes for the Board meeting to begin. Informing TTD Chairman Mr. Nagi Reddy that I would be back soon, I took Mr. Goenka in my car to the Padmavathi Guesthouse, which was under construction.

Mr. Goenka fell in love with the project the moment he saw the amenities being provided. The "Ananda Nilayam" shimmering in sunlight on one side and the beautiful Chandragiri valley on the other overwhelmed him with joy. Even as he was in a spell of ecstasy, I told him very quietly…

"This will be the largest guesthouse in Tirumala. It will be used only for VVIPs like the President, the Prime Minister and the Chief Minister. Such VIPs do not number more than ten. When they are not around, the guesthouse will be yours for the number of days stipulated under the donor cottage scheme."

He was going round the guesthouse even as he muttered, "yes, yes" to what all I told him. After rounds of hesitation, I told him, "If VIPs happen to be here when you choose to come, we will provide you alternative accommodation in a different cottage". I was apprehensive of his reaction but nothing showed up on his face.

"Prasad garu, the guesthouse is a thing of beauty. We have been thinking of going in for a cottage costing about Rs.5 lakh. Now that you say the guesthouse will cost Rs.20 lakh, I cannot take a decision alone here and now. I have to talk to my people".

I did not lose time. "Is that all? Speak to them right now". Before he could get over the astonishment, I called in my staff and arranged for his making lightning trunk calls.

"Goenkaji, we should resolve the issue this morning. Make the telephone calls and come to the Board meeting. We will take a decision in today's Board meeting itself. Until your arrival, we will discuss minor items on the agenda". Enthusing him thus, I sent him to my camp office along with my staff. My tension was yet to abate. If Mr. Goenka were not to agree finally?

Within 10-15 minutes of the start of the Board meeting, Mr. Goenka entered the Board Room, called me aside to ask me, "If it is okay with you, we will give you Rs.5 lakh now and the remainder of Rs.10 lakh in a month. We will take care of furnishing etc at our own cost".

What could I say? Overhwhelmed with joy, I embraced Mr. Goenka and told him, "You are great." I was swept by a wave of gratitude. Mr. Goenka had no clue to my emotional reaction. Announcing Mr. Goenka's decision in the Board meeting, I said, "He is the biggest donor under the cottage scheme." As the members clapped their hands in appreciation, Mr. Goenka felt a bit shy and embarrassed.

I sighed in relief, as the tension of the past few days vanished instantaneously and a complex issue came to an end. My mind became light, took to its wings, flew into the Tirumala temple and prostrated before the Lord and returned. I wiped my tear-filmed eyes.

After listening to my explanation on Padmavathi Guesthouse, all the Board members unanimously agreed to convert it into a donor guesthouse. They congratulated Mr. Goenka once again.

Padmavathi Guest House at the time of inauguration.

Mr. Goenka's eyes became wet. "I once thought it would be enough if you showed me a good site for a Rs.5 lakh cottage. I had come to the meeting to get a categorical reply to my earlier request. But now, by the grace of the Lord we have become the donors for a Rs.20 lakh guesthouse. We will make it the best, even if we have to spend much more money than the estimated Rs20 lakhs. What a miracle! (Whose miracle is that?)". Mr. Goenka appeared to be a picture of joy.

A few days later, the Endowments Minister told the Assembly: "It is not a fact that the TTD is squandering lakhs of rupees on the construction of a VIP guesthouse. The guesthouse is being constructed with a donation from the RPG group".

17

ANJANEYA RISES ON THE ANJANADRI

I rushed to the spot as soon as I heard that a woman had been murdered on the footpath to Tirumala Hills. What I saw filled me with a deep sense of dejection. The murder took place at the seventh mile, where the footpath and the *'ghat'* road traverse through dense forest.

Skirted by dense forest, the place would be enveloped in total darkness during nights. As stray lights en route were of little help, it provided a perfect setting for a crime like murder. Although murders were committed all over the country I could not reconcile myself to murder on the holy hills. The ghastly crime made me take special interest in the problems the pilgrims faced in walking up the hills. Shortly after I took over as Executive Officer, I did walk up like any ordinary pilgrim but in a different frame of mind.

× × ×

For generations, devotees had been trekking to Tirumala to have *'darshan'* of the Lord. They come by bus or train to Tirupati from distant places, but make it a point to take the nine-km-long journey to reach Lord Venkateswara's abode nestling amidst hills at an altitude of 3200 feet above sea level. Carrying their personal belongings on heads and their children on shoulders, the devotees keep chanting "Govinda, Govinda" to forget the stress and strain of climbing. Generally it is a journey they undertake months or years of taking a vow to visit the Lord.

As the number of pilgrims visiting Tirumala increased, the government constructed the 'ghat' road and introduced reliable bus service. As a result, there had been a gradual decline in the number of pilgrims going on foot to Tirumala. During nights, a sense of insecurity prevailed. The daytime journey too was not pleasant. As it is hot most of the year, pilgrims had to contend with scalding, uneven and steep granite steps. When it occasionally rained, pilgrims were drenched. Most people, therefore, opted to travel by bus. I wondered why the journey by foot to Tirumala could not be as pleasant as an excursion. So, I decided to walk up the hills along with my wife and children at least once a month at different times to understand the pilgrims' problems. I reckoned with the opportunity of spending three to four hours with the family and thinking of improving facilities for pilgrims.

When the TTD Executive Officer chose to walk, other senior officials naturally followed. We began to improve the facilities along the footpath, as we understood the pilgrims' problems one after another in course of time.

We got the uneven steps repaired and abutting shrubs cleared and improved drinking water facilities all along the route. We improved, illumination by installing more lights and reducing the distance between lights. We erected billboards with divine messages to help pilgrims focus their minds on the Lord. We thought we had done a lot. Yet there was not much improvement in the number of devotees walking up the hills. Only those who had taken a vow or those who could not afford the bus fares were going by foot.

I was determined to unravel the mystery of pilgrims keeping off the footpath. Once as I walked up, I saw a group of pilgrims panting as they struggled to walk up. The head of the family sported long hair and a thick beard apparently meant to be offered to the Lord. He carried a small trunk on his head and slung bags over his shoulders. In addition, he had a child in his arms. I noticed that he was often shifting the child from one arm to the other. His wife carried another trunk box. Breathless and sweating, because of the load and the strain, they chanted "Govinda, Govinda". But would Lord Srinivasa listen to their cries? Why should not pilgrims chant Lord Srinivasa's name with devotion and dedication instead of as an expedient to forget strain? At once I decided that pilgrims taking the footpath should be spared the drudgery of carrying luggage. I implemented the idea immediately. The TTD would transport their luggage free of cost to Tirumala if they deposited it at the Alipiri tollgate or in the choultries at Tirupati. By the time the pilgrims reached Tirumala by walk in three or four hours, their luggage would have arrived there safely. I learnt some pilgrims earlier used to go up the hills by bus, deposit their luggage in a choultry, and return to Tirupati by bus to undertake the journey by foot to fulfil their vows. That could be avoided now.

Provision of the free luggage transport facility led to an increase in the number of pilgrims using the footpath. Yet, the woman's murder on the footpath continued to haunt me. I pondered as to what else could I do for pilgrims trekking up the hills.

On my next trip along the footpath, it rained all of a sudden. Seeking shelter, the pilgrims on the footpath scurried to the nearby trees. But, I kept going unmindful of the rain. Although there were '*gopurams*' and '*Mandapams*' here and there, they were far away from each other and were of little help in such contingencies. I heard a group of pilgrims discussing as to when the rain would abate and enable them to reach the Hills and have '*darshan*'. The tree under which they stood did not spare them from the rain. I heard an annoyed pilgrim, half jokingly, hurling a challenge at the Lord. "If you deem us genuine devotees, why can't you protect us from rain or at least send us umbrellas?" I immediately wondered why there should not be a canopy all along the route to protect pilgrims from rain and shine? A permanent umberalla. I proposed to the TTD Board that a permanent cement shelter be erected all along the footpath.

The Board members laughed at the proposal. "Mr. Prasad garu, are you crazy? Erection of a nine-kilometre-long shelter on a plain road itself is difficult. How do you erect a shelter on 9 km-long uneven and zig-zag footpath up the hills? How can the materials be carried?" They did not intend to ridicule me; they genuinely felt that my idea was impractical. But the rain-drenched pilgrims' 'SOS' to Balaji for umbrellas kept flashing across my mind. Would it not materialise if Balaji willed it, I wondered. Undeterred by the initial opposition in the TTD Board I persisted in selling my idea, again at the next meeting. After some discussion, the Board finally gave the green signal. In the first phase, the shelter was to be constructed from Alipiri at the foot of the hills to the *'gopuram'* from which *'Srivari Namas'* are visible.

Even as the permanent umbrella began to unfold. I ordered that the footpath steps be set right so that they were not too steep and the slabs re-laid wherever warranted. I appointed Dr. Janardhan Naidu, a graduate in medicine wedded to social service, as the TTD Security and Vigilance Officer and asked him to focus on security all along the footpath. We posted two security guards per shift for every KM. We provided better illumination by changing the old lamps and we ensured the availability of healthy snacks all along the way. We constructed shelters abutting the footpath to enable pilgrims to take rest or to cook food. We opened a deer park on the way to provide relaxation to pilgrims. We arranged for the broadcast of Balaji devotional music. We installed telephones and opened first aid centers. We completed the half-finished "*gopurams*". All these measures saw the number of pilgrims using the footpath jumping from 400-500 a day to 4000-5000. Yet, the agitation in me since the day of the murder had not died down. I felt that something else needed to be done.

On another trip, I visited the cloak- room atop the hills where the luggage deposited by pilgrims at the foot of the hills is returned to them. Although the TTD vans transported the luggage from Tirupati to Triumala free of cost, pilgrims had to carry it once again from the cloak- room to their places of stay like choultries. Coolies exploited the pilgrims. I heard an elderly man asking his son, "Venkatesa, (or a similar name) you carry this piece of luggage". I wondered why Lord Venkateswara who received offerings worth billions of rupees from pilgrims could not spare them from the drudgery of carrying their luggage. Within days of the idea striking me, I arranged for free transport of pilgrims along with their luggage from any point to any point on the hills. (Who had provided it? Who had inspired me?) The free buses cover all the centres in the pilgrim town. Pilgrims have to wait hardly for a few minutes to catch a free bus.

But the disquiet over the murder would not leave me. What else should I do? I did not know. Who would enlighten me? Standing at the spot where the murder was perpetrated, I turned to the Lord Himself. " I have come here to serve your devotees. Tell me what else should I do now and rid me of the agony over the murder on the foot path".

× × ×

Accompanied by my wife Gopika and children Madhavi and Sanjiv, I set off for Kakinada by road. My schedule was to inspect the TTD kalyan mantaps *(marriage halls)* under construction at Nellore and Vijayawada, inspect TTD ghats under construction at Rajahmundry for Godavari '*pushakaram*' and then go to Kakinada, where another '*Kalyanamantapam*' was under construction. Incidentally, Kakinada was my wife's native place.

We halted overnight at Vijayawada and left early in the morning. We were scheduled to reach Kakinada by 11 a.m. But by the time we reached Rajahmundry, it was midday. The children were hungry. The TTD was constructing bathing '*ghats*' for pilgrims visiting Rajahmundry for the Godavari '*pushkarams*'. My batchmate Narayanan who was Collector, East Godavari, was waiting for me for joint inspection of the works.

Although I hurried through the bathing '*ghat*' inspection, it was past lunchtime. Gopika was impatient since her parents at Kakinada had been awaiting us for lunch. We at last set out from Rajahmundry to Kakinada hoping to reach there at least by 2 PM. En route at Peddapuram, I sighted by chance a 12-foot-high statue of Lord Anjaneya near the tank and signalled the driver to halt.

I got down from the car and walked towards the statue. Gopika, who had till then been fretting and fuming over the delay, could not repress herself from exclaiming, "What a beauty!" The well-sculpted statue had a divine halo around it. Something I had been searching for seemed to be within my grasp. But I had no idea what it was. Inquiries revealed the sculptor was Thogu Lakshmana Swamy, a resident of a nearby village. "I feel like visiting the artist right now", I told Gopika a bit hesitantly. She replied enthusiastically, "Let us go" . We travelled along a bumpy road for another hour looking for Lakshmana Swamy.

We found Lakshmana Swamy, in his 50's, making statues outside his small hut. He was surprised to see us come in the hot sun. I straightway asked him, "Can you come to Tirupati to build Hanuman statues like the one at Peddapuram?"

"Who are you?"

"I am the TTD Executive Officer"

Lakshmana Swamy's joy knew no bounds. He reminded me of Lord Lakshman. How would Lakshman have jumped up had Lord Rama sent word through a messenger asking him to come over to a particular spot and meet him. But Lakshmana Swamy had not stepped into the wide world barring a few neighbouring villages. I told him that I would make all the arrangements for his travel to and stay in Tirupati. He wanted to bring two of his assistants. I said 'okay'. We will come definitely, whenever you want us" was the excited answer of Lakshmana Swamy. As we got into the car, I felt relieved of the unknown burden, weighing me down.

× × ×

On return to Tirupati, I entrusted the responsibility of looking after Lakshmana Swamy to two dedicated officials–Executive Engineer Vaikhasanachari and Assistant Engineer Bellam Venkatramaiah. The first assignment I gave Lakshmana Swamy was the erection of an Anjaneya statue, bigger than the one at Peddpuram, in the park in front of the TTD administrative office (Huzur Office). Lakshmana Swamy built statues with cement and gave them a coat of mosaic to ensure that they lasted at least for a century without maintenance. However large a statue was, he paid attention even to minute details like flowing hair, nails, jewellery, clothing etc so that it looked natural and artistically appealing. I suggested that he produce Garuda and Anjaneya statues for

Garudadri and Anjanadri hills. Garudari is the first hill that comes into view at Alipiri, at the foot of the hills. But where is Anjanadri? I did not know. "But go ahead with Garuda. We will see later", I told the artist.

'Hanuma' Statue at the time of Pratistha

On my next trip to Tirumala by foot, I happened to halt at the seventh milestone the murder spot. The spot flooded my mind with memories. Somehow, I was not as agitated, at the spot as in the past. But, I was excited. I could not make out why. I shut my eyes and prayed to the Lord. As the statue of Anjaneya Swamy occupied my mind, I almost cried *'eureka'* The solution eluding me for long flashed across my mind. Electrified, I felt like jumping like a ten-year-old boy.

In response to my enquiries, pundits enlightened me about some slokas in *'Bhavishya Puranam'* mentioning the birth of Lord Anjaneya. Anjanadevi and Kesari came to Narayanagiri and did penance for 12 years to have a child. Anjaneya was the offspring of their penance.

Pampyaah poorva dhigbhage panchasa dyoja Nanamthare
Naarasimhasramam devi varthathe; vasudhatale

Thasya Dakshinadigbhage Narayana giree sthate;
Uttare swamythirthasya varthathe krosamatrake

Viyadgajeti Vikhyatha tatra gachaadhasukham
Tatrasnatwaadha kalyani dwadasabdham tapa schara

Tena punyena putro bhavishyati gunadhika
Matangye nyna mukhta mukhtasa narayanagirim yayo

Hanumantha mimam prahuvn munayo veethakalmasha
Anjana vratha masthaya putram prapa girisware
Tasma Danjarisai loyam lokoy vVikhyatakeerthiman

Without losing time, I showed the spot near the seventh milestone to Lakshmana Swamy where the Anjaneya statue was to be erected. The natural beauty of the place thrilled him. "I will spare no effort in sculpting a magnificent statue of Hanuman, who will be a source of strength to devotees. That way, I will make my life purposeful", he said, overwhelmed with devotion. It is the masterpiece of Lakshmana Swamy that devotees now see at the seventh milestone. What is significant is that the '*ghat*' road and the footpath converge at the point where the statue stands. By whichever way one goes to Tirumala, one invariably sights Anjaneya, the son of Anjani.

Only after the installation of the Bhadranajaneya statue in 1980, the agony and the void in my mind since the day of murder left me.

"Buddhirbalam yasodhairyam nirbhayatwam arogata
Ajadyam vakpatauvmcha hanumath smaranath bhaveth"

"He, who remembers Lord Hanuman, will be blessed with discretion, strength, fearlessness, good name, valour, good health, agility and eloquence".

I had visualised the installation of seven statues on the footpath representing the seven hills on the way to Tirumala (Venkatadri, Garudadri, Seshadri, Anjanadri, Vrishabhadri, Narayanadri and Anandadri). Anjaneya had risen where the unfortunate murder had been perpetrated. Since then, He has been inspiring and infusing the pilgrims with energy, valour and fearlessness.

'Garuda' at the Foot Hills

18

A SWAMI'S FAITH MOVES SEVEN HILLS

Chief Minister Channa Reddy was staring at me impatiently.

That he did not relish the idea of the TTD donating Rs.12 lakh to Ramakrishna Mutt in a hurry was writ large on his face. I was not interested in prolonging the dialogue, since I knew the outcome, going by my past encounters with him. Yet, there was no change in my stand that the Tirumala Tirupati Devasthanams should donate Rs.12 lakh to Ramakrishna Mutt, although, I had no illusions of Dr. Channa Reddy quietly nodding his head and telling me, "Prasad, go ahead and do what you think best".

As my determination got steeled - whether on its own or at the prompting of somebody else — I unleashed the last arrow in my armoury, "Sir, this is God's will. If Lord Srinivasa wills this to happen, who are we to say a 'no'?"

Dr. Channa Reddy lifted his head to pierce into my eyes. "Is that so?" he said sarcastically. I kept quiet.

"Look Prasad, don't try to mix spiritualism and administration with your half-baked philosophy. They don't go together".

It was now crystal clear. The proposal would not fructify. Concern clouded my mind. Flashing across my mind were Ramakrishna Mutt, the construction of which was grinding to a halt for want of funds, and Swami Ranganathananda, who, with single-minded devotion to the project and undying faith in Lord Srinivasa, was looking for the donation. My helplessness crushed me. I had already exhausted all my resources in trying to convince the Chief Minister. I was left only with patience to withstand the Chief Minister's barbs. Although, I was not sure to what extent.

"Are you a member of Ramakrishna Mutt?" the Chief Minister shot another question breaking the deafening silence.

"No sir, except for talking to Swami Rangathananda over phone I have not seen him so far."

"Then?"

The Chief Minister was apparently bent on ferreting out the reason for the urgency of the Rs.12 lakh donation (without waiting for the promulgation of the new regulations for release of funds from the Common Good Fund) and my personal interest in it. There were the hints of a slur on my personal interest and intellectual honesty. I had to convincingly explain the rationale behind the proposal?

× × ×

A few days before I met the Chief Minister, Dr. Channa Reddy, in 1979, Swami Ranganathananda of Ramakrishna Mutt had called me over the phone when I was in the TTD Huzur (administrative) office attending to some work. I had neither seen him nor talked to him over the phone earlier, although I had heard about him. He had earned a name for himself by developing Ramakrishna Mutt in Delhi.

I had heard of him as a repository of knowledge, spiritual philosopher, competent leader and eloquent orator who could cast a spell on his listeners by holding forth for hours on the noble purpose of human life. But I had not had the fortune of meeting him one on one.

When, therefore, Swami Rangathananda called me personally over the phone, I was excited. After exchanging pleasantries, the Swamiji broached the subject straightway. The Andhra Pradesh Government led by Mr. Jalagam Vengal Rao had assigned a sprawling place in the Lower Tank Bund area in Hyderabad for the construction of Ramakrishna *'Mutt'*. Construction of the mutt complex was under way then.

"We did not have adequate funds when we took up the *'mutt'* construction. But firmly believing that God would always facilitate a noble task, I plunged into construction. The complex includes an auditorium, guest rooms, monks' quarters, a prayer hall, a library, a book stall etc. Vindicating my faith, donations poured in from far and near. The first phase of the construction is almost complete. To complete the works on hand, we badly need Rs.15 lakh. Otherwise, the project work will come to a standstill. I have exhausted all sources of donations. If I persevere, I may mobilise Rs.2 lakh to Rs.3 lakh more. Where from do I get the remainder of Rs.12 lakh? It is against this backdrop, I felt that, barring Lord Venkateswara no one could extend a helping hand. As His representative, you should take the initiative and bale me out". This was Swami Rangathananda's plea.

I was shaken by the helplessness in his words. For want of Rs.12 lakh, such a big project faced the prospect of coming to a standstill. He would like the TTD to donate that crucial Rs.12 lakh. For the TTD, making donations was not an issue. In fact, the TTD had given donations to many such projects. The noble project for which the Swamiji sought funds was meant to serve the humanity. Ramakrishna Mission, promoted by Swami Vivekananda at Belur, has spread to several cities. It has demonstrated (in practice) over the years that "service to man is service to God". The relief and rehabilitation works undertaken by Ramakrishna Mission in times of natural calamities are legendary and invaluable.

But, even in normal circumstances, Rs.12 lakh was a big amount for donation. But when Swami Rangathananda phoned me, I found myself altogether in a different set of circumstances.

The Government felt that temple trusts had been doling out cash without any rhyme or reason depending on their whims and fancies resulting in abuse of funds. Therefore, it decided to rationalise funneling of funds through a Government administered Common Good Fund (CGF). Temple trusts, including the TTD, would have to make annual contributions to the CGF. All donations for renovation of temples and other charitable activities would be routed through the CGF. Individual temple trusts, including the TTD, were to be barred from making donations directly.

Swami Rangathananda had sought the donation four to five days before the new regulations were to come into effect. I was inclined to make the donation. But if I made the donation fully aware that the new CGF regulations were about to come into effect, both the Government and the Persons-in-Charge Committee (working in place of the Trust Board) would hold me guilty. The Persons-in-Charge Committee had met only two or three days earlier. It was unlikely to meet for the next one month.

Explaining all this, I suggested to the Swamiji, "Please meet the Chief Minister, the Endowments Minister, the Revenue Principal Secretary and the Endowments Commissioner once and put in a word. If they have no objection, I will immediately make the donation". My words disappointed the Swamiji. I could make out his disinclination to knock at Ministers' doors for funds. But I told him what I had to. Such was my plight.

"Prasad garu, we have taken up a good cause. And I firmly believe that God always blesses good deeds. My faith in Srinivasa's helping hand has not waned. Please take the initiative and try once. Let us leave the rest to Lord Venkateswara's grace", concluded Swami Ranganathananda.

To the extent I knew, Swami Rangathananda had never gone round politicians seeking donations. Therefore, I did not believe that he would heed my suggestion and call on the Chief Minister, the Endowments Minister, the Revenue Principal Secretary or others. But what was the basis for his supreme confidence? Would funds flow on their own and '*mutts*' get constructed, if one did not seek funds? Would God descend from the heavens to take up construction if he sat quietly reposing faith in God's benevolence? How much planning ought to have gone into the construction of such a massive project? How much effort should have been mounted to mobilise funds? The Swamiji now remembered the TTD out of sheer necessity. What would he have done had there been no TTD? Such unpalatable thoughts raced across my mind for a while.

But what should I do now? Twelve lakh rupees was not a small amount. The Persons-in-Charge Committee was not due to meet for the next one month. By that time, the new CGF regulations would have come into force. The new CGF committee would take at least a month or two to organise itself, process the cases and release the funds, if they are sanctioned. The Swamiji could not afford to wait for a month. As he needed funds very badly. If a donation for Ramakrishna Mutt were to be made, it had better be made at once. Release of funds a couple of months down the line might not be that fruitful. What would happen if I mustered the requisite courage made the donation and placed it before the Persons-in-Charge Committee for ratification? If the other members were to disagree? I shuddered at the prospect. I was hardly 38. The other two members of the committee were older, senior and occupied higher positions. They might conclude that I was irrational and emotional.

I was on the horns of a dilemma. The intellect told me, "Go ahead. This is a good project". Administrative experience warned, "Why do you want to take a risk?" I found myself getting up from the chair. I did not know why. The moment I turned aside, I saw the life-size portrait of Lord Srinivasa. "Lord, I am leaving the matter in your hands. Whatever you want me to do, I will do". I shut my eyes and began to ponder.

Then, all of a sudden cropped up the question: Was I sincere in entrusting the matter to the Lord? If I was sincere, why should I hesitate? The donation was meant for a good cause. The TTD could become a partner in the mega project of a dedicated mission which had translated its philosophy of "service to man is service to God" into practice and planned to foster a new culture in innumerable lives. There was no reason to waver when the cause was noble. There was then nothing wrong in praying to the Lord in total surrender that He take care of the consequences. I remembered Swami Rangathananda saying, "All depends on Venkateswara's grace". Without losing time further, I returned to my seat, called up the Financial Advisor and instructed him to straightway make out a cheque for Rs.12 lakh in the name of Ramakrishna Mutt. Collecting the cheque, I left for Hyderabad the next day.

Immediately after landing in Hyderabad, as a measure of abundant precaution, I spoke to the other two members of the Persons-in-Charge Committee – Revenue Principal Secretary Ramesan and Endowments Commissioner Chandramouli Reddy. Once they heard me, they sounded pessimistic of the donation being approved.

The gist of what both of them said was the same: "One need not doubt the service record or the integrity of Ramakrishna Mutt. Even the TTD contributing to a noble cause like theirs is not wrong. But you can be faulted for making the donation shortly before the new regulations of the Common Good Fund are to be brought into force. And doing it without the knowledge especially of the Chief Minister and the Endowments Minister might be inviting trouble. Think calmly..."

Even after listening to them, my mind would not waver. I felt that an invisible force was pushing me from behind. I was convinced that I should necessarily stand by a good cause and that the Lord would take care of other things.

However, heeding the suggestion of the Persons-in-Charge, I decided to meet the Chief Minister and the Endowments Minister. Hoping they would give an okay. The Endowments Minister was out of station. Finally, I tried and got an appointment to meet the Chief Minister that very evening. I talked about Ramakrishna Mission's project, the urgency and the appropriateness of the TTD making the donation. Yet...

× × ×

Dr. Channa Reddy deflated my fervent contention that I had the gift of the gab. If the Chief Minister were to say a 'no' even at this stage, I could not muster the courage to pass on the cheque to Ramakrishna Mutt under any circumstances. I indulged in self-flagellation: "I seem to have come here unnecessarily. Perhaps, I ought to have come here after handing over the cheque. At the worst, the Chief Minister might have blasted me. Now, it would not be possible to pass on the cheque if he says a 'no'. What am I to do? " I came back to senses once again. "Why am I torturing myself? Have I not laid the burden at Srinivasa's doorstep? He would ensure that whatever is destined to happen, happens". Once this thought struck me, my mind became clear and light. I was about to get up.

Finally, without any premeditation, I told the Chief Minister, "I am not so wise as to talk to you about faith in God and service to humanity. Lord Srinivasa has endowed you with enormous discretion to choose between good and evil, right and wrong. This project is coming up in Hyderabad. And Ranganathananda is not going to take it away. It benefits only local people. Please think it over. Whatever be your decision, I will abide by it". I got up.

Dr. Channa Reddy looked at me sharply. I did not know what he felt. He said, "Wait a minute, Prasad". He called up his private secretary; "You seem to have told me yesterday that Ramakrishna Mutt Swamiji had sought an appointment. Get him on the line; I would like to speak to him."

In a couple of minutes, the Chief Minister spoke over the phone to Swami Ranganathananda about the project and its present status and assured him that he would facilitate the requisite financial aid. I could not believe my own ears. Even before I could recover from the pleasant surprise, said the Chief Minister: "Okay, you send Rs.12 lakh to him. Going by what the Swamiji says, it is a mega project. We don't think it will be completed with this Rs.12 lakh. What will happen if the Swamiji cannot raise the extra money to complete the project?"

"Sir, what all the Swamiji told me was that he initiated the project with God's inspiration and that God would ensure its completion. If you don't mind, let me say one thing: If Lord Srinivasa showers his blessings, the project is bound to be completed. All those who extend a helping hand, including the Chief Minister, are incidental characters".

The Chief Minister smiled and commented: "You seem to have imbibed *'vedanta'* after going to the TTD".

Replying, "It is all God's grace", I came out. (Although the Chief Minister said that I need not wait for the Endowments Minister's clearance, I briefed the Minister over the phone on the subject. I recalled Swami Rangnathananda's words: "Whether this happens or not depends on Lord Venkateswara's grace".

In the next hour, Mr. Ramesan, Mr. Chandramouli Reddy and I met as Persons-in-Charge Committee and adopted a resolution on the Rs.12 lakh donation. As I had no time to hand over the cheque to the Swamiji personally, I entrusted the job to TTD Liaison Officer Prof. Sreerama Murthy and boarded the flight to Tirupati. By the time I landed at Tirupati, Swami Ranganathananda had already called me. When I called him back, he expressed his gratitude and said, "Prasad garu, Lord Srinivasa's greatness lies in making the impossible possible. He has willed that the project take shape. He, therefore, chose you ..(True?)"

I shared with him the doubt voiced by the Chief Minister. "What will you do if you run short of funds for the next phase of the project?" The Swamiji once again underpinned his faith in God. "He (The Lord) would decide whether this should go through or not. If He does not want it, we cannot execute it. If He wants it, no one can stop it. If necessary, I may have to come to Lord Srinivasa once again..".

A few days later, Swami Ranganathananda visited Tirupati and had *'darshan'* of Srinivasa. I was fortunate enough to spend some time with him. His erudition, clarity of thinking, incisive analysis and unflagging service-mindedness impressed me very much. He invited me to visit Ramakrishna Mutt and see how the project was shaping up. I visited the *'mutt'* within a week. Every brick there reflected the dedication of Swami Rangathananda, and his team members Paramardhananda and others. By then a crore of rupees had been spent. Asked how much it would cost further, Mr. T. Venkataramana Reddi, Director of Town Planning, who was acting as the architect, replied "another Rs.40 lakhs or Rs.50 lakhs". Unwittingly, I asked where from the Swamiji was going to get so much money.

The Swamiji's tranquil face lit up with a smile. "How has such a big project come up to this stage? Have I built it? Don't you know that the Great Power which has done this so far will take care of the rest also?" The Swamiji did not utter a word. But the realised soul made me understand a host of such feelings of his in a flash by merely pointing his forefinger at the sky. I could not but congratulate him on his immense faith in the Lord.

× × ×

A few months rolled by. One day all of a sudden Swami Ranganathananda asked me over the phone to go over to Hyderabad immediately to discuss an important matter. In response to my query, he said the matter concerned Ramakrishna Mutt lands being under the occupation of the Defence Department. Not knowing what to do, he wanted to seek my advice. It struck me that it had something to do with the project under construction. I agreed to visit Hyderabad.

My Hyderabad visit two days later only confirmed my surmise. The second phase of the project, when we met last, was estimated to cost Rs.40 lakh-Rs.50 lakh. Now with the decision to add a cellar to the prayer hall and go in for better flooring, the estimate had escalated by another Rs.15 lakh. He had exhausted all his resources and sources. If he persisted, he might get Rs.2 lakh to Rs.3 lakh more. What about the remainder of Rs.12 lakh? He would like to know whether the TTD could be of any help.

How? The Swamiji had a proposal up his sleeve. Ramakrishna Mutt had a sprawling seven-acre site at the Begumpet old airport, donated by a philanthropist. It had been under the occupation of Defence people for a long time. If sold in the market, it might fetch Rs.50 lakh to Rs.60 lakh. But the Swamiji was not prepared to sell the land for the sake of money to a real estate builder or a trust that would abuse it. He would like to transfer it to a reputed charitable or a religious institution. That was why he was not insisting on market value for the land. It would be enough if he got the Rs.12 lakh required.

As the Swamiji explained the situation, our Hyderabad liaison officer and Sanskrit College Principal Professor Sreerama Murthy drew me aside and whispered, " Why can't we take the land for our Sanskrit College". (The college had been located in the corridors of a Hanuman temple till then).

I could not lap up the Swamiji's proposal or the Liaison Officer's suggestion because of some built-in limitations. The TTD had been finding it difficult to manage properties donated by people at different places. On top of it, the TTD had no tradition of purchasing properties. Wherever necessary, the Government itself or donors gave land to the TTD. Still, at the insistence of Sri Rangathananda, I had but to go to inspect the land.

The land abutting the airport was highly precious. The city had already been expanding in that direction. In a few years, the land value would shoot up to crores of rupees. The Swamiji was not sure when the Defence Ministry occuping the property for its Atomic research activities for decades would vacate the land or how to get them vacate it.

"Prasad garu, leave aside the question of the value of this land. I need only Rs.12 lakh. I will transfer the land to the TTD. Since the transaction is going to be between two religious institutions, there is no scope or need for anybody to attribute motives. If you give me Rs.12 lakh, my project will be through".

I was caught in a dilemma. The site was beautiful. In the days to come, its value would definitely go up. But would the TTD Trust Board appreciate if I were to say that I acquired the land as Ramakrishna Mutt needed money. (A Trust Board had been constituted to replace the Persons-in-Charge Committee). In case the Board members were to question why I bought the land at a cost of Rs.12 lakhs for a college, which was being run free of cost in the Hanuman temple premises, what could be my answer? Assuming that I bought the land convincing the Board, what would happen if the Defence people did not vacate? Would it be possible to re-sell the land if necessary? A myriad questions of this type burrowed my brain.

The Swamiji seemed to have read my mind: "Look Prasad, don't view this as a commercial transaction. Consider it as an opportunity for the TTD to aid a noble cause. It may be difficult for me to get the Defence people vacate the land but not for you and the TTD", he pleaded once again. I could not decide. I felt I was getting sucked into an unnecessary controversy. Cautiously, I told the Swamiji, "Sir, give me a few days. I will think over and let you know". In fact, personally I was inclined to help Ramakrishna Mutt. Helping a good and just cause was a matter of privilege. Moreover, the appreciation in land value would be much more than the bank interest the TTD would get on Rs.12 lakh deposit. But the newly appointed Trust Board members might not agree. Having just been appointed, they would in all probability shoot down my idea, I reasoned.

When the Trust Board met, I wondered whether I should raise the subject or not. Then it struck me, "Why not I leave it to Lord Srinivasa". Then a member raised his voice to complain, "It is surprising that we don't have a good '*kalyan mantap*' in Hyderabad. The TTD has '*kalyan mantaps*' in Bangalore and many other places. We should give priority to the construction of one in Hyderabad".

"Oh! What a great idea", I told myself in delight. I cried "eureka". I took up where the member left off. "That is what I was about to say ..." and narrated how the TTD could acquire seven acres of land near the Begumpet airport dirt cheap for just Rs.12 lakh. I had answers to all their questions and doubts. I rattled off: "We can build a complex with four to five *kalyan mantaps*, a large prayer hall, a building for our Sanskrit College, etc., etc. So far as the Defence people are concerned, we could talk to the Prime Minister or the President when they visit Tirupati and get the Defence people vacate". The Board unanimously approved my proposal. (Was it mine?). I sent a cheque for Rs.12 lakh to the '*mutt*' and it transferred the land to the TTD.

Fifteen days later, Union Defence Minister Babu Jagjivan Ram visited Tirumala and had '*Sri Vari darshan*'. Immediately after the '*darshan*', I prayed to Lord Venkatewara and handed over my representation to the Defence Minister.

Mr. P.V.R.K. Prasad with Defense Minister Mr. Babu Jagajevan Ram

What a surprise? I received a reply in 10 days. The Defence Minister ordered that the site be vacated in a year. He himself

Rama Krishna Muth constructed by Swami Ranganadhananda in Hyderabad.

stipulated the deadline. At the end of the deadline, a senior defence official called on me and sought extension of the deadline by 15 days. As promised, they moved into the defence complex premises opposite Hyderabad Public School. Prof. Sreerama Murthy was a picture of happiness as the Sanskrit College had moved from the Hanuman temple verandah into its own building. Prof. Sreerama Murthy, who took me round the new college premises, praised me to the skies in his characteristic style and said, "Sir, but for you no one else would have ...".

I cut him short and said, "Do you know who is responsible?" He looked at me in wonder. Recalling Swami Rangathananda's gesture, I pointed my right forefinger at the sky.

19

ANNAMAYYA COMES TO MS's RESCUE

"Almost four hundreds years ago Lord Srinivasaa had willed that it should happen this way. What do you say, Mr. Prasad?" asked Mr. Atma.

Mrs. M. S. Subbalakshmi, the 'Queen of Music', (to quote India's first Prime Minister Pundit Jawaharlal Nehru), her spouse Mr. Sadasivam, two or three others and I were signing agreements in Mrs Subbulakshmi's house in Madras when Mr. Atma (son of Mr.Sadasivam and Secretary to MS) made this observation.

As I looked at him quizzically, Mr. Atma repeated his statement. I smiled and said, "Good joke", even as I continued to attend to the task on hand.

Mr. Atma would not leave me. "Don't dismiss my observation as of no significance. Listen to me for a while", he said, and travelled 400 years back in time. Listening to him, all of us there had a hearty laugh.

× × ×

Mrs. M S Subbulakshmi popularly known as MS is the only female musician who has earned the country's highest 'Bharat Ratna' award. She has been described as a 'sweet vocalist', a 'great musician' and even as an 'incarnation of Goddess Saraswati'. Music is her breath. An ardent devotee, she offers the nectar of music to the Lord every day. One wonders as to what makes her sweet voice cast a spell even on animals and birds.

There used to be a great musician called Tansen in Emperor Akbar's *Court.* Akbar believed that no one in the entire world could excel Tansen in music. As he was returning to the palace one day after a stroll, he heard a new voice singing magnificently. Akbar thoroughly enjoyed the singing by this stranger. The next morning, unable to contain his pleasure, he told Tansen, "I heard a wonderful voice last evening. If you don't get jealous, let me tell you that his is the best voice in the world."

Tansen smiled and said, "Oh, Emperor, what you say sounds incredible. Let me also have the privilege of hearing such a singer". That evening Akbar took Tansen to the spot where a man sitting atop a boulder singing. His sweet voice impressed Tansen also. A little later, Akbar asked, "What do you say now?"

Tansen smiled and said, "True Sir, I cannot hold a candle to that Sun of music. While my music is confined to singing the praises of the Lord of Delhi, he has dedicated himself to singing the praises of the Lord of the Universe".

MS belongs to that genre of geniuses dedicated to singing the glories of the Lord. Music lovers used to throng her concerts to have a dip in devotional music that flowed from her. M. S. had carved out a niche for herself in the hearts of all people ranging from lay persons to heads of States and religious '*mutts*'. Even Prime Minister Pundit Jawaharlal Nehru, captivated by MS's music, had once said "Who am I, a mere Prime Minister of India, before you, the Queen of Music?" It is no wonder that she has been conferred 'Bharat Ratna'.

The credit for spotting her talent, encouraging it, and earning her worldwide acclaim goes to her husband, Mr. Sadasivam. A Gandhian and a disciple of Rajaji, Mr. Sadasivam organised concerts by MS to raise funds for many charitable institutions. (Their daughter Radha too is a good musician). During 1960-1980, MS was the uncrowned queen of the music kingdom. Had she desired, she would have earned crores of rupees through her music concerts. But neither she nor Mr. Sadasivam ever thought of amassing wealth for themselves. She spread the fragrance of devotional music only in aid of charitable causes. Music concerts were a means to provide happiness to others and encourage good causes.

One day at the beginning of 1979, I received two urgent messages – one from Kanchi *'peethadhipati'* Sri Chandrasekharendra Saraswati Swami and the other from Puttaparti Sai Baba. The thrust of both messages was the same: "The TTD should somehow go to the aid of Mrs. Subbalakshmi".

I could not immediately make out what they wanted the TTD to do for the great musician, and why. In fact, the TTD had already appointed her an *'asthana vidwan'*. What else could the TTD do? Then I happened to read about the plight of the MS family in the morning newspaper.

The news report said that financial problems had forced the Sadasivam family to sell its bungalow in Kalki Estate in Chennai and move into a small house on rent near Valluvar Kottam. Mr. Sadasivam had already shut down his loss making 'Kalki' magazine. The news upset me.

Were she to ask, there were innumerable music lovers to offer financial assistance. But it was uncharacteristic of both MS and Mr. Sadasivam to seek monetary aid. They would not compromise on self-respect. They would neither stretch their hands for any assistance nor accept it even if it was offered unsolicited. Was the Queen of Music who had mesmerised millions of people go without a shelter of her own?

Agitated over their economic plight, I also felt that the TTD should do something. When I went to the temple that evening and stood before the Lord, MS came to my mind. "Can't you go to the aid of the musician who treats you as her *'Perumal'* and prays with her golden voice daily? Millions wake up in the morning to her melodious rendering of your *'Suprabhatam'*. Her chanting of *'Vishnu Sahasranama'* (your Thousand names) provides solace and inspiration to millions".

As I came out of the temple, I saw an old woman, amidst a group of devotees, singing in praise of the Lord. Swayed by devotion, the others in the group were playing *'talam'*. Then in a flash it dawned on me what I should do.

When I went to sleep that night, I was filled with happiness. At the break of dawn, I left for Kanchi and told Sri Chandrasekhara Saraswati Swamiji. "I have thought over your message. We are now taking Annamayya *'keertanas'* to the public through the Annamacharya project. If MS sings Annamacharya *'keertanas'*, we can record and release LP records throughout the country. Although the *'keertanas'* are in Telugu, every one will listen because MS is a great artiste gifted with a sweet voice and more importantly she sings with utmost devotion. That way, Annamayya's *'keertanas'* in praise of Lord Srinivasaa will get publicity and MS, a share in the revenue on sale of LP records."

The Swamiji commended the idea. He, however, counselled: "Prasad, MS and Sadasivam are not worldly-wise. They don't bother even about the next day. Whatever you do should not embarrass them. Work out something which will be useful and justifiable to the TTD while it takes care of the MS throughout her life."

Immediately on my return, I discussed the proposal with the Persons-in-Charge Committee. The committee liked the idea of projecting Annamayya *'keertanas'* through MS as they would get national and international recognition. Committee Chairman Dr. Ramesan, and member Chandramouli Reddy encouraged me by giving the "go ahead". Dr. Ramesan agreed to join me on my visit to Madras, to meet MS. We both left for Madras. The MS family was living in a small house on rent near Valluvar Kottam. On arrival, we presented a very good replica of Lord Srinivasaa to Mr. Sadasivam.

Initially Mr. Sadasivam was highly enthusiastic when I explained the project. But soon he started to express his misgiving: "Annamayya's *'keertanas'* are in chaste Telugu. But we are proficient only in Tamil. MS has no problem in singing Tyagaraja *'keertanas'*, also in Telugu, because she has been practising them since childhood. Asking her in her sixtieth year to learn and sing so many Annamayya *'keertanas'* in Telugu without the Tamil slang will be next to impossible".

These were reasons for his reservation. MS would not like to render any *'keertana'* without understanding its meaning and spirit. It would take at least a week for her to understand the meaning of each *'keertana'* and capture the diction in Telugu.

We were planning to produce five long play records. It would mean recording of 50 *'keertanas'* spread over 50 weeks or almost a year. No wonder, Mr. Sadasivam pursed his lips as if to convey, "This is something that cannot happen".

I was disappointed. We had come all the way to somehow assist the family. Why was he responding like that? Were we to tell him openly that "it is only to help you that we have taken up this project", he might shoot down the proposal altogether. I remembered Kanchi Swamiji's words, "They do not look for charity from anybody". How could I convince him?

I remembered Lord Srinivasaa once again and left it to him as I could not do anything. Meanwhile, MS dropped in. The moment she saw the picture of Lord Srinivasa, which we had presented earlier, she prostrated before the Lord and went into a rapture saying, 'Perumal, yennakkaga neengale vanduttela?" (Oh Lord, have you yourself come for my sake?).

What an ecstasy she experienced! Her face, radiant with continuous practice of devotional music, seemed to mirror her deep and unflagging belief that "Perumal alone will liberate" her. It was reminiscent of an event I had witnessed a few months earlier.

× × ×

A few months after I had taken over as TTD Executive Officer in 1978, I visited the TTD Leprosy Hospital & Rehabilitation Centre. Dr. Bhaskara Rao, the Centre's in-charge, introduced the leprosy patients one by one to me. As he introduced me to a young man called Veerachari, I felt like knowing more about him.

Veerachari was hardly 25 and a bachelor. His family, belonging to Bomanahalli near Bellary, was adept at carving pictures on wooden planks, their traditional occupation. Veerachari used to turn out masterpieces even as a child. By his teens, he had earned recognition as an expert craftsman.

One day he noticed some white patches here and there on his body. Gradually, they spread to his entire body. The white patches on his fingers and nose began to grow in size. Fearing that it could be a skin disease, he consulted doctors in the city. They diagnosed it as leprosy. The moment he was branded as a leprosy patient, all the villagers began to keep a distance from him. He cried uncontrollably for days and nights over the social boycott and prayed to the Lord. One Dr. J. S. Narayana, who spotted the artist in Veerachari, took the initiative and started the treatment and later sent him to the Tirupati TTD Leprosy Eradication Centre.

After four years of treatment, the doctors could prevent leprosy from spreading to other parts of his body. But, the disease, had already eaten away his fingertips that carved masterpieces. That could not be reversed. The TTD doctors had treated him to the best of their abilities and could do no better.

On introduction, Veerachari, a benign man of few words, saluted me and stood aside. I was sad to notice that leprosy was slowly consuming and eclipsing a talented craftsman.

"Have you stopped carving pictures?", I asked him unable to restrain my curiosity as I saw his fingers. He was supremely happy that I showed interest in his work. "Just a minute, Sir", he said. He ran into his room and fetched four or five beautiful pieces, which he carved after the disease had struck him. A carving depicting Lord Srinivasaa was one of them.

What a superb workmanship! What great skills God had endowed him with! As I keenly watched the Lord on wood, I forgot myself. Noticing my interest, Veerachari said in a low tone, "I have travelled thus far. God willing, if the disease does not eat away the remainder of my fingers, I am eager to carve out many such pieces."

Undeterred by leprosy that targeted his fingers, he continued to carve out marvellous pieces. He sincerely believed that Lord Srinivasaa would bail him out. His deep faith in the Lord moved me. I felt that society should not lose such a talented artiste. As if pushed by somebody, I used my position and influence as TTD Executive Officer to organise special treatment for him by a visiting German specialist at Vellore CMC for a few weeks.

Veerachari was full of gratitude. On the eve of my transfer from Tirupati, he presented me a lively *'Gitopadesam'* wooden carving depicting Krishna and Arjuna on the chariot engrossed in discussion with intricate details of the horses, decoration on the chariot etc. It is a rare masterpiece. "Why do you take all this trouble?" I asked him. "The Lord has revived my art through you. He has granted me the fortune of serving Him by giving me a job (in the TTD artificial limbs centre) and staying here itself."

Yes, I clearly remember, as per the rules of the rehabilitation centre, hewas expected to go back to the village once he was discharged following cure. He met me to represent that he would like to stay on in Tirupati serving the Lord. He did not want to go back to his village as he was not sure whether the villagers would accept him wholeheartedly. He wanted a job in the TTD so that he could spend the rest of his life in the service of the Lord. TTD employment regulations did not permit the EO or even the Board to give employment, without reference to the Employment Exchange. Creation of all new posts had to be approved by the Government.

Already, I had been engaged in a fight with the Government by giving jobs to about 20 Bal Mandir inmates who had reached 18 years. That was a peculiar case. The TTD had been running an Orphanage, adopting orphans and providing them all facilities – such as shelter, food, clothing, education etc upto the age of 18 years. When an inmate attained 18 years of age the Bal Mandir would discharge him/her from the institute. These orphans did not know where to go and what to do. They also did not know as to how to continue studies, if they had not completed their education.

I felt that the moment TTD gave shelter to an orphan, it was the responsibility of the TTD to take care of him till he is properly rehabilitated. I felt that these children should be provided employment in the TTD, depending upon their skills, aptitude and qualifications. No qualification rules would be relaxed but other general employment rules regarding reference to Employment Exchange, putting out open advertisements, providing for open competition, rules of reservations etc should not apply. On that basis, I had rehabilitated about 20 inmates who had completed 18 years of age. The Government had not so far ratified the appointments as the recruitment was not as per rules, though the philosophy and principle behind the policy was appreciated.

Similar was Veerachari's case. As I was not doing anything for personal benefit, I had appointed Veerchari as a Carpenter supervisor in the Artificial Limb Centre, which I started on behalf of the TTD for the benefit of polio affected and other disabled persons. Veerachari was referring to my relaxing all the rules, without waiting for authorisation to rehabilitate him.

× × ×

I recalled Veerachari's devotion to and faith in the Lord when I saw MS in her rapture.

As I tried to persuade Mr. Sadasivam and MS to accept my proposal, I looked at the benign picture of Lord Srinivasaa, who seemed to be smiling. I assured Mr. Sadasivam that I would make available the services of the Annamacharya Project Officer and Telugu Professor, Mr. Kamisetti Srinivasaulu Setti, to explain and guide MS in the language, style and the meaning of the *'keertanas'*. Then, MS, who had been keenly watching and listening to us said in Tamil, "For the sake of *'Perumal'*, I will practise the *'keertanas'* however difficult they are". Finally, taking a bold and determined stand, she said to her spouse, "Accept the proposal". For me, her acceptance was a miracle. I wondered how *'Perumal'* entered her mind at the crucial moment.

Finally, we decided to limit the number of Annamayya's telugu *'keertanas'* to three LP records. On the remaining two LP records, we decided to record popular Sanskrit compositions like *'Ganesa Pancharatnam'*, *'Madhurashtakam'*, *'Gita Govindam'*, *'Nama Ramayanam'*, *'Hanuman Chalisa'*, *"Lakshmi Ashtotram'*, *'Sri Venkateswara Karavalamba Stotram'*, *'Govindashtakam'*, *'Kanakadharastavam'*, *'Durga Pancharatnam'*, *'Ranganadhagadyam'*, *'Dwadasa Stotram' and 'Sishtashtakam'*. We thus ensured that the *'stotras'* from the scriptures and great compositions of Adi Sankara, Ramanuja, Madhwacharya and other great saints were covered.

So far so good. But MS would not evince any interest in discussing the terms of payment. She stepped aside saying, "When the singing is for *'Perumal'* what is the point in discussing payment?". Mr. Sadasivam also was highly embarrassed to talk about it. What the Kanchi *'Peethadhipati'* told me reverberated in my ears. "If we just indicate, several rich industrialists will support them for life and extend any other assistance. But MS and Sadasivam won't accept any such proposal. They won't agree if you say the project has been conceived to help them. They are the last persons to seek charity from anybody. Only Lord Srinivasaa should go to their aid".

Mr Ramesan, our Chairman, clinched the issue. HMV company would meet all the recording expenses including the fees for support artistes. The TTD would deposit Rs.7 lakh in the joint account of the TTD and MS in a bank. She would be entitled to the interest on the deposit all through her life. After her death, the TTD would get the capital back. The TTD would be entitled to the royalty on the sale of the cassettes, payable by the HMV Company. But responding to MS's suggestion, we made a slight change in the agreement before wrapping it up. Under the amended agreement, the TTD would make joint fixed deposit of Rs.4 lakh in MS's name, Rs. 2 lakh in Mr. Sadasivam's name and Rs.1 lakh in their daughter Radha's name. The monthly interests on the deposits would go to them as long as they live. The TTD would get back the deposit on their death.

× × ×

As we signed the agreements, Sadasivam's son and MS's secretary Atmanadhan smiled.

"Perumal seemed to have a foreboding of MS's economic plight 400 years back itself. He made Annamacharya write thousands of *'keertanas'*." Atmanathan's comment made all of us laugh. But MS recalled *'Perumal'* and went into ecstasy. I noticed tears of joy flowing down her cheeks. The TTD's *'Balaji Pancharatnamala'* cassettes and LPs and CDs now available in the market are the products of the soulful music that flowed from MS out of this venture.

After all this, one doubt continued to trouble me. What was the role of Mr. Sadasivam in the entire project? Inclusion of Radha could be justified as she was the co-vocalist. We had made a joint deposit of Rs. 2 lakh to benefit Sadasivam. How could I justify it?

"How shall we go about the project?". I asked Mr. Sadasivam, seeking his guidance. *"Perumal'* will take care of every thing", he replied. Perumal possessed Sadasivam. It was a treat to watch the organisational abilities of Sadasivam. He had an amazing network. The way he motivated and coordinated the activity to meet the deadline was phenomenal. Mr. Sadasivam got the LP records of Balaji Pancharatnamala released in a magnificent and unprecedented manner, always attributing all his new ideas to 'Perumal'.

Mrs. M.S. Subbalakshmi being honoured by Mr. Anjaiah, Chief Minister Endowments Minister Mr. Chowdhay & Mr. P.V.R.K. Prasad are also in the picture.

President Sanjeeva Reddy released one LP and Prime Minister Mrs. Indira Gandhi, another. State Governors released one LP in all States at the same time. On the day the Prime Minister released the LP in New Delhi, The Chief Ministers released the same in the State Headquarters. Senior Peethapadhis and Swamijis like Swami Ranganadhananda of

Ramakrishna Mutt, Satya Sai Baba of Puttaparthi, Sankaracharyas, Srivaishnava, Dwaita and Saiva Acharayas released the other cassettes simultaneously. I was amazed at Sadasivam's subtle publicity and marketing strategy. I could comprehend the contribution of Sadasivam in moulding MS into a 'Bharat Ratna'.

By the time the last LP was released in about a year, the TTD had earned Rs.10 lakh as royalty thanks to the promotional effort of Mr Sadasivam, MS's devotional music and TTD's name. Even before the project was completed, the TTD got back much more than it had spent. The TTD also had the satisfaction of popularising Annamayya *'keertanas'* all over India and abroad. Assisting a famous musician in her hour of need, of course was a God sent opportunity. The Kanchi seer was happy in that he had played a role in helping a devotee of *"perumal"*. Sri Satya Sai Baba subtly remarked, while releasing the LP, "This project has achieved all the objectives".

How had all these become possible? Which Power orchestrated it?

20

THE LONG AND SHORT OF THE BROAD AND NARROW 'NAMAM'

Right in front of the Tirumala Srinivasa temple, I had to reckon with a rain of stones once.

It was for the first time in the history of the temple that people had pelted the Tirumala Tirupati Devasthanams Executive Officer with stones. Even before I could collect my thoughts on how to respond to the untoward and unanticipated development, Vigilance Officer, Dhilleswara Rao and a security guard had been injured as they tried to come to my rescue. The TTD security staff immediately threw a security cordon around me and whisked me away from the crowd into the temple. The fracas resulted in the *'darshan'* of Lord Venkateswara being suspended and the *'maha dwaram"* (main entrance) of the temple being shut. This happened in 1982.

The abrupt halt to the *'dharma darshan'* under way and closure of the *'maha dwaram'* happened for the second time during my association with the temple. During 1981, the TTD staff and the police had clashed near the *'maha dwaram'* as the devotees walking in line watched. When the clash turned serious, the *'maha dwaram' was* shut and the *'darshan'* halted.

There seemed to be a connection between these two incidents.

× × ×

Lord Venkateswara of Tirumala appears with a broad, white *'karpoora namam'* (camphor symbol on the forehead). During the *'darshan'* after *'pulangi seva'* (flower decoration) on Thursdays the size of the namam is reduced considerably, and during the Friday morning *'abhisheka seva' (sacred bath)*, the Lord appears without the *'namam'*. Devotees then have what is called *'netra darshanam'* and *'nija pada darshanam' (opportunity to see the eyes and the feet of the Lord).*

This *'namam'* seeks to combine the traditions of the two *'Vaishnavite'* sects (*'vadagalai'* and *'tengalai'*). It is neither in 'Y' shape nor "U' shape but a combination of both. The *'namam'* carries *'kasturi tilakam'* in its middle portion. The application of the *'karpura namam'* as a combination of 'Y' and 'U' shapes is a skillful operation. Once applied, on Friday morning the *'namam'* has to last a week until the next *'abhishekam'*.

When I was Executive Officer, many devotees, known and unknown used to draw my attention in person and by way of letters to the *'namam'*. Acquaintances even entered into a debate. The thrust of their argument was that the *'Srivari namam'* had grown so broad over the years that it virtually covered the Lord's eyes. It is possible to see the Lord's eyes to some extent during the Thursday *'pulangi seva'* when the size of the *'namam'* is reduced considerably. The Lord's eyes can be seen fully bereft of the *'namam'*, and the feet, bereft of decoration, only during the Friday morning *'abhisheka seva'*.

All those who drew my attention to the *'namam'* showed me ancient paintings of Lord Srinivasa to drive home the point that the *'namam'* was not so large in the past. They questioned as to why the old practice could not be restored. I did not bother about the matter in 1978 when I had just taken over as Executive Officer. As the number of people who pleaded for a smaller *'namam'* increased, my interest in the subject grew.

During 1980-81, I studied the *'namam'* issue at length. I keenly looked at pictures, paintings and drawings that were available with the TTD and devotees. In most of the old pictures, the *'karpoora namam'* was narrow and small. In some, the Lord's eyes could be clearly seen in full and in some others, to a large extent.

Then I inquired as to when the broad *'karpoora namam'* came to be applied. Priests, *'mirasidars'* and *'Jiyyangar'* said they were not aware of the lean *'namam'* as shown in the old paintings. They categorically declared that as far as their memory went, only the broad *'namam'* was being applied. But why did the old pictures depict a narrow *'namam'*? Their conjecture was that painters depicted the Lord's *'namam'* as it appeared to them or as they liked it. Photographing of the statue was not permitted since the advent of photography. So, the interested artists used to sit near the sanctum sanctorum and drew paintings.

I was not satisfied with their explanation. I, therefore, wrote letters to 'Acharya Purushas' and Agama pundits to enlighten me on the issue. It produced no results.

As the news of my inquiry into the origin of the broad *'namam'* became public, some devotees represented to me, "It is not fair to permit only a few to have the privilege of *'srivari netra darshan'* during *'pulangi seva'*, *'abhishcka seva'* and *'abhishekanantara seva'*. You should enable all devotees, at least during your TTD stewardship, to have *'darshan'* of the Lord's eyes to some extent at least on all days of the week. To me the logic seemed appealing and convincing. But, the point of usage and custom has to be answered.

I discussed the matter with *'Jiyyangar'* and priests. Showing them the old paintings, I asked why the *'namam'* could not be narrow and lean. It would enable devotees to view the Lord's eyes. In addition, a narrow *'namam'* could be applied in half the time required for the broad *'namam'*. The 15-20 minutes thus saved could be added to the *'dharma darshan'* timings enabling 500-600 more pilgrims to have *'darshan'* of the Lord. I kept questioning them frequently on these lines. Having heard me, they did not feel like raising any objections. "We will leave it to you", they said. I decided to reduce the size of the *'namam'*. Yet, I could not muster the courage to implement it straightway. I tried for old records to get a clue whether there was any reference to the increase in the quantity of camphor for the namam so that I could link it to the change of the size of the namam. No luck.

Finally, one Friday at the beginning of October 1981, I asked the priest in charge on Friday. "To apply a small *'namam'* after the *'abhisheka'*. *'Vijaya Dasami'*, came on October 8,which happened to be the last day of the *'Brahmotsavas'*. The Lord's *'chakra snanam'* (Holy bath to the sacred disc) in the *'pushkarini'* (temple pond) scheduled that day was getting completed. That marked the completion of Brahmostavams. There was a heavy rush of pilgrims. Having spent an hour in the temple overseeing Darshan arrangements, I went back to the camp office at Tirumala by 10 AM.

Around 10-30 AM, some one from the temple informed me over the phone that some trouble was brewing at the temple. As I rushed to the temple, I found the situation was terrible. The *'darshan'* had been suspended and the main entrance shut. As I got the main entrance opened and entered the temple, TTD employees, who had been on a sit-in protest, surrounded me. They gave vent to their ire and spewed hatred and revenge against the police.

According to them, a Reserve police officer on deputation for *'bramotsavam'* duty had tried to enter into the temple through the *'maha dwaram'* along with his family to have *'darshan'* of the Lord. He was infuriated when the staff asked him to produce the pass. All deputation duty staff members were expected to obtain darshan passes. He abused and pushed the staff aside and tried to barge in. When temple staff joined hands and thwarted him, he perceived it as an affront, and withdrew. Later he came with a number of reserve police personnel to the *'mahadwaram'* and had beaten the TTD staff on duty. They then marched into the temple with their shoes on and indiscriminately thrashed with lathis every TTD employee they sighted. Even as they were having a free run within the temple, the news spread like wild fire throughout Tirumala, and the staff outside rushed in and took on the reserve police personnel. The two groups fought bitterly. Ultimately, the police had to beat a retreat, as they were unable to withstand the onslaught from the TTD staff.

As a protest against the police attack, the TTD staff shut the *'maha dwaram"* and went on a sit-in demonstration inside the temple.

I was disturbed when I heard the story. My immediate concern was that the *'darshan'* should go on uninterrupted. For that to happen, the *'maha dwaram'* had to be re-opened. For the doors to be thrown open, the temple staff had to be persuaded. But they were in no mood to listen. They demanded immediate suspension of the concerned police officer. Sri Sampath was the Collector, and Mr Venkatarama Reddy was the Superintendent of Police. They also rushed to the temple, hearing about the incident. As District Magistrate and Collector, Mr.Sampath had ordered a joint inquiry by the Joint Executive Officer and the District Police Superintendent into the incident. Assuring the staff that the inquiry would be completed by that evening, we persuaded with great difficulty the staff to open the *'maha dwaram'*. The *'darshan'* resumed 15-20 minutes later. The inquiry was over by the evening. Action was also taken against some of the guilty. However, for many days the relations between TTD staff and the police were strained. I was distressed and disturbed over the incident and the bad publicity in the media, bringing down the image of the institution and the administration. Why did it happen?

Months passed. I continued to get letters on the *'namam'* issue. I was rudely reminded of the issue when a devotee angrily wrote, "Why don't you reduce the *'namam'* size despite many requests?" I told myself, "It is true, I have already instructed the priests to reduce the *'namam'* size. Why have they not implemented it?" Again on the first Friday that followed, I told the priests, "Reduce the size of the *'karpoora namam'*. The Lord's eyes should be visible to the devotees all through the week". They nodded their heads.

From the temple, I went to inspect the demolition work going on. The High Court had vacated the stay against the widening of Sannidhi Street the road opposite the main entrance of the temple. That very Friday morning, TTD's Revenue and Engineering Departments started demolishing structures on Sannidhi Street. The demolition was proceeding briskly. Standing near the *'maha dwaram"*, I was personally supervising the operation. Even as I felt that every thing was going on as planned, a stone flew past me suddenly. As I looked in that direction, I saw a group of persons suddenly entering the Sannidhi street pelting stones. Irked by the demolition of shops for the widening of Sannidhi Street, shopkeepers and Tirumala residents joined hands to pelt stones at me.

Noticing that the stones were aimed at me, Vigilance Officer Dhilleswara Rao and other security personnel rushed to save me. In the process, Dhilleswara Rao and one more security guard were hit by stones. The stones also struck a few pilgrims who were standing in the queue. The temple reverberated to the cries, shouts and slogans. The TTD security staff fired into the air to disperse the crowd and halt the stone throwing. The *'darshan'* queue was stopped and the *'maha dwaram"* was closed to protect the pilgrims. Within a few minutes the police and the security staff reported that all the miscreants had been driven away, the *'maha dwaram'* was reopened and *'darshan'* resumed. The demolitions were also resumed.

But this incident shook me. I could not reconcile myself to such unsavoury developments at the sacred place, as the shower of stones in front of the *'maha dwaram"*, the firing by security staff, the closure of the *'maha dwaram'*, and the halting of the *'darshan'*. The more I thought, the more distressed I became. I did not know how long I stayed in the temple in that disturbed state. There was no reason for the shopkeepers and residents to be agitated. Most of them had agreed to part with their properties on the understanding that they would be given shops of the same size at the same place, of course with a setback of 50' feet when the road was widenned. Other than one or two disgruntled elements, we had received consent from all shopkeepers and residents.

I could not get a satisfactory answer - Why did it happen? What mistake had we committed?

Finally, to get some relief as if in search of an answer I went into the sanctum sanctorum to have *'darshan'* of the Lord. I was about to ask the Lord, "Why has this happened". Then I noticed the Lord's narrow *'karpoora namam'*. It was for the first time that one could *have 'netra darshanam'* of the Lord on a Friday evening as I desired. Yet, I did not feel happy. Agitation continued and I felt more disturbed.

Agitated and confused I was looking at the Lord particularly the namam – the eyes. I had a feeling that I was getting some message. Observing my predicament, the priest came to me and whispered: "Sir, we reduced the *'namam'* size some months ago as instructed by you. Within a few hours, there was a clash between the temple staff and the police. We had to shut the *'maha dwaram'* and halt *'darshan'*. Thereafter, without informing you, we reverted back to the old *'karpoora namam'* size'. Today, once again, we reduced the *'namam'* size as directed by you. Within hours this unfortunate attack on you had taken place. We had to shut the *'maha dwaram'* and halt *'darshan'* again. That's why..." His voice trailed off into silence

As I listened to his words, quiet realization dawned on me. Gradually, my agitation began to subside. I did not say anything more to the priests. I returned home mulling over the happenings. The priests immediately restored the status quo of the *'namam'* (as it appears today). I have not discussed the subject with anybody, anytime. Am I sure whether there was a connection between the namam and the incidents?

21

'PRASAD—DOWN-DOWN'

"Down, Down, Anti-Poor Prasad", "Transfer, Transfer, Enemy of Cows", "Long Live CM, Long Live Anjaiah, Jewel of the Poor".

Raising such slogans vociferously, 400 to 500 Tirumala residents besieged Chief Minister T. Anjaiah at the Tirumala guesthouse one day in 1980. Mr. Anjaiah was visiting Tirumala for the first time after taking over as Chief Minister. Endowments Minister P. V. Choudary, TTD Trust Board Chairman Nagi Reddy and some officials accompanied the Chief Minister. As all of us watched, the crowd led by local leaders raised the slogans targeting me. All the so-called "victims" of my decisions happened to be Tirumala residents.

The demonstrators included those who:

- Lost their places of residence skirting the temple following the Master Plan execution
- Were about to lose stalls and shops because of Sannidhi Street widening, then under way
- Were dead set against licences for hawkers
- Rearing cattle on the Hills, and
- Earned their bread solely through begging

As the Chief Minister arrived at the guesthouse, the leaders of the protesting crowd choked him with garlands and shouted slogans like "Long Live, Chief Minister" and "Long Live, Saviour of the Poor". Some even prostrated before the Chief Minister describing him as their last refuge and requesting him to come to their rescue. Mr. Anjaiah, himself coming from humble beginnings, was considered to be the friend of the poor, and a "pro-poor Chief Minister". Overwhelmed with joy, he assured them, "Why do you worry? I am here to solve your problems".

The Chief Minister's blanket assurance to the milling crowd in the midst of the demonstration puzzled me. Anticipating the shape of things to come, I was getting ready to bow to the inevitable. As some one said, "Be prepared to face the worst; any improvement over the worst, ultimately gives you some solace". As far as I could think, the pro-poor Chief Minister had three options before him to live up to his reputation:

1. Throwing me out of Tirumala straightway to oblige the local crowd
2. Ordering me to concede to all their demands
3. Upbraiding me in public to placate the protesters

Whichever option he chose, I could not escape humiliation. As my mind fathomed the depths of humiliation and getting ready to face it, the slogan shouting acquired a higher pitch. Observing the demonstrators, I spotted local leaders in the front and hawkers in the rear. The hawkers sold trinkets like "vaddi kasulu", photos, flowers, books and eatables without any licence in Tirumala. All of them seethed with anger and revenge against me because I had proposed that all hawkers atop the Hills should be identified and the eligible, given licences. I hit upon the licensing system to rescue pilgrims from unscrupulous hawkers, who took gullible devotees for a ride by palming off trinkets at inflated prices under some false pretext or the other. Introduction of the licence system, we felt, would also make hawkers accountable. It would stabilize the Tirumala population as we could be able to control the flow of a large number of people coming to Tirumala to eke out a livelihood.

We had decided that only those who had been doing business in Tirumala for a minimum of three years and had a local residence were eligible for the licence. Their names should have figured in the house-to-house survey conducted in 1979 for Master Plan purposes, or the 1971 census records or at least in the voters' lists. Obviously, those whose names were not to be found in any of these documents had come to Tirumala in the recent past searching for livelihood.

The eligibility criteria were designed to curb Tirumala's growing population. The TTD was finding it difficult to meet the basic needs of the then existing population and the ever-increasing flow of pilgrims. If the steady in-flow of people into Tirumala in search of livelihood continued unabated, the administration would have a tougher task on its hands in time to come. Tirumala faced water crises frequently and the roads were already choked. I also decided to evict all beggars in the interest of pilgrims.

When we started implementing the decisions, there were murmurs of protests from the aggrieved. The local leaders, who were bent upon retaining and improving their hold over the local people, took advantage of the situation to whip up a campaign against me. It was true that my actions did cause hardship to them. But was it not my responsibility to make the stay of pilgrims comfortable and pleasant? After all, they come from remote villages carrying offerings to the Lord, enduring a lot of stress and strain and incurring huge expenditure.

How could I present my viewpoint unless the Chief Minister asked for it? Such a prospect, however, appeared dim. Hyderabad news reports indicated that the new Chief Minister would not tolerate anything that harmed the interests of the weaker section. Against that backdrop, I felt that the Chief Minister might concede to the agitators' demands. The dice, indeed, appeared loaded against me.

As the leaders got themselves photographed, garlanding the Chief Minister, the sloganeering continued unabated. "The Demon of the Cow that Lord Krishna Loved", "Down, Down Prasad, the Cow Slayer".

The slogans once again depressed me. I could not understand what crime I had committed against these cow lovers. It was true that I had tried to prevent the Tirumala residents from unleashing cows and buffaloes for free roaming and feeding atop the Hills.

The TTD Dairy, supplemented by the Vijaya Dairy, met the milk requirements of the temple, the canteen and temple employees. As their supplies fell short of demand, local residents who raised cows and buffaloes met the requirements of coffee stalls, some staff and pilgrims. But since the milk vendors did not have spacious houses to accommodate the cows, they let them out into the streets. Acting as live speed-breakers on Tirumala roads, the cows survived on offerings made by devout pilgrims. The streets were littered with cow-dung and urine. Some residents did not bother about the upkeep of cows at all, as pilgrims attended to their feeding. Their love for the cow began and ended with milking. Observing the lucrative business line, even some TTD staff ventured into dairying. Their unhygienic surroundings sparked protests from neighbours and 'SOS calls to the TTD. Rogue animals goring pilgrims resulting in their hospitalisation and the TTD offering lame explanations had become routine.

If the cows were not to be seen on streets, they would be in TTD forests grazing. The TTD, which owns the forest within a 10.5 km radius of Tirumala, had been striving hard to preserve and promote its forest wealth. The cowherds returned home from forests, not merely with the cows but also with the firewood collected without authorization for local sale. The forests thus became victims of firewood hackers and hawkers. The cowherds occasionally triggered forest fires too by hurling burning cigarette or bidi butts into bushes.

As a result, Cows and buffaloes had unwittingly turned Tirumala into an insanitary and unhygienic place. There were protests from unwary pilgrims hygiene-minded staff and people who cared about afforestation. I did not know how long such a situation had been prevailing but I felt I should not remain a mute spectator.

The Master Plan for Tirumala envisaged maintenance of hygiene, roads and greenery. If the greenery were not maintained, the temperatures in Tirumala too would shoot up. Pilgrims had to be saved from cows and buffaloes.

As the Master Plan was being implemented, Mr. Shravan Kumar, Revenue Principal Secretary, happened to be the

Chairman of the TTD Persons-in-Charge Committee for a few months. Having had rich experience as Prl.Secretary (Forests) earlier, he evinced a lot of interest in the preservation and promotion of forest wealth atop Tirumala Hills. Under his guidance, we prepared a bio-aesthetic plan. The entire TTD forest within the 10.5-km radius was divided into 18 sectors or zones and drew up plans to promote different species of trees or plants in different sectors. Sectors were earmarked for promotion of firewood plantations, horticulture, floriculture, medicinal plants, spices etc. We constituted a Forest Division under the leadership of a competent conservator (Mr. Rajasekhara Reddy) to promote afforestation on systematic lines. Our idea was nothing short of re-creating the legendary "Nandana Vanam" in five years in Tirumala. In addition, we undertook development of parks and gardens by planting hundreds of species of flower and ornamental plants, under the leadership of committed and knowledgeable Garden Superintendent Dr.Tammanna. The flower gardens continue to be a feast to the eyes and a special attraction to one and all at Tirumala.

Many were the obstacles that stood in the way of the realisation of our dream. Unfortunately most of them revolved around the cow.

Incidentally, the cow had caught my attention in a strange way. When the Lord was being bathed with milk during a Friday *"abhisheka"*, I wondered how milk was procured for the *"abhisheka seva"* in ancient times when there was no habitation around Tirumala. Then the story of Lord Brahma incarnating as cow and visiting Tirumala every day to bathe the Lord in the snake pit with milk struck me. The Lord seemed to have prodded me, a servant of the Lord, to do something to preserve Tirumala's cow population. I lost no time in opening cowsheds and directing that all cows be kept in the cowsheds only. For a nominal fee, the TTD would provide fodder and feed, water and medical aid, and maintain hygiene and sanitation in the sheds. As a result, the cows stopped grazing on plants and trees in TTD gardens. The roads were rid of cow dung and urine. Complaints from staff quarters ceased. Those local residents who raised cows out of their attachment expressed happiness over TTD measures. The TTD measures, however, angered those who abandoned the cows for feeding by pilgrims but lived on milking them. Collection of the nominal fee and the ban on the free movement of cows irked them. (The TTD Executive Officer, in his capacity as Tirumala Panchayat Officer, could ban cow movement).

In addition, we prohibited hacking of trees in TTD forests. With the cooperation of the Forest Department, we got firewood depots opened to preempt complaints about firewood scarcity. With the support of the Union Petroleum Ministry, we promoted the usage of cooking gas in place of firewood in the Tirumala canteen, private hotels, *"kalyana katta"* and TTD quarters. We installed solar water heaters in choultries, *"kalyana katta"*, cottages and guesthouses. We ensured round-the-clock milk supply with the help of Vijaya Dairy. Pilgrims welcomed the measures. But private milk vendors and firewood hawkers were unhappy because their incomes were hit.

Local leaders, keen on retaining their hold over the public, gathered the disgruntled milk vendors, firewood hackers, people displaced by road widening and even beggars and went into action during the Chief Minister's visit. They bombarded the Chief Minister with allegations against me. In fact, these leaders should have had no grievance against TTD policies over cows or hawkers' licences because they did not concern them directly. The TTD earned their wrath by trying to evict them from religious *mutts* and TTD sites that they had occupied without authorisation.

My self-confidence stemmed from clear conscience. After all, we had initiated these measures in the interests of pilgrims and the development of Tirumala. But all those who flocked to the Chief Minister hated me. There were no pilgrims or local people, who appreciated my actions, to defend me.

The slogans grew louder. "Drive out Beggar Starver", "Prasad, Down, Down". Drawn by the slogans, the Chief Minister asked in wonder, "Are you being starved?" and invited the slogan shouters to brief him. The beggars vented their anger against me. "Brother, we have been living and begging here for generations. Now this Prasad has driven us away to Tirupati. He has robbed us of our livelihood". Some of them prostrated before Mr. Anjaiah.

True. When I took over as Executive Officer, there were hundreds of beggars who harassed pilgrims in Tirumala by seeking/demanding alms. Alms-giving was a short-cut to salvation, they harangued the pilgrims. Pilgrims visited Tirumala to have "darshan" of the Lord and offer prayers in a quiet and sacred environment. There was a flood of complaints from pilgrims against beggars. As Executive Officer, I felt, I should look after pilgrims but not beggars who earned their livelihood with ease but without any investment. That was why I banned begging atop Tirumala Hills. I instructed my staff that any one seen begging should be removed to Tirupati immediately. The then Vigilance and Security Officer Janardhan Naidu implemented my directive ruthlessly. No wonder, the beggars treated me as a villain of the first degree. Two or three local leaders acted as their advisors. They told the Chief Minister: "This Executive Officer drove away the poorest of the poor without food or shelter in an authoritarian and inhuman fashion. He is a cruel demon who deprived pilgrims of sacred deeds like alms giving. You alone can rescue the poor by transferring him".

Their pressures and prayers amidst slogan shouting pinned down the Chief Minister. He appeared to be moved by their plight. It was not even ten days since he became the Chief Minister. The moment he stepped into Tirumala for the *"darshan"* of the Lord, the local leaders and their followers, affiliated to the ruling party, encircled him with their tales of woe. My self-confidence began to erode. Endowments Minister Mr. P. V. Choudary and TTD Chairman Mr. Nagi Reddy were aware of the rationale behind my decisions. But they too appeared helpless in coming to my rescue if the Chief Minister succumbed to the pressure mounted by the demonstrators.

When the news of the Chief Minister's Tirumala visit became public, the TTD Chief Security Officer and the

Additional Police Superintendent, Mr. Janardhan Naidu and Mr. Ramachandra Reddy alerted me that local leaders were mobilising all disgruntled people to lodge a complaint against me.

"They are planning a big protest demonstration, Sir. The local leaders are getting ready for a trial of strength and resolve the matters once and for all. If we don't ban the demonstration, you may land in trouble," they advised me. I decided against the ban after thinking about the matter deep and long. "What all I have done is to provide a conducive atmosphere to pilgrims to have '*darshan*' of Lord Srinivasaa. If my decisions are wrong, I will undergo the punishment to be meted out by the Lord. If my actions are right, the Lord will look after me. Why should I then bother about processions or demonstrations?"

I told the security people. "Let people represent their grievances to the Chief Minister. After all, in a democracy they are entitled to present their problems and grievances to the Chief Minister. Who are we to dismiss their cases as unjust or baseless? Our objectives are different. Incidentally, they are affected. We have not initiated the measures only to cause them any loss or harm. We don't harbour any ill-will against them. Let us, therefore, not prohibit the demonstration". The result was I had to stand as an accused in public court. What should I do?

Fearing such embarrassment, Endowments Minister Choudary and TTD Chairman Nagi Reddy had thought of explaining the facts to the Chief Minister earlier. Even though they travelled with the Chief Minister from the Renigunta airport to the guesthouse atop Tirumala Hills, they did not get an opportunity to raise the subject. By the time the Chief Minister arrived at the guesthouse, the demonstration had already been in full swing.

Once the slogan shouting abated, the Chief Minister invited a delegation into his room. In the presence of the District Collector, the Endowments Minister, the Board Chairman and me, the representatives unfolded their tale of woe. They narrated how I had harmed hawkers, harassed cow owners, deprived beggars of their livelihood and hated the locals. They made allegation after allegation with emotional ferocity, "Our poor people here cannot survive so long as Prasad is here. Shift

Prasad and save Tirumala", they said in unison and shouted "Anjaiah Zindabad" again. The outside crowd picked up the cue and shouted, "Prasad, Down, Down".

Depressed over the turn of events, I could not utter a word. Observing my plight, the Endowments Minister (who knew the facts) whispered into the Chief Minister's ears, "Don't take any decisions in haste..." The Chief Minister cut the Minister short with a wave of his hand. My last hope too had ebbed away.

I felt as though I was sinking with humiliation as the ground slipped from under my feet.

P.V.R.K. Prasad with Mr. Anjaiah, Chief Minister.

Chief Minister Anjaiah looked seriously at the local leaders and said; "I have known Prasad since he worked as Secretary to Chief Minister Sri. P. V. Narasimha Rao", and looked at me.

Was he adding fuel to the fire by bringing in political equations, I wondered. Who would now save me? I recalled Lord Srinivasaaa and said to myself, "The very Power who brought me here should save me. The Lord is my last refuge".

The Chief Minister continued, addressing the local leaders: "So don't tell me anything against Prasad. If Prasad cannot do you justice, no one else can. I am passing on all your representations to the Executive Officer".

I could not believe my own ears. The Chief Minister placed all the petitions in my hands, looked at me with a benign smile and told the leaders: "When a good, useful, developmental activity is undertaken, it may occasionally inconvenience some people. On that score, we cannot say that development shall not take place. I am aware of all the good things being done by Prasad. Go away and talk to him later".

The leaders looked at each other in puzzlement. By the time the significance of the Chief Minister's remarks sank into their minds, he had set out for the Lord's *"darshan"*

Tears welled up in my eyes. Moments ago, the ground appeared to be slipping from under my feet. Now I seemed to be soaring into the skies.

Who had empowered me?

Tammanna, Garden Superintendent of TTD Gardensreceiving 'Best Organisation Cup' in Horticulture Development from Mrs. Indira Gandhi, Prime Minister, Mr. Sravan Kumar, Chairman and Mr. P.V.R.K. Prasad are also seen.

22

EXPERIENCE IN DARKNESS

Once a year, a silk sari goes as a gift from Lord Srinivasa of Tirumala to Godadevi of Srivilliputtur in Tamil Nadu. It is presented with temple honours on the occasion of Godadevi's "kalyanotsavam". The tradition had its origin in a strange experience I had on a dark, stormy night amidst heavy rains and strong gales.

× × ×

Sri Venkateswara of Tirumala and Godadevi of Srivilliputtur have been linked for centuries. Godadevi is said to be an incarnation of Bhudevi, wife of Lord Maha Vishnu. According to historical sources, Vishnu Chitta, a great devotee of Lord Vishnu, found a female baby in his *(BASIL) 'Tulasi'* garden. Overwhelmed with joy over what he regarded as a divine dispensation, he took the baby home, named her Godadevi and brought her up. The child's speaking faculty began with her lisping the word "Ranganatha". Intensely devoted to Sriranganatha of Srirangam, it culminated in her marriage with the Lord. The lyrics she had sung extempore out of her devotion to Ranganatha are today known as *"Tiruppavai"*.

Sriranganatha of Srirangam and Sri Venkateswara of Tirumala are one and the same – Lord Maha Vishnu. When muslims invaded the southern States, the Srirangam temple was shut and the processional deities and valuable ornaments of the Lord had been removed to Tirumala for safe custody. Thus Sriranganatha happened to be in Tirumala temple for a number of years. When the invasion threat abated, the deities and ornaments were taken back to Srirangam. That is why the place Sriranganatha occupied during his sojourn in Tirumala is even today known as "Ranga Mantapa". To the extent we know, at least for a century, Vastram (A piece of cloth) and garlands are sent in the name of Godadevi from Srivalliputtur temple to Lord Srinivasa during Lord Srinivasaa's *"brahmotsavams"*. In return, a sari and *'prasadam'* are handed over as a return gift from the Tirumala temple.

After I took over as TTD Executive Officer in 1978, I visited many temples in South India but could not visit Srivilliputtur. I was scheduled to go to Guruvayur in 1981 in connection with the construction of a *mantap* in Venkateswara temple there. According to my schedule, I was to return to Madras touching Tiruvananthapuram, Tiruchendur, Courtallam, Madurai, Tiruchi and Srirangam. Shortly before I left on my Guruvayur trip, Pare Pattedar Seshadri suggested that I visit Srivillipuutur and have *'darshan'* of Godadevi en route to Sirangam. (The priests of Srivilliputtur on a visit to Tirumala had invited me to visit the temple earlier). I sincerely felt that I should have *'darshan'* of Godadevi to seek her blessings. Noticing my interest, Seshadri explained the route I should take to reach Srivilliputtur and offered to alert the priests there if I could tell him the date and approximate timing of my arrival there. But I myself did not know on which day and at what hour I would be there. I told him, "Leave it to me; I will go there". I got into the car and proceeded on the long journey.

Once the job at Guruvayur was over, I reached Courtallam via Tiruchendur. I had already been behind schedule by a day. As my schedule was upset for one reason or the other, I was keen on returning to Madras and back to Tirupati as soon as possible.

I could not leave Courtallam early in the morning as planned. As I set off after some delay in the afternoon, there was a sudden change in the weather. In the wake of a depression in the Bay of Bengal, it started raining heavily. I was supposed to reach Madurai by 5-30 p.m. but going by the weather, I was not sure whether I would land there even by nightfall. The sky was heavily overcast and darkness encircled us. Driver Gopal an energetic and efficient young man could hardly see ten yards ahead. The going was very tough and frustrating.

I was not unnerved as the national highway was very good. I felt that we could reach Madurai in an hour and half or two, even it made slow progress. I began to boost Gopal's confidence. "It is all right if you slow down. The road is good. See to it that we keep moving so that we can reach Madurai somehow or the other". The driver obliged with a hesitant nod.

Gopal applied brakes all of a sudden, as the headlights, piercing through darkness and heavy rain unfolded a breach in the road hardly a few feet ahead Gopal applied brakes all of a sudden. The Highway was breached. I complemented him for his quick reflex avoiding a major disaster. I got down, holding an umbrealla to take stock of the situation. The road was breached and the water was gushing through the breach. We could not proceed further even by an inch. Determined to reach Madurai, I asked the driver to reverse the vehicle. After traveling some distance, we spotted a roadside tea stall open. In response to my query, the tea stall operator suggested that we go back two more km, take the left turn and proceed till we reached a village en route and after crossing the village, we should take a left turn again to join the main road beyond the breach.

We travelled back two km and took the left turn. We entered the village in darkness as there was a power breakdown. As we reached the middle of the village the car broke down. I was annoyed. "Why is this trip going haywire?" As I held the umbrella, the driver Gopal opened the bonnet and focussed the torchlight on the engine. He fiddled with the engine for a few minutes in vain. He could not locate the problem. He attempted to start the engine twice or thrice, without any result.

Suddenly, the rain and winds came to a stop. Although it was pitch dark, we were relieved that the rain had abated. I enquired of the villagers as to where we were.

Surprising. We were in Srivilliputtur. There was a flash of lightening. As I looked up, I could see the Godadevi temple tower piercing into the sky. Then I recalled Seshadri's suggestion that I visit Godadevi and pay her my respects. How was it that I forgot what I planned to do? Yet I landed here. How could the car break down exactly opposite the temple?

I did not bother to seek answers to such questions. I wanted to have *'darshan'* of Godadevi. With Gopal following me, I stepped into the temple. As we entered the temple, the power supply in the village was restored. The priests identified me and took me into the temple affectionately. I got *'archana'* done for Godadevi and had prasadam. I forgot myself as I saw her pleasant, glowing countenance. I felt that the compassionate Godadevi herself fulfilled my wish when I went astray and brought me to her.

When I went back to the car, Gopal while enquiring about a mechanic, casually switched on the engine of the car. It started. We were surprised as we did not know the reason for its stopping and the reasons for its starting. We returned safely.

I was thinking of these happenings for several days – Far two many coincidences, why did they happen? How could they happen? — No rational explanation – what was the significance of all this—

Perhaps because of the experience, I proposed that every year on the occasion of Godadevi Kalyanam on the day of *Uttara nakashatra* in *Phalgun* month, a silk sari and other presents should be sent with temple honours from Lord Srinivasa. The TTD Board approved the proposal. Since then, this practice has been going on, for the past three decades.

23

WHEN I PLEADED GUILTY

A year or a year and half after the mass religious conversion of Hindus at Meenakshipuram in Tamil Nadu, the State Government issued me a show-cause notice. The notice asked Why action should not be initiated against me for disrupting communal harmony. I had no alternative to 'bowing my head' for thc 'crime' I had reportedly committed.

× × ×

When I took over as Executive Officer of the Tirumala Tirupati Devasthanams in 1978, the Hindu Endowments Act covered all the temples including the Tirumala temple in the State. As Tirumala began to attract more pilgrims resulting in its income shooting up and activities increasing, the Government felt that the TTD needed separate legislation. The then Chief Minister, Dr. Marri Channa Reddy, took keen interest in the matter. Dr. Ramesan, Chairman of the TTD Persons-in-Charge Committee, Mr. Chandramouli Reddy, Endowments Commissioner, and I, as EO Member Secretary, undertook the task of drafting the new legislation.

As per the new Act, the major responsibilities of TTD were broadly as follows:

(*a*) Conduct of '*sevas*' to Lord Srinivasa

(*b*) Maintenance of temple

(*c*) Provision of amenities to pilgrims at Tirumala and Tirupati

(*d*) Protecting and promotion of ancient Hindu '*dharma*'

(*e*) Extension of assistance to organisations engaged in similar activities

(*f*) Construction of prayer halls and '*kalyana mantapams*' at different places, and (*g*) Conduct of religious, educational and social activities.

The Act also stipulated that the TTD provide free medical, education and social facilities only at Tirupati. While drafting the provisions, the committee thoroughly discussed TTD's role in protecting and promoting Hindu *'dharma'*.

× × ×

The British, who ruled India, did not interfere in Hindu religious customs or traditions. They, however, promoted the setting up of Christian educational and medical institutions and construction of churches, and contributed to the spread of Christianity in India. The British ruled a large part of India. Hindu and Muslim kings in their respective kingdoms encouraged their own faiths as per their personal beliefs. In the few Hindu states, there was some encouragement for Hindu religious activities. When the patronage of kings diminished, a void developed, despite the activity by some interested groups with their limited resources. In such a setting, the responsibility of protecting Hindu *'dharma'* fell on the shoulders of a few Hindu religious organisations, *'mutts'* and temples. Even these institutions confined themselves to the observance or conduct of routine rituals, fairs and festivals. Not much thought was given to propagate Hindu *'dharma'* Thus, there was a gradual decline in the understanding and appreciation of the Hindu philosophical thought. More and more emphasis was laid on routine rituals, and not on the spirit behind them.

The situation became worse after the country gained Independence. With the adoption of a secular Constitution, the Government felt that it was not appropriate to encourage any one religion. As a result, there was no organised effort to protect the Hindu religion, although *'peethadhipatis'* made sporadic and feeble efforts here and there. Simply put, the context did not permit promotion of Hindu religion in a systematic manner as there was no organisational structure or accepted hierarchy. There was neither a common agreed plan, nor a meeting point for organisations interested in such activities.

Many people argue that Hinduism is not a religion but only a way of life. To whichever Hindu sect one belongs, all Hindus agree on this proposition. Adi Sankara, the propounder of

'Adwaita' philosophy, Ramanujacharya of *'Visishtadwaita'* and Madhwacharya of *'Dwaita' philosophy* – all accept *the* Vedas and ancient *'dharma'* as eternal truths but interpret them differently. Most of the religious *'mutts'* are affiliated to these schools of thoughts. The leaders of the *'mutts'* tried to propagate spirituality, customs and traditions according to the school of thought to which they belonged. That was felt necessary to further the interest of their 'mutts'. They did not initiate any programmes in mutual cooperation or undertake foccused religious and spiritual activities through any accepted organisational structures. In other words, most religious activities were individual efforts. As a result, new *'swamijis'* proliferated, each propagating his own school of thought, although everyone swore by *'sanatana dharma'*. Each also tried to safeguard his own turf or *'mutt'*, to prevent any erosion in his support base, area of influence and source of income.

There are a large number of temples, some with reasonable resources. Most of these temples have come to be known as the appendages of some *'mutt'* or *'peetham'* either because of local conditions or the proclivities of the persons in management committees. Yet, the local committees had total sway over the management of these temples. They focused on organising fairs and festivals in the name of traditions and on siphoning income from temples and temple properties. They were not too concerned about providing amenities to pilgrims or protecting and promoting Hindu religion. Hindu religious activities in temples and *'mutts'* were further crippled with the promulgation of the Inam Abolition Act and the Tenancy Act, resulting in the temples loosing their vast landed properties, which was providing a regular source of income.

Thanks to the secular Constitution, the country's traditional system of education emphasising Hindu spiritual and ethical values gave way to English language-based education emphasizing Western materialistic value systems. As a result, the age old teaching of spiritual and ethical values, which had stood as the bedrock of the Indian way of life, faced the threat of extinction. In addition, with the advent of movies and the television, the traditional age old exposure tospiritual awakening through art forms *like 'puranas', 'bhajans', 'harikathas', 'burra kathas'*, and puppet shows began to recede.

What stood out starkly at the macro level was the absence of a *'mutt'* head or a *'swamiji'* acceptable to all Hindu sections, for systematic promotion of Hindu *'Dharma'*. Non-Hindu institutions worked in unison and received funding from external agencies to spread their clout throughout the country. It was in such a scenario that weaker sections among Hindus became victims of religious conversions.

The Andhra Pradesh Government was one of the earliest to regulate temple maintenance through the Endowments Act. Former Prime Minister P V Narasimha Rao, way back had served as the Law and Endowment Minister in Andhra Pradesh, introduced sweeping reforms in the management of temples, their funds and properties. However, during implementation the provisions relating to organisational arrangements to advise the Government in temple administration by autonomous religious councils did not materialise as the Government did not want its authority to be eroded. Adequate attention was paid to protecting temple lands, other properties and incomes, but not to the promotion of *'dharmic'* matters. When a separate law for the Tirumala Tirupati Devasthanams was contemplated, such gaps in the system were expected to be addressed.

× × ×

The Assembly passed the TTD Bill, formulated by the Persons-in-Charge Committee, in 1981. The Act stipulated that a certain portion of the temple's income be spent every year on the protection and promotion of Hindu *'dharma'*. A *'Hindu Dharma Rakshana Sanstha'* was constituted as part of the TTD. Initially, an Advisory Committee comprising Sri Jayendra Saraswati of Kanchi Kamakoti Peetham, Sri Viswesa Teertha Swamiji of Pejavar Mutt and Sri Tridandi Narayana Jeeyar Swami was constituted for the *'Sanstha'*. These three headed the *'peethams'* of the three different Hindu sects of *'Adwaita, Dwaita and Visisthadwaita'*.

Against this backdrop, I received a message one day from Sri Chandrasekharendra Saraswati Swamiji of Kanchi

Peetham, who was on a vow of silence at Satara in Maharashtra. He broke his 45-day-old vow of silence to discuss for about five hours the need for the TTD formulating schemes for protecting the Vedas and ancient '*sastras*'.

He wanted The TTD:

1. To provide employment and regular monthly incomes to Vedic scholars so that they could be attached to temples to recite the Vedas for eight hours a day;
2. To encourage the '*gurukula*' system by providing financial assistance to '*gurus*' to teach the Veda '*sastras*' to interested students in places convenient to the '*guru*'.
3. To give assistance to scholars of repute under the '*kumara adhyapaka*' scheme in the '*gurukula*' system so that they can pursue higher studies and research; and
4. To give assistance to organisations involved in such activities.

Executive meeting of Hindu Dharma Rakshana Samstha—Sri H.H. Srimannarayana Peda Jeyar, H.H. Visweshathirtha Swamiji of Pejawar Mutt, H.H. Sri Jayendra Saraswathi Swamiji of Kanchi and H.H. Madhira Adhinam, Executive Officer, P.V.R.K. Prasad and Dr. Arka Somayaji, Secretary, HDRS.

I got all the '*swamiji's* proposals implemented in a few months by *the 'Hindu Dharma Rakshana Sanstha'* with TTD funds. We also launched a scheme to appoint full time organisers (missionaries) under the Hindu '*Dharma Rakshana*' programme. But most of the senior *swamijis* wanted their own disciples to be appointed as full-time workers. They were more interested in spreading their own areas of influence under the TTD while promoting Hindu '*dharma*'. This embarrassed the TTD. These full time organisers had set their eyes on having permanent employment with the TTD and not on propagating '*dharma*' with missionary zeal. A year after the experiment, I decided to look for alternatives.

It was during this period there was the news of mass religious conversion of Hindus at Meenakshipuram in Tamil Nadu. Pricked by the astounding news, beamed across the nation by the media, many Hindu religious institutions and elders assailed the TTD for not playing its due role in protecting and promoting Hindu religion.

I had no idea as to what the TTD could or should do. As an ad hoc measure, I handed over some vehicles and Hindu '*dharma*' propaganda material to some *swamijis*. Not satisfied, many '*dharmic*' institutions and '*swamijis*' pressed the TTD for funds to promote Hindu '*dharma*' under their auspices. They insisted on the TTD supporting them in their mission to protect Hinduism in the wake of the Meenakshipuram conversions. Since the TTD is a Hindu religious institution, they believed their demands were reasonable.

I was in a dilemma. Although I could not question their integrity, I had no idea of their capabilities or commitment to judiciously spend the money offered by millions of devout pilgrims to Lord Srinivasa.

How could we, therefore, release funds directly? Even if funds were released, what recognition would the TTD get for its service? The TTD, which worked under Government regulations, could not encourage any particular institution or patronize a particular swamiji. To how many institutions could the TTD release funds? What should be the basis for selection?

The alternative was to get the job done directly by TTD employees. But how could we get the mercenary employees, who worked for monthly wages to have missionary zeal and match their counterparts in non-hindu religious organizations.

Being Government officials, we had Conduct Rules. But would they apply when we worked in an institution like the TTD? If so, to what extent? Should I be loyal to the TTD or to the secular Government? Should I not discharge my obligations to the TTD when I drew salary from it? Why should I invite problems? Would it not suffice if I simply maintained status quo i.e., by not doing anything?

Assailed by such questions, I used to visit the Lord to pray for an answer: "Oh Lord, What should I do? Who should shoulder the responsibility of promoting Hindu philosophy and faith in God and protection of ancient Hindu spiritual values? What is TTD's role in it? What is my role? Will my actions be '*dharmic*'? How should I proceed?"

As I stepped out of the temple after such a prayer one day, I heard the Bhagavadguta '*sloka*' rendered by Ghantasala.

"Karmanyevadhikaraste maphaleshukadachana

Makarma phalahethurbhuma te sajnostya karmani"

"Do your duty without an eye on the outcome. Do not get disinterested in discharging the duty cast on you". The verse, which seemed to directly address my dilemmas, enabled me to formulate a course of action.

Lord Srinivasa is acceptable to every Hindu irrespective of his sect, caste, creed or the school of thought. Similarly, the TTD is held in esteem by all '*mutts*' and '*swamijis*' and religious organisations. How would it be if I assembled all like-minded people at one place, drew up a minimum action plan acceptable to all and got it implemented by heads of institutions with TTD support?

The moment such a thought struck me, I acted at lightning speed and sent invitations to all like-minded people. In all, 51 organistional representatives - chiefs of various Hindu '*mutts*' and many senior *'swamijis'* took part in the conclave. Senior *'swamijis'* from Kanchi and Pejawar and Jeeyars, who were also members of the advisory council of the *'Hindu Dharma Rakshana Samiti'*, were present. Others included Sri Veerendra Hegde of Karnataka, Swami Chinmayananda, Sri Vidya Prakasananda Swami of Suka Brahma Ashram, Malayala Swamiji Yerpeda Peetham, representatives of the Viswa Hindu Parishad, the Sadhu Samaj and Brahma Kumaris, Ramakrishna mutt and Sivananda Ashram. Many chairmen of major Hindu temples and established religious organisations also attended.

As anticipated, we could draw up a minimum action plan acceptable to all the participants to promote Hindu *'dharma'*. Activities were to be initiated in the four southern states, as a first step. We formed a Steering Committee. Research, drafting and printing of material was to be undertaken as directed by the Steering Committee. The TTD would open offices in the capitals of all the four southern States and act as the coordinator for the distribution of promotional material as suggested by the Steering Committee. The TTD would supply the material including stickers either free of cost or at nominal charges to all the member organisations. The TTD would not have grassroot level workers. The man power of all the member organizations would work for this programme, with intellectual and infrastructure support by the TTD. The programme took off in a few weeks. The literature in Telugu, Tamil, Kannada and Malayalam began to reach the public at large through hundreds of *'dharmic'* institutions.

In addition, the TTD took up a number of major activities like :

- Publication of books on spiritual subjects and their supply at subsidised rates to the public
- Extension of financial assistance to authors of spiritual books to publish their works
- Organisation of training programmes, including training of trainers for the spread of Hindu religion through art forms like *'puranas'*, *'bhajans'* and *'kolatams'*

- Implementation of schemes like *'Veda Parayana'* and *'Veda Rakshana'*
- Training of school teachers in *'dharmic'* matters
- Holding of competitions among students to promote their knowledge of Hindu *'dharmic'* literature
- Getting authoritative literature drafted to counter mischievous and misguided criticism of Hindu *'dharma'*
- Construction of temples/prayer halls in *'Harijanwadas'*
- Encouragement of *'bhajana mandals'*
- Free supply of microphone sets to temples
- Establishing a *'purana'* school to prepare pracharaks, requisitioning the services of eminent scholars like Sri Malladi Chandrasekhara Sastry and Sri Sribhashyam Appalacharyulu to train students.
- Promotion of spiritual lectures by established and accepted orators of Hindu philosphy.
- Tape-recording of all the *'sakhas'* of all the Vedas with the assistance of erudite scholars and building a core library.

Gradually, these measures gained momentum, and started making an impact.

To help Hindus protect themselves from mass religious conversions, we got "*simha garjana*" (lion's roar) posters printed in south Indian languages and ensured that they reached all sections of people in every village and hamlet. The posters carried the slogan, "Our *'dharma'* is like the Ganges water; the alien *'dharma'* is a mirage". Stickers with slogans like "*Dharmo rakshati rakshitah*", (Save *'dharma'*, by following it, you will be saved) and round stickers with the *'omkara'* symbol were distributed from house to house. On all TTD *'prasadam'* sachets, we published the minimum action programme agreed upon at the conclave and the do's and don'ts for a Hindu.

We organised *'Geeta gnana yagnas'* in Telugu at a number of places by Sri Vidya Prakasananda Swami of Suka Brahma

Ashram near Srikalahasti. Tens of thousands of people attended each *'gnana yagna'*. We recorded the discourses in audio and video tapes and released them to the public. We arranged discourses on Hindu *'dharma'* and Bhagwadgita by Swami Chinmayananda in many towns. Thousands of people attended his discourses at all places with great enthusiasm, although he spoke in English. Thanks to the TTD, the talks by Swami Chinmayananda and Sri Vidya Prakasananda, hitherto confined only to a limited number of the educated, reached lakhs of common people.

The TTD, in another initiative, brought about some sort of coordination in *the 'Ganesh nimajjanotsavam'* function in Hyderabad. It helped in bringing about cohesion among all Ganesh Samitis and laid out a route for the procession. During the first year the TTD supported the planning and coordination by providing material and financial support for *'pandals'*, public address systems, buntings and *'dharmic'* literature. All these activities earned the TTD widespread acclaim for rousing the hitherto dormant devotion and spirituality among the people.

× × ×

The police Intelligence reported all these activities to the Government in a distorted form. Acting on those reports, the Government issued me a show-cause notice in 1982. It said:

"The Government has received reports to the effect that you, as a Government official and TTD Executive Officer, have been abusing your position to disrupt communal harmony in the State. Why should not disciplinary action be initiated against you for indulging in such unlawful activities?"

I was stunned as I read the notice. I found myself in a slough of despondency. While everybody was congratulating me on "defining the TTD's role and doing a good job", the Government was pointing a finger accusing me of misconduct. I could not digest. It haunted me day and night. To whom should I represent and what should I say? Who would stand by me in this hour of distress? Had I taken up these activities as a mere Government servant, I could be faulted under Conduct Rules. But I had undertaken them in my capacity as

TTD Executive Officer. Was I not expected to discharge my role requirements?

Distraught, I knelt before Lord Srinivas. I bowed my head like a guilty person. Recalling the show-cause notice, I questioned repeatedly, "Am I at fault? Am I guilty?" Who had inspired me to take up such activities? Who had given me the courage? Had not the Lord's words, *"...makarmaphala hethurbhuma te sajnoswakarmani"*, entered my mind, would I have done all these things? Then how had I become a criminal? Had not the Lord said, "Discharge your duty?". Didn't I act on the Lord's counsel? How had it become a crime?

As I watched the resplendent Lord, I thought on those lines once again. Suddenly something struck me. As I recalled the *'sloka' "Karmanyevadhikaraste"*, I got the answer. Unknowingly, tears of joy rolled down my cheeks.

I drafted my reply to the Government notice on these lines: "The Government has not explained how I disrupted communal harmony. According to the Tirumala Tirupati Devasthanams Act, 1981, protection and promotion of Hindu *'dharma'* are among the primary responsibilities of the TTD. What the TTD has done now is to make every Hindu proud of his or her religion, by propagating the Hindu culture, its values and its greatness. The appointment of an IAS officer as TTD Executive Officer does not mean that the Government has turned the Tirumala temple into a national secular institution. When I was appointed, I swore in the presence of the Lord that I would abide by TTD objectives under the Act. Had I not acted according to TTD objectives and had I taken no interest in protecting and promoting Hindu *'dharma'*, the Government could have taken action against me for failure to discharge my duties and contravention of the TTD Act, 1981. But unfortunately, the Government is now holding me guilty for discharging my duty as TTD Executive Officer. As long as I continue to be TTD Executive Officer, it is my duty to accomplish its objectives. Under these circumstances, neither the TTD under my leadership nor I personally have exceeded our limits in any manner. I, therefore, do not feel it necessary to offer any explanation to the Government". (Who had given me the courage to draft such a reply?) I added: I personally feel that the Government cannot fault me on this count. My conscience is clear that I have done the correct thing. It is my duty to do what I have done. If the Government is not happy with my performance, it has the authority to transfer me and post me elsewhere. However, I would like to reiterate that my loyalty will be to the TTD and its objective as long as I continue to be its Executive Officer?

President Dr. N. Sanjeev Reddy being shown the Books published by TTD by P.V.R.K. Prasad, Chairman, Dr. Nagi Reddy and Endowments Minister Chowdari are also seen.

Within two days of my letter to the Chief Secretary, I had a call from him asking me to meet the Chief Minister immediately. When I called on the Chief Minister, Sri. Bhavanam Venkatram, he had called the Chief Secretary, Director General of Police and the Inspector General of Police (Intelligence) for the meeting, The Chief Minister spoke to me politely, and said, "I have nothing personal against you". He explained how the Intelligence reports had called for putting a halt to my activities. He indicated that I should sort out the matter with the Chief Secretary, the Director General of Police and the Inspector General, Intelligence. The Chief Minister implied that I sit with them and sort out the matter. But, I contended that there was nothing to be sorted out. The *'Gita sloka'* *"karmanyevadhi karaste maphaleshu kadachana..."* continued to ring in my ears. The IG, Intelligence, on whose reports the action had been initiated, drew the attention to TTD's role in the Ganesh procession. The TTD had never taken up such a role earlier. The united action by all the Hindu organisations might result in conflicts here and there. He was particularly worried about the volatile situation in Hyderabad.

TTD publication stall in Godavari Pushkarams.

I spoke out my mind with courage and conviction. "As TTD Executive Officer, I have not undertaken religious conversions. All I have done is discharge my duties under the TTD Act, 1981. Is it a crime to ask the Hindus to be proud of their heritage? Is it objectionable, if a Hindu religious institution sings the glory of Hindu philosophy and scriptures? What were the police doing when Hindus were tempted, coaxed and even at times bribed to convert into other religions? If a Hindu organisation is not expected even to enlighten Hindus, what else is it expected to do? As long as I continue to be Executive Officer there, I will continue to act like that. If the Government does not like my work, it is welcome to transfer me. It is a shame that the Government that could not act against forces harming communal harmony through mass religious conversions is trying to harass those discharging their duty, based on false reports". With my knowledge, I was worked up and became emotional.

Chief Minister Bhavanam Venkatram listened to me with rapt attention. Then he patted me affectionately and admiringly, and declared that he was closing the matter.

Performance of my duties did not subsequently result in any bitter outcome. I was also not transferred out for this reason. Even today, this conflict is there for a Government servant posted to a religious institution like TTD - Should He be loyal to the secular Government or to the religious institution?

Bhagavadgita

24

NAHAM KARTA HARIH KARTA

My collegues and I were stunned when the news was conveyed to us. It was as sudden as it was shocking. It had come to light that the flag mast (Dwajastambham) in Lord Venkateswara temple atop Tirumala Hills was rotten inside.

The mast, sheathed with gold plates, was so decayed that it was not to be found for a few feet from above. But the flag, clinging to the mast's gold plating continued to jingle. For the pilgrims, the flag mast appeared normal. But we realised that the gold plates, hugging the partly hollow mast, could collapse any moment. The prospect sent shudders down my spine.

But, how did the mast last so long? Which power had propped it up? What could be done? Such questions swamped us in early 1982 when I was the TTD Executive Officer.

× × ×

Those were the days when we launched a number of renovations in the Tirumala temple. These included the polishing of the gold plated *'Ananda Nilaya'* (the temple tower), reconstruction of the kitchen (*'potu'*) to meet the demand for *'laddu'* and other *'prasadams'*, renovation of many small temples within the complex, construction of a *'kalyana mantap'* for the Lord's wedding ritual and installation of specially designed brass grills on either side of the queue lines. As part of the renovation programme, reguilding and polishing of the gold plates of the flag mast and the *'sacrificial altar'* (*'bali peetham'*) abutting it and replacement of gold plates wherever warranted were planned.

As one enters the temple through the '*maha dwaram*' (main entrance), one sees the six-foot-high 'sacrificial altar' and the flag mast piercing through the roof into the sky. One could make out that the roof was laid long after the installation of the flag mast since it left enough room for the flag mast to go through the roof. Atop the 50-foot-high flag mast, there was a gold plated wooden panel with a number of small bells, which jingle whenever there is breeze. As the flag portion appeared to be tilted, I ordered that it also be repaired.

One day, as the works were under way, I had a frantic phone call from the Engineer Venkataramaiah, who was overseeing the renovation works. I could make out the anxiety and urgency in his voice as he wanted me to rush to the temple. As I arrived at the temple, Mr. Venkataramaiah took me to the top of the flag mast along the makeshift wooden scaffolding. As he removed the flag set-up, I could not immediately sight the mast supporting it. I was shocked. Not until we removed four rungs of gold plates did we notice the wooden mast. But it was shriveled and decayed. The flag continued to be in place propped up by the gold plates and not the wooden mast.

What was to be done? Some officials counselled that we leave the flag mast untouched and take up only the polishing of gold plates. In their view, it was impossible to replace such a tall flag mast with a new one and, therefore, it should be allowed to last as long as it would. The engineers removed the gold plates gradually to the bottom of the mast as directed by me. That the mast was rotten to the core and there was a yawning gap between the gold covering and the post was starkly revealed. I was stunned. Normally, gold plates are fixed all around the mast. Now, the gold plates remained intact while the wooden mast inside lay decayed and ruined. The gold plates had a circumference of seven to eight feet at the bottom and three and half feet at the top.

That the mast had been decaying for a few years had come to light only now. Had we not noticed it, it would have decayed totally and the gold plate covering it might have come crashing to the ground one day. Installation of a new 80-foot-high mast in place of the ruined one, however, was not easy as it was not something like gold that could be bought in the market. *'Brahmostvams'* were hardly four months away and the great ritual would start ceremoniously with the hoisting of *'Garuda flag'* on this mast. Could we meet the deadline?

My conscience would not permit me to leave the rotten mast untouched and attend to outside renovation. As if some power had possessed me, I grew emotional. I announced, "We are going to get a new mast and install it" and put an end to further discussion.

× × ×

The magnitude of the problem dawned on us subsequently. The mast was 50 feet high from the ground and 30 feet below the ground level. There was a seven-foot-high stone platform around the mast. Unless all the gold plates were removed and the soil excavated up to the base of the mast, the mast could not be pulled out. That also called for the dismantling of the 'sacrificial altar' in front of the mast. It meant the digging of a big pit right in the temple in front of the main entrance. Engineers estimated that it would take a week. Even assuming that the old mast could be removed, from where was the new mast to come? This was the second issue. We thought a perusal of old records might shed some light on the year of its installation and the source of the trunk used for the mast. But there was no reference to the installation of the mast in the 180-190-year-old records available to us. Perhaps, the mast was too old. Tall trees might have been available those days on the hill itself nearby. The *'mandapam'* and the outer *'Prakaram"* might have been constructed after the erection of the mast. We went back to the temple records in *'modi',* script also with no success. We abandoned the search for an answer in the records and focussed on searching for a new mast. But a mast, according to *'agama sastras'*, has to have certain characteristics. It should not have any openings or cracks, be straight and without any branches. In addition, what we required was at least a 75-foot-high mast with minimum 8' ft diameter at the foot and 3' feet at the top. For it to last long, it should be a teak trunk. There were murmurs that such a trunk might not be available, as we would have to look for a 300-year-old flawless teak tree. But I did not lose hope. Immediately, I contacted

State Government forest officials. The forest experts, after a discussion, concluded, "It is impossible to locate such a teak tree within the State. If we are lucky it might be found in the Western Ghat forests in Karnataka or Kerala – where some areas remained untapped in hill ranges due to their inaccessibility.

As these discussions over the phone took place, many priests, '*mirasidars*' and press reporters gathered around the flag mast. They were freely sharing what they felt they knew. In the olden days, when the temple was under the control of '*mahants*', and prior to that, there was a strong rumour that there could be a treasure trove under the mast. The flag post renovation once again sparked rumours that there could be a treasure trove. There were already anxious inquiries from the Chief Minister, the Endowments Minister and other important people. My answer to all of them was 'The flag mast is rotten and, therefore, it is being replaced".

Although I answered such queries as a matter of fact, the tension within me was palpable. As I wracked my brain over locating a suitable teak trunk for the flag mast, I had to grapple with the treasure trove rumours. The flag mast was located right in front of the second main entrance and between the first two '*prakarams*'. The pilgrims' queue into the temple abutted the flag mast. '*Prasadams*' from the kitchen too had to come into the temple along that way. The Lord's idols, used for processions and for paid '*sevas*' were taken in and out only through that entrance. If excavation were undertaken to remove the decayed mast, pilgrims would definitely be inconvenienced. And the people were eager to watch the treasure trove being unearthed. It was a complex situation. Forests in Kerala and Karnataka had to be searched for the right trunk for a new mast. What could we do if such a tree having a trunk of the stipulated characteristics and dimensions was not to be found? Even if it was found, how was it to be brought to the temple atop the hills? Even if it was brought, how was it to be installed? I had already completed my three-year term as Executive Officer. I might be transferred any moment. Could I get the flag mast installed before I moved out?

'Brahmotsavams', are due to take place in four months, and should begin with flag hoisting. Would the flag mast be in place by then? Thoughts on all these aspects merely aggravated my tension but provided no solution. Finally, I concluded, "The very Power which brought me here would provide a solution".

As I was about to leave the temple with such thoughts around 10-30 in the night, there was a call from a Bangalore devotee, Mr. H. S. R. Iyengar. I had not heard of him earlier. As I lifted the receiver rather impatiently, he spoke non-stop. "Sir, I heard over the radio that you are planning to replace the flag mast. A teak tree should be 280-300 years old for providing a flag mast of the size required. It might be available in Dandeli forests of Karnataka. I have wide contacts in Bangalore. The Chief Conservator of Forests here is a good friend of mine. If you permit, I will get the forests scoured and locate a suitable tree with his assistance. Please write him a formal letter. Leave the coordination to me. Treat it as my service to the Lord and permit me to do the job." The next moment, I formally called up the Chief Secretary and the Chief Conservator of Forests of Karnataka to seek their assistance. By 11 p.m I had completed my telephone calls. At last, calm returned to my troubled mind as a result of assistance from strange quarters.

× × ×

We started dismantling the base of the *'Dhwajastambham'* and *'Balipitam'* and began excavation work the very next morning. It took us almost a week to go to the base of the mast. Meanwhile, I appointed a committee comprising of retired officials, vigilance officers, police and media representatives, local elders and some devotees to closely observe, and record anything found during the excavation with a view to scotching rumours about hidden treasures. Round-the-clock monitoring teams were constituted. Media was allowed free access. What we found at the base of the flag mast were only a few gold and silver pieces and coins. We noticed that the mast had decayed almost up to its base, which was 30 feet below the ground level.

In that one week, at the instance of Mr. Iyengar in Bangalore, the Chief Conservator of Forests had deputed search parties into the interior forests, got nearly a hundred potential teak trees examined and short-listed 16 trees on Dandeli mountain slopes. That very week, Karnataka Chief Minister

Mr. Gundu Rao, Chief Minister, Karnataka being taken for Darshan by P.V.R.K. Prasad.

Mr. Gundu Rao and his family happened to visit Tirumala. When I told him of the flag mast issue, Mr. Gundu Rao said, "Please take the trunk for a new flag mast as Karnataka's donation". Before the weekend, my engineers and I, accompanied by Mr. Iyengar and the Chief Conservator of Forests, examined the 16 short-listed trees. Of them, only six trees seemed to have the stipulated features. Two of the trees had trunks taller than what we needed for the mast. Keeping in mind TTD's needs, I sought all the six trees. We could not, however, testify to their quality going by their appearance. The trunk should be seasoned and perfect. There should not be any holes or cracks or bends. The Chief Conservator said that nothing could be said about the quality of the trunk until a tree was cut down. I was overtaken by anxiety. "What if the trunk were not be found perfect after so much of effort...?" Instantaneously, I relaxed by concluding, "The very Power which has led me so far will take care of the rest".

Surprisingly, when I met the Chief Minister and the Chief Secretary at Bangalore on my way back, they declared that all the six trees would be donated. As the felling of the trees started, one more complex issue cropped up.

The trees happened to be at different places on high mountain slopes in deep forests and away from roads. The trunks, after cutting, had to be carried for distances ranging from two to eight km to the *'ghat'* road. The Chief Conservator arranged for the clearance of bushes and trees en route. Normally, when trees are cut for timber, they are sliced and transported. But the trees we chose would be useless if they were cut into pieces. What was to be done? Once again, I concluded, "The very Power who needs the mast will look into such aspects".

× × ×

Meanwhile, forest workers of the Somani paper mills noticed our hectic activity. Soon, to our pleasant surprise, representatives of the paper mills management and staff turned up and pleaded, "Sir, leave this job to us treating it as our contribution to Lord Srinivasa". So saying, they took over the responsibility. Within a week, they cut the trees and transported the trunks with the help of chains, ropes and pulleys to the *'ghat'* road virtually inch by inch.

I heaved a sigh of relief. The difficulties in transporting the trunks to Tirumala Hills, a few hundred km away, had not struck me then. Mr. Iyengar once again took the initiative and hired a 16-wheel truck-cum-trailer. The truck operator said, "It may take four or five days to transport these six, long logs up to Tirupati as we have to negotiate many curves and some railway crossings, old bridges and difficult turnings. But we don't know how long it will take to move from Tirupati to Tirumala as the entire stretch is a ghat road having innumerable sharp curves. . We may get stuck at a sharp curve on the *'ghat'* road and we don't know for how long. So, please pay us hire charges on KM basis up to Tirupati, and later on the time taken to reach Tirumala from Tirupati. They felt that it could take a few days to cover the 20 KM *'ghat'* section between Tirupati and Tirumala.

The truck carrying the trunks reached Bangalore in two days. At the Vidhan Soudha, the State Secretariat, the Chief Minister arranged a *'puja'* programme, formally announced the donation of the logs and handed them over to me. As I laid my hands on the trunks in the presence of thousands of people, a wave of joy beyond words electrified me. (Why so?) The truck reached Tirupati by 4 p.m. the next day. At the dairy farm on the Tirupati outskirts, thousands of men and women gathered to offer *'aarti'* to the sacred trunks, chanting, *'Govinda, Govinda'*. In the next one hour, the truck touched Alipiri, where the *'ghat'* road starts.

At the time of installation of new 'New Dhwaja Sthambam'

Till then, there was all-round happiness. The driver got down from the truck and took a sharp look at the hills. He was apparently mulling over the problems that lay ahead — the 20 km-long *'ghat'* road and the large number of hairpin bends. Those days even long chassis buses were not allowed on the *'ghat'* road. Only special small chassis buses plied. He finally approached me and said like a man in a trance, "Sir, I have set out on a great adventure in my life. My ambition is to drive up the hills nonstop. Only then would I be satisfied. En route, the *'ghat'* road parapet wall may get damaged, and boulders, hit by the trailer, may roll down. I don't know how much time it will take; but I am determined to make it".

I assured him, "You will not be held responsible even if the parapet walls get damaged or boulders roll down...We will take care of all such aspects." (Could we really say that we were doing every thing and every thing was happening because of our capabilities?).

The tree trunks, destined to become the flag masts, began their journey along the second *'ghat'* road as the twilight sun shed his golden rays. This *'ghat'* road has less hairpin bends than the first ghat road and bends also are not as sharp as on the old road. This road is used for going up and the old road for coming down the hills. (We had diverted all pilgrim and vehicular traffic to the old *'ghat'* road. Pilots and escorts with all engineering recovery equipment including cranes/pullies, ropes etc had been organised on either side of this log-laden, heavy and long vehicles. Labourers were mobalised, to undertake pushing or pulling or arranging support if required. It had become a big convoy of vehicles. With the full throated *'Govinda, Govinda,'* chanting of all those present, the convoy moved.

As feared, whenever the truck negotiated a turn, the trunks hit the abutting hill slopes and trees resulting in boulders rolling down and tree branches crashing. At some turns, the parapet wall collapsed. At some others, the trailer wheels hit the parapet wall and jumped across the valley. The engineers and I, travelling in a car behind the truck, missed a heartbeat or two as we witnessed the incidents. At one or two turnings, half of the trailer had gone beyond the road and seemed to be hurtling into the valley. Seized with tension, we often shouted "Oh, Oh". We were afraid of the vehicle as well as the logs rolling down into the valley at one of the turnings. Highly tensed up, we felt as if we had been travelling for hours.

× × ×

But, it was not true. In less than an hour – 55 minutes to be precise —, the truck carrying the trunks reached Tirumala without halting anywhere. Tirumala Hills reverberated to the cries of "Govinda, Govinda" raised by thousands of joyous pilgrims and TTD employees as they saw the truck entering Sannidhi Street. Tears of happiness rolled down my cheeks.

What a miracle? The truck that started at Alipiri a little before the sunset arrived at Tirumala by the time the sun sank into the western skies. The truck owner, who was following all through in a car said, "I have had the great fortune of serving the Lord this way. I feared that it might take a few days for us to reach Tirumala with many halts in between. I do not know what made the driver drive non-stop unmindful of the hazards till he reached Tirumala. Only God has made it possible. That's why, I don't want to take a single paisa as transport charges for the entire operation. This is my service to the Lord" (Wherefrom did he get the inspiration?) How could we pay for something that transpired between them and the Lord. We had arranged a good '*darshan*' of the Lord to Mr. Iyengar, the truck owner and the driver and honoured them with '*sesha vastra*' as pundits recited Vedic verses and invoked blessings. They knew that the Lord had already blessed them by utilising their services.

The logs were unloaded opposite the temple on Sannidhi Street, which had been widened from six feet to 100 feet by then. Without such a wide road, it would have been impossible for the logs to reach the temple. Even if they had been brought through Mada streets, they could not have been taken inside the temple without using sannidhi street. We felt that the widening of Sanndhi Street had been done only to facilitate this activity (who planned it?). After thorough inspection by pundits, engineers and others we selected the best log for the flag mast in Srinivasa temple. To ensure that it lasted for at least a couple of centuries, we got it chemically treated. To prevent insects and worms from burrowing into the mast, we decided to shield the mast with a tin sheet and then only go in for gold coated rings. These activities took a few days. At last, I thought the flag mast was ready for installation. At this point, another problem bothered me.

Engineers had concluded that the '*mantap*' above the old flag mast had to be dismantled if the new 75-foot-high flag mast were to be installed. The alternative, they suggested was the lifting of the flag mast with a crane and its planting through the hole in the '*mantap*'. That was of course, not possible unless the main *'prakaram'* wall was dismantled to accommodate the crane. That would call for sacrificing either the *'potu'* (temple kitchen) or the *'kalayana mantapam'*. Both were out of the question. I was not inclined to demolish the *'mantap'* . As, no heavy machinery could be taken inside the temple, deploying a crane was ruled out. If both the alternatives were not

New Dhwjasthambam after installation

acceptable, how could the flag mast be installed? We wracked our brains in vain until midnight that day and adjourned in sheer exhaustion for the next day. But I could not go to bed. 'why are we making such a big fuss over installation after having brought the trunks here braving many hardships for three weeks? Can't the competent engineers accomplish a small job?". If I am destined, I will get the flag mast installed. If not, I won't be doing it. Let me leave it to the Lord and closed my eyes to sleep.

× × ×

Nothing contrary to my intuition happened. As we resumed our discussion the next morning, some one said, "Let us bring the trunk inside the temple through the *'maha dwaram'* in a slanting position. Once it comes to the *'mantap'*, we will insert it through the existing hole in it and straighten it. We will take the assistance of engineers and workers building the Papanasanam dam". What a splendid idea! (Who was behind it?) Engineers plunged into action by taking measurements and concluded the idea was feasible if a deep sloped pathway is cut from the *'maha dwaram'* to the pit, already dug up for removing the old *'Dhwajasthambham'*. This digging to whatever depths from the *'mahadwaram'* to the sacrificial altar should not inconvenience pilgrim lines. Yes – it is difficult, but possible.

Without losing time, we decided on an auspicious moment for launching the work. With the help of HCL engineers and workers, we took the chosen mast from Sannidhi Street via Golla Mantap and the *'maha dwaram'* into the temple. Stands

Mr. P.V.R.K. Prasad and with Gopika performing 'Gopula near Bali Peetham' in connection with the installation of New Dhwajasthambam and Balipeetham

were erected to prop up the mast in a slanting position. As the workers pushed the smaller end of the mast gradually from the *'maha dwaram'* to the sacrificial altar along the deep pit, its crest touched the hole in the *'mantap'* from below. With a little more effort, the mast was made to go through the hole and slowly pushed and guided gradually to stand erect facing the sky. The engineers' strategy had paid off. The teak tree trunk from Dandeli forests was ready by that evening to be installed as the flag mast in the Tirumala temple without any damage to the *'mantap'*.

There was one final twist to the tale. Pundits quoting the *'sastras'* said that the nine types of gems and the nine types of grains should be placed in the foundation. We followed the advice by depositing them in two boxes and placing them at the base of the mast. Involuntarily, I pulled out the gold chain with the Lord Srinivasa medallion from my neck and deposited in one box. Within seconds, the priests, *'mirasidars'*, VIPs,

New Dhwajasthambam with the Gold Covering. Chief Minister Mr. Bhavanam Venkataram and Mr. P.V.R.K. Prasad leading the procession.

temple employees, Board Members. and many pilgrims, who had gathered there, came forward to make their own contributions. One more big box overflowed with devotees' goldrings, chains, bangles and other ornaments. Though there was no *'nidhi'* when we dug up, we ensured that there was a *'nidhi'* at the bottom before we closed. Once the boxes were placed at the bottom, concrete was poured. Then the flag mast, standing erect in 90 degree position, was installed as ordained by the *'sastras'*. We got the old flag mast immersed in the Papanasanam reservoir. Within a month, construction of a platform around the flag mast, its gold plating and raising of a new *'bali peetham'* (sacrificial altar) in front of the flag mast were completed. Once all the renovation works, including the polishing of gold plates of the *'Gopuram, Balipeetham'* and the flag mast were completed, we organised a mini *'brahmotsavam'*. As the Tirumala Hills reverberated to the pundits' Vedic chanting and blessings, the flag mast and the *'bali peetham'* were consecrated on June 10, 1982. A week later, I received my transfer orders.

As I left Tirumala on transfer, I stood at the *'Dwajasthambham'* and *'Balipeetham'* to look at the concealed (by gold rings) teak trunk that had metamorphosed into the flag mast. The bells atop the flag mast seemed to be whispering to me. A strange feeling enveloped me. An official beside me commented, "Sir, what was impossible could be accomplished in two months, thanks to you. But for you..."

As I was listening to him, I heard the voice of an old pundit chanting.

"Naham karta harih karta
Tatpuja karma chakhilam
Tadapi matkruta puja
Tatprasadena na anyadha"

(I am not the doer; it is Lord Sri Hari who does, and gets everything done. Still, if I happen to perform any puja or good deed, it is possible only because of Lord's grace. Not otherwise).

How true!

25

VOWS AND WOES

Perhaps for the first time in the history of the Tirumala Sri Venkateswara Swami temple, the *'palabhishekam'* came to a standstill during a Friday morning *'abhisheka seva'*. Large containers of milk were brought in but the *'ksheerabhishekam'* Would not take place. The moment I came to know the reason, I suspended the Dairy Superintendent. But was he responsible for the lapse?

× × ×

The Friday morning *'abhisheka seva'* is the most important of all *'sevas'* in the Tirumala Venkateswara Swami temple. Devotees taking part in the *'seva'* experience an unforgettable bliss. As the space is limited, only 130-140 people can take part in the 'seva' and have *'darshan'* of the Lord during the ritual bath. The ritual lasts for an hour to an hour and a half.

The significance of the *'seva'* lies in the fact that devotees can see the Lord in his unadorned form during *'abhisheka'*. During this *'seva'*, the garlands, ornaments, silk clothes and all other adornments are removed.

Devotees go into an ecstasy as they see the resplendent Lord in His youthful glow and vibrant form, which evokes devotion and surrender. They can view the Lord from the head to the toe only during *'abhisheka'* as He is bereft of any decorations during this phase. During the rest of the period, the Lord's eyes and forehead are covered with *'karpoora namam'* and *'kasturi tilakam'* and the entire body is richly decorated. Except for a part of the face, the entire idol is covered with either cloth, ornaments or flowers. Devotees bring in perfumes like *'punugu'*, *'javvadi'* *'kesari kasturi gandham'* and offer them for use in the *'abhishekam'*.

When I joined TTD, the temple administration used to offer new silk cloth to the Lord only on four occasions during a year. The same were cleaned, washed and used again and again to dress up the Lord.

The silk cloth is long and specially woven and used to cost about Rs.8000 in the beginning of the 1980's. I felt that every week, after the holy bath *'Abhisekham'*, on Fridays, the Lord should be adorned with a new cloth. The temple certainly could spend the Lord's own money for this. This also could be converted into an *'arjita'* (paid seva). I felt that only a few could afford that. But the *'melchat seva'* that I introduced received good response. A devotee taking part in *'melchat seva'* occupies the position next only to that of the Executive Officer during the *'abhisheka seva'* and has *'darshan'* of the Lord from close quarters.

After the *'abhishekam'*, the Lord is adorned with the silk cloth offered by the devotee. In the first year of the introduction of the seva, devotees came forward to offer a silk cloth during most of the weeks. Now, the devotees have to book the slot years in advance to take part in the *'seva'*. One who wants the booking for the first *'vastram'* can take part in the *'seva'* only in 2032. Every Friday, there are so many devotees willing to offer clothes that their number has to be restricted because of space constraints in *'Sayana Mantapam (Kulasehkarapadi)'*. Only, the rich can take part in the *'Melchat seva'* as the fee is now Rs. 12500/-. Even this seva is entirely booked upto 2020.

But a large number of devotees can take part in *'ksheerabhishekam'* by offering milk for the *'abhisekham'*. Devotees bring in milk and pour it into a large container near the temple main gate. Along with milk supplied by the temple, milk offered by devotees also is used for the Lord's *'Abhisekham'*. The *'ksheerabhishekam'* lasts about ten minutes.

Although it had been three years since I took over as TTD Executive Officer, I could not offer milk for the *'abhishekam'* even once. Whenever my wife Gopika and I took part in the Friday *'abhisheka seva'*, we would resolve that we should offer milk at least the following Friday. But invariably we forgot to bring Milk, and remembered it only when we were in the midst of the *'seva'*. Many Fridays passed without our offering milk for *'Abhishekam'*.

× × ×

But during the 1981*'brahmotsavams'*, Gopika firmly resolved that 'come what may' she would offer five litres of milk for the Friday *'abhisheka seva'*. For four days prior to Friday, she told herself every day (lest she should forget) that we would be offering milk for the *'seva'*.

Normally, during *'brahmotsavams'*, the Executive Officer stays atop the Hills with his family and relatives visiting invariably to have *'darshan'* of the Lord. Traditionally, the Executive Officer and his wife take part in every *'seva'* in which the Lord is taken in a procession during *'brahmotsavams'*. Once the idols complete their journey around the temple's four *'mada'* streets, *'srivari tirumanjanam'* is performed. The Executive Officer and his wife take part in that ritual also. Thus, Gopika used to be fully occupied from morning to evening running between the temple and the cottage on those days to take part in the *'sevas'* on the one hand and attend to relatives visiting Tirumala, on the other. As she was pre-occupied with numerous tasks, Gopika feared that she might forget the Friday milk offering. Therefore, she repeatedly prayed to the Lord, "Let us have the good fortune of contributing some milk for the *'abhishekam'* at least this Friday".

That Friday finally arrived. After taking part in the Lord's early morning *'Abhisekham'* procession, we went into the temple and squatted in front of the sanctum sanctorum. After a short while, the curtain was lifted to enable the devotees to watch the *'abhisheka seva'* to the Lord whom millions revere as the God of the *'kaliyuga'*. The moment the curtain was raised, I noticed the *'Jiyyangar'* and head priests whispering among themselves. Without initiating the *'abhishekam'*, they drew back the curtain again. Perhaps, they were attending to some minor preparatory work, I thought.

Meanwhile, two large containers were brought out and taken away from the sanctum sanctorum. A little later two large containers were taken in. The *'peshkar'*, the priests and other temple staff were moving about anxiously. Noticing all this, I asked the staff, "What is the hitch in starting the *'abhishekam'?*" "Nothing sir, it will start in a couple of minutes", they replied. I was surprised because the Lord's *'sevas'* took place on time. Delays were very rare as the TTD had a well-oiled machinery in place. The priests and other staff were given to collecting and checking and double-checking all the material for every *'seva'* well in advance. The office of the Executive Officer procures the materials, the *'Jiyyangar'* and his staff take care of the quality and quantity of materials and the priests use them only after they are satisfied.

I couldn't understand why there was such a delay in the performance of the *'abhishekam'*. I called the priests once again and inquired. "Nothing Sir, we will be initiating it in a few moments" they said. After the containers came in and went out for the second time there was anxious waiting for some more time. Finally, the head priest rushed in and the *'abhishekam'* was started. *'Ksheerabhishekam'* was carried out to the Lord with the priests pouring milk with conches. I noticed with surprise that the priests used only three conches of milk completing the *'Ksheerabhishekam'* in a few seconds. There should have been at least 250 litres of milk. This milk *'Abhisekham'* was over within a minute whereas it ought to have gone on for about ten minutes. Rest of the *'Abhisekham'* went on as usual for an hour.

Unable to restrain my curiosity on coming out of the sanctum after the *'Abhisekham'*, I asked the *'Jiyyangar'*, priests and *'Peshakar'* , "Why was the *'abhishekam'* delayed?" Then they disclosed the reason.

The milk supplied by the dairy farm for the *'abhishekam'* had turned sour. The priests noticed it after the milk had been brought into the sanctum sanctorum. Immediately, they requisitioned milk from the TTD canteen atop the Hills. The milk looked good at the canteen but went sour the moment it was brought into the sanctum sanctorum. Even the milk brought in by devotees and poured into the container turned sour when it was taken inside. In other words, there was no milk at all for the *'abhishekam'*.

I could not contain my indignation over the mess. Immediately, I announced the suspension of the Dairy Superintendent. Was he not expected to keep an eye on the quality of milk? How could he have been so irresponsible?

Meanwhile, my wife Gopika came out of the temple. She went into a tizzy the moment she heard the milk episode. I asked her what had happened. "Look, even this week we failed to get milk for the *'abhishekam'*. Though, I had bought five extra litres of milk from the dairy, and kept it in the fridge, I forgot to bring it here. What a sin have I committed', she said and started sobbing.

The *Peshakar* intervened. "Madam, as all the milk here had turned sour, we had to requisition the five litres of milk sent by the dairy to your cottage and used it for the *'abhishekam'*. Today the Lord had *'abhisekham'* with only five litres – that too your five litres. We did not know that you had bought the milk for the *'abhishekam'*. We could not disclose this in the presence of the devotees" he said. As tears of joy streamed down her eyes, Gopika dashed into the temple to express her gratitude to the Lord. As I began to reconstruct the whole chain of events, its full impact dawned on me.

Later, the Dairy Farm Superintendent explained that the milk was good when it left the farm and arrived at the temple. The five litres of milk sent to our cottage too was from the same lot. He said that he was not derelict in his duty of maintaining quality.

I cancelled the suspension order when I realised that the Superintendent was not to blame. How was it that only the five litres of milk that Gopika requisitioned from the dairy remained unspoiled while all the remainder went sour? Is there any answer? If there is, will it stand rational scrutiny? Is there any limit to the grace of the Lord?

26

OPERATION RESCUE BY MYSTERY COUPLE (STRANGE!)

After waiting for four to five hours at the guesthouse atop Tirumala hills, movie distributor Krishna Murthy and his wife at last caught hold of me around midnight that day. Wracking my brain over an intractable issue, I had by then lost all energy and patience. So my response was curt: "Let's meet at office tomorrow". But they would simply not heed. They virtually pinned me down in the verandah and unburdened themselves. As I listened, my eyes overflowed with tears of joy.

× × ×

As the Tirumala Tirupati Devasthanams Executive Officer in 1982, I had to get a new flag mast (Dhwajastambham) installed in 'Srivari' temple. Simultaneously, we took up works like reconstruction of the *Bedi Anjaneya* Swami temple, widening of Sannidhi and Mada Streets, refurbishing of the gold plated *'Ananda Nilayam'*, installation of continuous cleaning system for the *'pushkarini'* (temple pond), renovation of the *'potu'* (kitchen) and restoration of the *'bali peetham'* (sacrificial altar). We were keen on early completion of all the works, initiated in February 1982. We also wanted to undertake *'ashtabandhanam'* of the *'mula virat'*. (*'Ashtabandhanam'* refers to the firming up of the Lord's statue on the lotus platform). Once all the works were completed, *'samprokshana'* had to be performed, as according to *'agama sastras'*, only then the sanctity of the temple would be restored. We wanted to celebrate the rare event on a grand scale by organising a mini *'Brahmotsavam'*. We had invited 300 *'rithviks'* and Veda pundits from all over the country for conducting *'samprokshana'* and other rituals as stipulated in the *'sastras'*. As the tasks were numerous, the temple staff meticulously planned everything and assembled all the needed materials well in advance.

For undertaking any repairs in the sanctum sanctorum, the divine energy in the statue has to be first transferred and inducted into a holy *'kalasa'* (container) and kept securely at a separate place. All the daily *'sevas'* and rituals would be performed to the Lord in the *'Kalasa'* when the repairs go on. Once the repairs are over, the divine energy is restored from the sacred container to the statue by following the procedures laid down in the *' agama sastras'*. Then the *'ashtabandhanam'*, which involves the placement of special binding materials around the statue to firm up the base, is performed. That marks the completion of re-installation. *'Agama Sastras'* say that the nine gems (*nava Ratnas*) have to be deposited at the place where *'ashtabandhanam'* is carried out. Since similar *'samprokshana'* programmes were planned at the temples of Bedi Anjaneya Swami, Yoga Narasimha Swami, *'dhwaja stambham* '(flag mast), *'Balipeetham'* etc the staff procured the required sets of *'nine gems'* (n*avaratnas).*

After darshan of the Lord, while leaving the temple, on my way to attend the TTD Board Meeting, a day prior to the *'ashtabandhanam'*, I inquired from the priests as to how the arrangements were progressing. A senior priest *'mirasidar'* informed me that one more set of nine gems (*navaratnas*) might be required. I casually asked him to discuss the matter with the *'Peshkar'* (temple officer) who will organise, and left for the meeting. After the Board meeting was over at 8 PM, accompanied by my wife Gopika, I went to the temple for *'darshan'*. As we came out, the priests informed me that everything was going on as planned, except for one item i.e., *'navaratna'* set . All the gem sets procured had been utilised in other temple structures and there was a shortfall of one set for the *'ashthabhandanam'* of the statue of Lord Srinivasa in the main temple. I was annoyed. After all, we had procured the gem sets as per priests' estimates and the Deputy Executive Officer delivered them to the priests. Why was there a shortfall now?

That too for the *'mula virat' (main deity)*? I realised after a review that the renovation of the Varahaswamy temple - planned as an afterthought led to the shortfall. The idol of Varahaswamy in the temple near the *'pushkarini'* (temple tank), was at a low level and was not visible to the devotees. Whenever the priests were moving inside the sanctum, I observed once or twice, that the dhoti (dress worn by the priest) was brushing the idol. I resolved to reinstall the idol in an elevated position. Priests and *'Agama'* pundits, were initially hesitant to disturb the idol from that centuries old position. Hence, we dropped the idea. But when I broached the topic again everybody agreed on renovation involving the idols reinstallation on a higher platform at the same place. That renovation work was over. The last gem set had been used for *'Varahaswami'* temple. Somehow, procurement of one more *'navaratna'* set had not been done. Every one forgot about it. All renovation works and *'samprokhana'* programmes involving the use of the nine or ten *'navaratna'* sets procured had been completed. One more set was required for the final and the most important *'astabhandanam'* of the *'moola vigraha'* (main idol of Lord Srinivasa).

It was about 9.00 p.m. I was annoyed that the temple staff and priests had been casual about it. I was not worried. Since the Executive Officer enjoyed wide powers, I felt procurement of another set of gems would not be a big deal. From the temple itself, I called up the Deputy Executive Officer at Tirupati and asked him to open the treasury and arrange to send another set of nine gems immediately. But the treasury could not be opened as the official who had the second key of the double lock had gone to Madras. All the precious things in the treasury are kept under double lock – with two different keys kept with two different senior officers. Unless both are present, the treasury cannot be opened. That was not expected... Still, we should be able to manage. There were so many jewellery shops in Tirupati and most would keep stocks of *'navaratna'* sets as they are generally in great demand for most of the foundation ceremonies connecting with *'bhoomi puja'*. The set would generally cost Rs. 1000 or Rs. 1500/-.

I asked our staff to scout around jewellery shops in Tirupati for a gem set and send one set through a special messenger. The staff went round Tirupati at lightning speed. Some shops had been already been closed. In the shops that were open, gem sets were not available. It was nearly 11-30 p.m and I was getting only negative news from Tirupati. It was time for *'Ekanta Seva'* before the closure of the temple for the night. My wife and I were still in the temple. We never expected that we would not be able to get one *'navaratna'* set in almost four hours in place like Tirupati. The time was running out. The chances of procuring a set now had almost become bleak with the midnight approaching. We had still five hours to go for the *'ashtabandhanam'* programme. But, what was the use of all that unproductive time. Many *'ritviks'*, scholars and *'mirasidars'* too were anxiously waiting with us. Would the *'ashtabandhanam'* go awry?

I began to introspect. What sin had I committed to face such a predicament? Where had things gone wrong? Was I derelict in my duty? Did I fail to take seriously the priest mentioning though casually of the shortfall in the gem sets before I left for the board meeting? Such thoughts aggravated my anguish but offered no solution. I agonized: "What a paradox! An Executive Officer with vast powers could not accomplish a small task. Have I fouled up a sacred event that comes not even once in a lifetime – may be once in a century or centuries. Frantically, I asked my wife and others for individual gems.

Even priests and *'mirasidars'* had all unsuccessfully tried desperately to collect the nine gems at least separately. Some persons use *'navaratna'* rings on their fingers. We cannot use for such auspicious occasions, gems already used. I was crestfallen, as I failed in my duty. Efforts to procure one sete through our manager at Madras too failed. We came to the conclusion "We cannot get the nine gems tonight and collecting them before 5 a.m. tomorrow is impossible".

Seeing my plight, the priests tried to console me, "Sir, don't worry; we will manage the situation somehow". What did they mean by 'managing somehow'? Would they use a *'navartna ring'* worn by somebody or would they complete the ritual without using '*Navaratnas*'? What a shame! I had squandered a lifetime opportunity to serve the Lord that too with His own money. Barring the seeking of the Lord's pardon for my infraction, there was little that I could do. I slapped my cheeks in penitence and prayed to the Lord. "I don't know how the rest of the programme goes. Pardon me for my lapse. I cannot forgive myself for this irresponsible behaviour. I shall die of remorse. Pardon me – have mercy. Please save me Lord... I leave the responsibility at your feet". (Weighed down by anxiety and with tears in our eyes, my wife and I stepped into the guesthouse past midnight when we saw a middle-aged couple. Staff told me that they had been waiting for the past three to four hours. I was annoyed that they had turned up at the wrong time. Yet, as they had been awaiting me for a long time, reluctantly I returned their greetings. He introduced himself as Krishna Murthy, a movie distributor from Madras. I said impatiently, "What is the great urgency? What is the idea of waiting up to midnight? Let us meet at the office tomorrow". But they too were in no mood to listen. Krishna Murthy and his wife began to tell me why they had come.

"....We have read in newspapers about your plans to carry out '*ashtabandhanam*' to the '*mula virat*'. Learning that you use the nine gems in '*ashtabandhanam*', we thought of doing that '*seva*' to the Lord. We personally scoured the Madras market, hand-picked the best available and costly gems at the rate of one for each category. We got them embedded into a gold base. Our ardent desire and wish is that this set should be used for the Lord's '*asthabhandanam*'. We know, you must have already made arrangements for '*navaratna*' sets and many would be willing to donote for such a cause. We, sincerely, request you to use '*our*' set for the Lord... so that we have the satisfaction that the Lord indeed accepted our service..." For me, it was like sunrise at midnight. "Am I hearing, Am I dreaming? .. 'O' Lord... how compassionate...." Tears rolled down my cheeks. I just hugged Krishna Murthy and lifted him. He was perplexed - Just as I did not know his anxiety, he did not know my agony and esctasy...Only the Lord knows...how..what...why...things happens like that. I profusely thanked the couple and invited them to be present in the temple to offer the set to the priests themselves early next morning at the muhurtam of *'Asthabhandhanami.'*

The certain disaster was averted thanks to the timely gift from the devoted couple. Before the next day's pre-dawn *'seva'*, the *'ashtabandhanam'* and restoration of divine force to the *'mula virat'* had been completed in all glory.

Why did it happen? How did it happen? Was it a mere coincidence?

Mr. P.V.R.K. Prasad and Gopika leading the procession at the time of Astabandhanam

P.S. in the Telugu version, I had wrongly written the name as 'Subba Rao' subsequents it was brought to my notice that the gentlemans name was 'Krishna Murthy' and not 'Subba Rao'. The mistake is regretted.

Prasad
Author

27

AGONY AND ECSTASY

My wife Gopika was stunned when she heard the news.

"Why has this happened? Hadn't Mr. Kumaraswamy Reddy told you that he would be handing over charge in Lord Srinivasa's presence? Why is the venue being shifted to Hyderabad? Won't you assume office in the Lord's presence?" She pounded me with such queries in despair and despondency.

I could understand Gopi's agony. In fact, I was trying to deal with my own disappointment. It was not that my transfer from TTD to take over as Managing Director of the Andhra Pradesh State Cooperative Bank (APCOB), was an unexpected development. She was upset because I was being deprived of the pleasure and privilege of taking office of Managing Director, APCOB, in the temple precincts - sitting in front of the Lord.

How could her reaction be any different? During the four years (1978-82) that I served as TTD's Executive Officer, she had taken part in most of the temple rituals along with me with deep faith in the Lord. Every time she was in the presence of the Lord, she felt exhilarated and energized. She used to take part in every ritual with great enthusiasm.

× × ×

Transfers from one post to another in Government service are routine. The transfers are very common, particularly for IAS officials who are moved frequently from one post to another. Lasting three years in a post is quite unusual when the average tenure of an IAS officer in a post is hardly one year. The tenure of TTD Executive Officer had been fixed as three years in the TTD Act. Against such a backdrop, the Government retained me as TTD Executive Officer for four years. That was done for two reasons: First, the Government felt that there was need for continuity in administration in the twilight period when the new TTD Act, 1981, contemplating many changes, was coming into force. Second, Endowments Minister P. V. Chowdary and TTD Board Chairman B. Nagi Reddy requested the Chief Minister that I should not be disturbed pending the completion of some important projects under the Master Plan, on the ground that I had already completed three years in TTD. Installation of the new flag post (*Dwajastambham*) under way also delayed my transfer. Since the transfer was inevitable, it had come as expected.

Within a week of the new flag post (*Dwajastambham*) being installed in Lord Srinivasa's temple, I received the transfer orders in June 1982. The State Government posted me as APCOB Managing Director and Mr. G. Kumaraswamy Reddy working as Managing Director APCOB, was posted as TTD Executive Officer. By then, I had already been selected for a post-graduate programme in Development Studies at Cambridge University under a British Government fellowship. I was due to join in Cambridge in August. Although the Executive Officer too is a State Government employee, under the new TTD Act, 1981, stipulated that the Executive Officer has to assume office in the presence of the Lord inside the temple – symbolizing the declaration of the loyalty to Lord Srinivasa and not to the powers that be in the Government. Since there was no such provision in 1978, I did not have the privilege of taking charge in front of the Lord from the Endowments Commissioner, Mr. Anandarao Mudaliar, who was acting as I/c Executive Officer. I had taken charge in Hyderabad.

Since, Mr. Kumaaswamy Reddy, with whom I was exchanging places had to take charge from me in the precincts of the Lord under the new Act, he would handover charge simultaneously. Naturally, my wife and I were delighted. Although I could not take over as Executive Officer in the temple, Gopika was happy that I could take charge as APCOB MD in the temple at least on leaving the TTD. I too had looked forward to the unusual previlege.

Although I had held many important positions including that of Information Advisor to the Prime Minister, in my 33 years of service, I derived the greatest satisfaction and pleasure as TTD Executive Officer. I had the fortune of being the TTD Executive Officer at a fairly young age (37), and that too for four years. As Executive Officer, I enjoyed all creature facilities like a bungalow, a car, servants etc. But the greatest fortune, of course, was having *'darshan'* of the Lord whenever I wanted. In whatever way one looked at it — material comforts, social status, spiritual quest and the challenge of leading an unique organisation with 37 departments and 15000 employees - working as Executive Officer was a rare privilage.

In fact, I faced many hurdles in implementing what I thought were good decisions in pilgrims' interest. Devout pilgrims come to Tirupati braving many hardships to fulfil their vows. I believed that service to pilgrims was service to God. I had not encountered so many impediments and affronts in discharging my duties in any other job as I had faced as Executive Officer. Yet, the satisfaction I derived in TTD service was unique, extraordinary and beyond words.

During those four years, Gopika had immersed herself in the worship of the Lord. As the wife of the Executive Officer, she had the opportunity to have frequent *'darshan'* of the Lord and take part in Lord's *'sevas'* (rituals). Although she was aware that such a privilege and pleasure were not permanent, my transfer unsettled her. Her four-year-old attachment to Tirumala and the Lord might have enmeshed her in the illusion of there being no end to such privileges. Even for me it was not easy to reconcile myself to the unpleasant news of the transfer... in one way announcing that I had exhausted my accumulated *'punya'* (virtuous deeds).

But, I tried to console her: "Gopi, What is there in it to regret? Transfers are an occupational hazard in Government service. Being posted at Tirupati for four years itself is great. Our 'Punya' (Virtuous deeds of ours) would have entitled us only to this length of stay. Let us accept that we have run out of our luck. But, let us not forget that. I would take charge for the new post in the temple and in front of the Lord. In the gloomy situation, she saw a silver lining:

Gopika recovered appreciating that I would enjoy the rare privilege of taking charge in the precincts of the Lord as APCOB Managing Director. All the more important to me as I did not enjoy that pleasure and privilege even when I took charge as TTD Executive Officer. Had the Government posted me in any other position, I would not have had such an opportunity.

Gopika reconciled herself to the situation, arguing: "Because of Lord's blessings, you have been appointed APCOB MD. Otherwise, why would you have been shifted precisely to that post two months before you are to leave for Cambridge?" Believing that God willed it that way, she looked forward to my handing over and taking charge in the temple precincts. I was also immensely happy for that opportunity.

The auspicious moment for the mutual exchange of places between Mr. Kumaraswamy Reddy and me had been fixed. In fact, I had a week's time to go to Hyderabad after handing over charge.

A day before the scheduled muhurtam (auspicious moment) to hand-over charge, Mr. Kumaraswamy Reddy called me over the phone from Hyderabad.

"Mr. Prasad, the APCOB Board has been convened for this weekend to discuss a crucial subject. The Chairman is insisting on my presence. I will, therefore, be coming to Tirupati tomorrow morning to take charge as Executive Officer and shall return to Hyderabad immediately. Since you anyway have joining time of about a week, I will hand over charge to you in Hyderabad immediately after the APCOB Board meeting here i.e., at Hyderabad. In case you are still there at Tirupati I can even handover charge at Tirupati".

What could I say? I mumbled, "As you wish it". I felt deflated and depressed.

× × ×

There was nothing unusual in Mr Reddy's proposal. It was quite natural in his position to suggest as he did. It would be unusual for me if I had requested him to handover charge in the temple whenever he decided to hand over. Hence, I did not express my desire. When Gopika heard this news from me, she was crestfallen and a personification of disappointment. " We seem to have run out of the Lord's blessings. That is why we are being robbed of this privilege". We tried to reconcile ourselves to the inevitable, believing in destiny. But, ill luck continued to haunt us.

As planned, Mr. Kumaraswamy Reddy arrived at Tirumala the next day. I handed over charge to him in front of the Lord.

Mr. P.V.R.K. Prasad handing over charge to Mr. Kumaraswamy Reddy in front of the Lord.

As Lord Srinivasa watched (did He?), the charge handing-over ritual took place strictly as per the procedures laid down, in the presence of TTD Chairman Nagireddy and Endowments Commissioner Rajagopala Raju and Board members. My wife and children too attended the event. Immediately after Mr. Kumaraswamy Reddy took over as Executive Officer, tears welled up in my eyes as the event marked the end of my being the first servant of the Lord, having the fortune of daily *'darshan'* of and service to the Lord. I felt as if every one was watching my fall from grace. Turning aside, I wiped my tears. But I did not attempt to wipe out the tears that streamed down my eyes half an hour later. In fact, I did not feel like wiping them.

Once I handed over the charge, the priests presented me the *'melchat Seshavastram'* cloth in front of the Lord as TTD Board Chairman Nagireddy and Commissioner Rajagopala Raju watched. *'melchatt'* cloth is one that has once adorned the Lord. According to temple traditions, only VVIPs like the President and the Prime Minister are honoured with *'melchatt'*

Mr. P.V.R.K. Prasad being given a ceremonial send off after handing over charge

cloth as Vedic pundits invoked Lord's blessings. Such an honour can take place only when there is a Board resolution. I wondered as to why was I being honoured on the eve of my departure from Tirupati. Who conferred on me the eligibility? Without my knowledge, the Chairman, the Commissioner and Board members had reportedly resolved to honour me with *'melchatt'* cloth (Did they? They kept it as a secret to spring a surprise on me. Who prompted them?). That was not the end of the story.

As we came out of the temple, well-decorated temple elephants were awaiting us at the main entrance *('maha dwaram')* to bid us an affectionate farewell. As my wife, children and I walked to the guesthouse, the temple elephants piloted us to the accompaniment of *'mangalavadyams'* (*'Sahnai/Sannai'* Music) while hundreds - TTD Board members, officials, friends, locals, well-wishers and acquaintances followed extending their greetings. The march to the guesthouse went like a grand procession. Tears of joy streamed down my cheeks as I experienced people's love, affection and admiration in abundance. That was why I did not feel like wiping the tears of joy.

But all these provided little consolation to my life partner. The moment she entered the guesthouse, she burst out in tears. "Why has the Lord, whom you have served till now sincerely in thoughts, words and deeds, turned unkind towards us? Why has He robbed you of the opportunity of at least taking charge as APCOB, MD in His precincts? What crime have we committed to be thrown out of the TTD and being left jobless?" I had no words as she sobbed.

Her agony and anxiety were not about my post. She too was aware that in Government service, no post was permanent for anybody. But having developed a deep attachment to and faith in the Lord through participation in every *'seva'* during the previous four years, she was now disturbed over the imminent end to her good fortune, like any other human being. She had come out of her disappointment, however, when she learnt that I was to take charge in the precincts of the Lord. The Lord who had provided such opportunity out of the way as an extraordinary blessing, had snatched it away at the last minute!

Yet, restraining myself, I spoke in a philosophical vein to console her. "Look, it is because of Lord's blessings that, unlike any previous Executive Officer, we have been honoured with the *'melchatt'* cloth, in the Lord's presence. Had there been no blessings of the Lord, how is it that so many people had bid such a splendid farewell to us? The TTD Board would have seen us off with temple honours? We owe all these to Lord's grace. There is no reason why I should take charge as APCOB M. D. here. Had it happened, it would have been a bonus".

However much I tried, I could not console her. In her view, we were guilty of some indiscretion or the other. That was why the Lord had denied me the opportunity of taking charge in His precincts. I told her: "Gopi, you are agitated, and so you are over-reacting. No APCOB MD takes charge in the Tirumala temple. Even if one wants to, it does not happen. Such a possibility had arisen, but it has not fructified. Is it fair to blame the Lord just because we have lost an opportunity? Had it been destined, it would certainly have happened. What is the point in getting distressed over something that was not destined?"

When you ardently want something to happen in a particular fashion, you are also concerned over that not materialising. We have read about the link between wishes, eagerness, fear, despair, attachment and end of discretion in the Bhagavadgita.

"Dhyayato Vishayn pumsum sanghstheyshypajayathe;

Sanghyasthaingyathekamaha kamathe krodhobhi jayathe;

Krodhodbhavathi sammohaha sammohath smruthi vibhramaha;

Smrithi brahmsath buddhinaso buddhinasathpranasathi"

"The man dwelling on sense-objects develops attachment for them; from attachment springs up desire, and from desire (unfulfilled) ensues anger.

"From anger arises infatuation; from infatuation, confusion; from confusion, loss of reason; and from loss of reason, one goes to complete ruin".

Yet that was her frame of mind. Her overriding anguish at that moment was that the Lord had purposely created an opportunity only to snatch away and that I would be able to take charge in the temple precincts only if we still have Lord's blessings. Finally, I told her, "Gopi, we still have a week to report. Meanwhile, pray to the Lord. If we are destined, it will happen. Otherwise, it won't happen. But get mentally reconciled to the fact that it may not happen. There is little beyond this that we can do..." I saw no possibility of my taking charge in the temple. Meanwhile, innumerable farewell meetings were organised for me in Tirumala and Tirupati.

× × ×

We decided to leave Tirupati, after attending *'anivari asthanam'* which was due to take place six days later in the Tirumala temple. After talking to devotees in Bangalore, we arranged for the first time for a jasmine-bedecked huge 'vahana' (Chariot) to be brought for the Lord's procession on *'anavari ashanam'* day. All arrangements had been made for the procession. I told Gopika, "We will return to Hyderabad the day after *'anivari asthanam'*, ritual. She nodded her head reluctantly.

Two days after taking charge as Executive Officer, Mr. Kumaraswamy Reddy returned to Hyderabad to take part in the APCOB Board meeting. As per our understanding, I was to take charge from him in Hyderabad after the APCOB Board meeting.

A day before *'anivari asthanam'*, Mr. Kumaraswamy Reddy phoned me up to say that he was coming to Tirupati as he had been told that the Executive Officer's presence during the ritual was a 'must'.

"I am planning to meet you at the Executive Officer's bungalow at Tirupati at 7-15 am tomorrow, hand over charge and then leave for Tirumala to take part in *'anivari asthanam'*. What do you say?"

What was there for me to say? I verified whether the timing of 7-15 a.m. was auspicious, and then told him, "As you wish ".

The moment she heard the dialogue, Gopika began to cry. "Why is God so unkind to us?

When he (Mr. Kumaraswamy Reddy) is coming to Tirupati, can't he hand over charge in the temple?".

Pursing my lips, I smiled philosophically.... Why should he? How could he?

Mr. Kumaraswamy Reddy had arrived that very night. He called me at Tirupati and said, "Sorry Prasad, I have to make a small change in the schedule. I am in the temple at Tirumala Hills. Priests tell me that I do not have adequate time to drive to Tirupati to hand over charge at 7-15 tomorrow morning and return to Tirumala to take part in the *'anivari asthanam'* programme. Let us do one thing. Come straight to the guesthouse at Tirumala tomorrow morning. I will hand over charge at the agreed, auspicious time. Then all of us will go to the temple to take part in *'anivari asthanam'*." Having already been accustomed to saying, "As you wish", I had no reason to change my reply. Atleast, I would have the privilage of having darshan of the Lord soon after my taking over the new assignement.

Gopika's agony was beyond description. "We are going up to the Hills tomorrow but the charge taking over won't happen in the temple". How could it happen? As I ran out of words of consolation, I prayed silently to Lord Srinivasa. "If not for me, at least for her sake, can't you ensure that the wish is fulfilled?" So praying, I slipped into sleep, fully convinced that the prayer was neither possible nor appropriate.

By 7-00 the next morning, few minutes earlier than scheduled, accompanied by my wife and two children I arrived at the Tirumala guesthouse. The Executive Officer was not in the guesthouse. Soon after we arrived Mr. Kumaraswamy Reddy phoned me. "Sorry, Prasad. I am right now in the temple, for *'anivari asthanam'*. I may not be able to come to the guesthouse. If you don't mind, come straight to the temple. I will hand you over charge of the APCOB Managing Director in the temple itself. What do you say?" What could I say"

I jumped with excitement. This time, I did not say, "As you wish it". Instead, I told him, "We are on our way" and hopped into the car along with Gopika and children.

The import of the news dawned on her. As if to wash the feet of the Lord whom she had blamed till then, she began to shed tears of joy copiously. "Has the Lord really beckoned us, really beckoned us?" Filled with gratitude, she leaned on me.

Within five minutes, we reached the temple. As *'anivari asthanam'* was under way, Mr. Kumaraswamy Reddy handed me over the charge of APCOB MD in the presence of the Lord, the very spot where I had handed him over the charge of Executive Officer. I felt that Srinivasa, the living God in this 'kali yuga' and the Supreme Lord, was watching and showering His benign blessings on us as I took charge.

The waves of joy that surged from our hearts seemed like the oceanic waves trying to kiss the sky on a full-moon night. Our ecstasy was beyond words.

Even to this day Gopika and I still debate, "How did it happen that way?"

28

(NO) CRIME AND PUNISHMENT

"Prasad garu, you are accused of three crimes. They are not petty crimes but crimes of corruption. What have you to say?"

The person who pinned me down with this blunt talk was the Chief Minister, Mr. N. T. Rama Rao (NTR). I was dumbstruck. That was the welcome the State Government accorded me on my arrival from the U. K. after a one-year post-graduation programme at Cambridge. I had gone to the U. K. after serving TTD as Executive Officer for four years and Managing Director APCOB for two months.

NTR had taken over as Chief Minister a few months earlier. Being away in the U. K., I was not fully aware of the administrative changes that had taken place after the fall of the Congress Government and assumption of power by NTR led Telugu Desam Party. The rumour doing the rounds on my return was that I might not get immediate posting orders. In course of time, I learnt from friends that the Government had already suspended some and was about to suspend 25 to 30 officials. Determined to root out corruption from the administration, the Chief Minister felt he should sternly deal with corrupt officials first.

When I heard that my name too reportedly figured in the list of the 25-30 people I was stunned. I told myself that it could only be a rumour but not a fact. I was doubly shocked when persons close to the Chief Minister confirmed that I figured in the list of the corrupt officials and that facing the *"Dharma Mahamatra"* – an institution created by NTR to deal with corruption – was inevitable. I agonised over the turn of events. "As TTD Executive Officer, I believed that every paisa dropped by pilgrims in the hundi belonged to Lord Srinivasa and utilising it purposefully and effectively was my bounden duty. What a paradox! I am now being branded corrupt!"

I might have been indiscrete in some instances occasionally. Even then, I believed that some inexplicable power made me act that way. It was also a fact that some TTD Trust Board members were not happy with me. Beyond this, I did not give scope for any corrupt practices either knowingly or even casually. Why was then the Government dragging me into this vortex of corruption?

Ignorance about the rationale behind the Government's move and the rumours doing the rounds depressed me. The Chief Minister and many of his ministerial colleagues were new to administration and inexperienced. From the Chief Minister downwards to the junior most Minister, all believed that the previous administration was mired in corruption and cleansing it was their foremost task. Many Ministers were yet to understand who was what among officials.

Against this background, there was none to listen to me. Even if there was one, he was not prepared to believe and appreciate what one was told.

I found myself directionless. Leaders who knew me and my style of work were not in positions of power and those in power did not know me. Moreover, all of them firmly believed or at least suspected that all those who worked in the previous Government had sullied their reputation. Senior officials, who knew me through and through, were not bold enough to take up my cause and speak to the Chief Minister.

The campaign that my name figured in the list of the corrupt made me despondent. I felt like shouting from housetops that "I am not corrupt, not corrupt...". Those who knew me could not speak to the Chief Minister. And I could not take the initiative because the Government had not served any memo on me on the charges. Again, there was no guarantee that the Chief Minister would grant me an interview if I sought one without knowing the specific purpose. NTR those days was not in a mood to grant an interview to one branded corrupt? Darkness descended on me.

Some collegues offered many suggestions. "Why do you want to meet the Chief Minister? When a senior official, Mr. X, like you, wanted to offer an explanation, the Chief Minister refused to see him. Let us see what happens. You can cross the bridge when you come to it. Let the charge-sheet be filed before the *"Mahamatra"*. If you are denied a posting and if something more happens, are there not good advocates to take up your case in courts?"

Those who offered such advice did not understand my agony and anguish. I was not bothered about courts and cases. I did not know what crime I had committed. But the disinformation campaign against me had been consuming me mentally.

"Akeertim chapi bhutani kathayishkanti tevyayam
Sambhavitasyacha keertirmarana datirichyate"

— Bhagavadgita

"People always talk about your infamy. For a self-respecting person infamy is more unbearable than death".

As long as I worked in Tirupati, I used to walk into the temple and represented to Lord Srinivasa whenever I faced a problem. True to tradition, I saluted the Lord from Hyderabad, and sent my joining report to the Government. Whether posting orders would be given or not should be clear soon. The joining report went from the Chief Secretary to the Chief Minister.

Breaking my anxiety over the shape of things to unfold, there was a call from the Secretary to Chief Minister, Mr. Mohan Kanda (the present Chief Secretary) informing me that the Chief Minister wanted to speak to me. Puzzled at the call, I went to meet the Chief Minister the next day.

As I entered the Chief Minister's office in the middle of the Secretariat, his personal staff ushered me into his chambers. "What is he going to broach? Now that allegations have already been made against me, what is there for him to ask? In case he does not seek any clarification, should I raise the subject on my own or not". As I debated these questions within myself, the Chief Minister entered the chambers. As I got up to greet him, he asked me to be seated and took his place in a sofa.

In a serious tone, he started the conversation. "Prasad garu, we have heard a lot about you".

"Favourably or unfavourably, Sir?"

"Both ways"

"Sir, I am not eager to learn the good aspects of mine which you may have heard. If you have no objection, I would like to know what bad things have been said about me". Although I uttered those words nonchalantly, I was apprehensive of what I might hear. For a moment, I shut my eyes and visualised Lord Srinivasa. From then onwards, there was a change in his conversational tone and tenor. Although his language was polite, his questions were sharp, straight and unequivocal.

"We understand you have committed three big crimes. The first complaint against you was that you doled out lakhs of rupees of the TTD to thousands of Brahmins indiscriminately?"

I suppressed a smile, and said, "Sir, may I give an explanation?"

"Certainly."

"This allegation is partially true. Some Brahmins did indeed benefit because of certain schemes taken up by the TTD." Mr. Rama Rao suddenly lifted his head to look at me sharply.

"As Executive Officer, I introduced two schemes to preserve and promote the Vedas and the *'sastras'* called *"Veda Rakshana"* and *"Sastra Rakshana"*. Those who have studied the Vedas for 12 to 16 years and earned the titles of *'kramapathis'* and *'ghanapathis'* are paid a monthly honorarium of Rs.600 to Rs.800 if they recite the Vedas in the temple nearest to them for eight hours a day for the welfare of society. The TTD implemented the scheme on the advice of Sri Chandrasekhara Saraswati Swami of Kanchi Peetham and with prior State

Government approval. It was for the first time such a scheme had been launched in the State. The Endowments Commissionerate, with the approval of the State Government, was to have implemented a similar scheme even two to three years prior to my joining the TTD. But the commissionerate, for some reason, could not implement. The job was transferred to TTD for execution when I was there. I implemented it with all sincerity and seriousness. If I had committed any crime, it lay in implementing Government orders in letter and spirit".

As I paused, Mr. Rama Rao let out a thoughtful "Oh".

"Sir, I forgot to tell you one important point. The '*kramapathis*' and '*ghanapathis*' who are eligible to draw the Rs.600-800 honorarium under the "*Veda Rakshana*" and "*Sastra Rakshana*" schemes do not run into thousands. There are just 370. A peon in Government service who is not even a matriculate earns more than Rs.2000 a month. In contrast, these scholars have spent 16 long years studying the Vedas, which is equivalent to doing post-graduation in a subject. What we pay these scholars – who recite the Vedas at the top of their voice for eight hours a day straining their vocal cords in the interest of society – is a paltry, monthly honorarium of Rs.600 or Rs.800. All these facts are on record. You can requisition the files and take a look at them. If this is the crime that is brought to your attention, I plead guilty".

There was no change in the Chief Minister's demeanour. He merely uttered a "yes" and asked me about the second "crime".

"We heard that you collected lakhs of rupees as bribes from the contractors of the Papanasanam dam at Tirumala after amending the contract terms to benefit them".

I could now understand the background to the allegations. Some one, out of jealousy or anger, had prepared a list of corruption charges against me according to a plan and handed it over to the Chief Minister. That too, when I was not in India. The matters being raised by the Chief Minister had in-built potential for distortion of facts.

The Papanasanam dam story is just an instance. Construction of the Papanasanam dam had been cleared by the time I took over as TTD Executive Officer in 1978. Tenders, based on the estimates prepared by an Engineers' Committee had been invited and the contract already awarded to the Bomaby-based Hindustan Construction Corporation (HCC). When the company was about to begin work after moving construction equipment, material and labour to the project site, the TTD issued "stop work" orders following some second thoughts. Some experts had suggested that the dam be constructed 100-150 metres downstream as it would increase the reservoir's storage capacity by three times and take care of Tirumala's water needs for two to three years. Work on the project, therefore, came to a standstill. The Engineers' Committee studied the suggestion for the change in location and found it feasible and desirable in the over all interest of Tirumala. The HCC thus could not initiate any work for three and half months.

Okay, the dam could be constructed downstream involving additional expenditure. When the estimates went up, tenders had to be called afresh. But what would be the fate of the HCC, which had mobilised equipment, material and men but could not take up construction because of TTD orders? Would the company keep quiet if the agreement was scrapped? If it were to go to a court of law against the loss inflicted by the TTD and obtain a stay on the construction of the dam itself ? The TTD would lose both money and time and pilgrims face water problems with the dam not materialising on time.

As the debate was going on, on these lines, I took over as Executive Officer (1978). I thoroughly reviewed the Papanasanam dam issue and the Engineers' Committee recommendation that it be completed early in the context of the frequent water crises in Tirumala. I placed the factual situation before the Persons-in-Charge Committee. As the members were fully aware of Tirumala's water scarcity and pilgrims' plight, they decided that old contractor should construct the dam at the new place without any further delay. As directed by the committee, I issued the orders to the contractor.

Papanasanam Dam During construction

Even as the dam construction was under way, we appointed a committee of five Chief Engineers of the State Government to decide on any changes in rates following the change in the dam site. The committee was asked to submit its report to the Persons-in-Charge Committee, which in turn would send it to the State Government for approval. I made it clear to the HCC that bills would be paid only according to the old rates and the new rates would become effective only after Government clearance. The company agreed to the terms and conditions and started construction. As a result, the dam, which was scheduled to take two years, could be completed in a year and half. It was even inaugurated in 1980.

I narrated the story in detail to Chief Minister NTR.

"Sir, because of my initiative, the dam could be completed fast and in record time without the work getting stalled or embroiled in litigation. Yet, the rate issue is still pending with the State Government. The contractor will be paid extra only if the State Government clears the revised rates. Beyond the old stipulated rates, we have so far not paid a paisa more to the contractor. If you regard completion of the dam construction in record time and without any interruption a crime or sin, I plead guilty to the charge".

Silence reigned between us for some time after my explanation. But NTR would not stop at that.

"But what about the misappropriation of diamonds in the name of getting a diamond-studded crown manufactured for Lord Srinivasa? It seems you spurned diamonds offered by the Customs Department and struck deals with private parties. We understand that a raid on your house will expose hordes of diamonds secreted in mattresses and pillows..."

This time, I could not help laughing. The Chief Minister was a bit shocked. The allegation was funny because I had been shifted from the TTD even before I had an opportunity to go to Holland to buy diamonds. My successor, Mr. G. Kumaraswamy Reddy, had the privilege of taking part in the diamond purchase. However, I had the unique fortune of tendering an explanation now.

Remembering Lord Srinivasa for whom the diamond-studded crown was designed, I explained the background at great length to Mr. NTR.

It was true that I was the architect of the plan to get a diamond-studded crown made for Lord Venkateswara. We got dummy models of the crown manufactured. We got the cost estimates prepared and selected highly skilled artisans to embed diamonds in the crown. We appointed a committee of jewellery experts to supervise the job amid foolproof security arrangements. All that remained was procurement of diamonds. The crown needed thousands of diamonds.

When Prime Minister Mrs. Indira Gandhi happened to visit Tirumala at that time, I showed her the diamond crown models and requested her to make available for the crown some diamonds seized from smugglers by the Customs Department. The TTD was ready to pay for the diamonds. She passed on instructions to her secretary and within days orders conceding our request were issued.

Mr. P.V.R.K. Prasad showing the 'Dummy Model of Lord's 'Diamond Crown'

Within a week of the issuance of orders, Prime Minister's Principal Secretary Sri. Krishnaswamy Rao Saheb, called me over the phone and advised me against using smuggled diamonds seized by the Customs Department. I was puzzled.

As I narrated the story up to this point to Mr. Rama Rao, my mouth went dry. I helped myself to a glass of water, saying, "Excuse me sir".

Mr. Rama Rao could not restrain his curiosity. He asked, "Why were you advised against using Customs' diamonds?"

"Sir, according to Rao Saheb, smugglers carry diamonds in their private parts to avoid detection. He wanted me to ponder whether such unclean diamonds should adorn the sacred crown of Lord Srinivasa. The matter went to the notice of the Prime Minister and she too opposed the proposal, according to Rao Saheb".

"Is that so?", said Mr. Rama Rao and shut his eyes for a few moments. He appeared to be praying. (Whom?). Once he opened his eyes, I narrated the rest of the story.

I was depressed when Mr. Rao Saheb advised me against using smuggled diamonds. Not knowing what to do, I requested him to suggest a solution because the TTD did not have the expertise or skills to choose diamonds or strike deals. He invited me to go over to Delhi.

The Principal Secretary to the Prime Minister took the initiative and arranged a meeting with the Managing Director of the Hindustan Diamond Corporation (HDC), a Government of India undertaking. During the meeting, the HDC agreed to buy the diamonds on behalf of the TTD. After a thorough and detailed discussion, we finalised matters regarding transparent selection of diamonds and quality checks, price evaluation by a third party, and transport, security and insurance.

"Sir, the arrangements were so thorough and perfect that it was not possible for any one to misappropriate a single diamond or change the rates under any circumstances. Fortunately or unfortunately - I don't know - by the time the purchase team in which the Executive Officer was a member could go to Amesterdam and Antwerp in Holland to finalise the selection and purchase of diamonds, I had been shifted from the TTD. As a result, I had no occasion even to see the diamonds. Even if I had an opportunity, I would not have stooped so low as to rob the God and stack my mattresses and pillows with diamonds. I pray to the Lord to ensure that even such thoughts never crossed my mind".

As I spoke thus, my hitherto repressed emotion was straining to burst out. After all, my integrity had been questioned and honesty doubted. With allegations of my robbing the God's diamonds and the TTD of funds for Vedic scholars in the very name of the Lord whom I had faithfully and sincerely served for four years.

Mr. NTR had by then stopped shooting further questions and was lost in thought. But my blood continued to boil. I was held guilty of a crime, which I did not commit and that too without verification. As I mentally kneeled before Lord Srinivasa and asked, "Why am I being subjected to such an ordeal", I felt a ray of light, emanating from the Lord, bathing me. Suddenly, I was all charged up. I stood up and said, "Sir, I don't know who told you what about me. Neither am I anxious to know. As long as I worked in the TTD, every cell in my body was dedicated to the Lord every moment. My conscience knows that whatever I did, I did it with the Lord's inspiration, with noble intentions and sans self-interest. I have not committed any wrong willfully. Whenever I felt inspired to do good deeds, I carried them out as my bounden duty as Lord's directive, but did not think of Government rules and regulations. As long as Lord Srinivasa reposed faith in my integrity and honesty, this Government cannot touch me whatever be the number of allegations and inquiries. I had the Lord in every thought, word and deed of mine. And I believed that God was the architect of whatever I did or could do. If you believe that I am a criminal…", I said as my voice trailed off - I was looking like a man possessed, "I am prepared to undergo any punishment, I would deem that also as a God's benediction. No one can save me from such a punishment – if it were to be Lord's wish".

NTR was perplexed to see me in that condition. Recovering quickly, he stood up, came to me and held my hands affectionately and said, "What is this? Mr. Prasad - Relax"

Placing his hands on my shoulders and pleasantly looking into my eyes, he said, "We never told you that whatever we said represented our opinion. They were all allegations brought to our notice by somebody. After all, we are new to administration. We have to trust somebody. Many have said many good things about you in glorious terms. I was one of those who were charmed by your work in the TTD before I entered politics. But once in administration, I could not shut my ears when I hear allegations against you.

Mr. Rama Rao then recalled how I got the construction of a choultry at Kandimallayapalle expedited to help him produce the movie, *"Veerabrahmendra Swamy"*. Mr. B. V. Mohana Reddy (subsequently a Minister) had drawn my attention to the movie crew's problems for want of suitable accommodation in the village. I took the initiative to get the TTD choultry (then under construction) completed in two months instead of the scheduled 12 months, and to facilitate housing for the movie unit in that remote place.

Still, I must have been looking worked up. Noticing it, Mr. Rama Rao once again clasped my hands and said, "Don't think we believe all these allegations. Our Secretaries Mohan Kanda and Banerjee repeatedly suggested that I first listen to what you have to say, instead of keeping the posting orders in abeyance and ordering an inquiry. That was why we decided to speak to you and get our misgivings dispelled." My eyes became wet once again, this time because of Mr. N. T. Rama Rao's straightforward and plain talk.

Without keeping quiet, I said, "Sir, order an inquiry into my conduct and give me a posting only after you are satisfied with its findings. Exoneration from allegations is more important than a posting for me".

Mr. Rama Rao smiled, patted me on the shoulder and bade me goodbye.

Surprise!

In the next one hour, I received the posting orders. The Government re-appointed me Managing Director of the Andhra Pradesh State Cooperative Bank, a post held by me before I left for the U. K. More surprisingly Mr. Rama Rao sent for me after two months to congratulate me. He told me that an inquiry, ordered in the wake of allegations against me in a magazine – *'rajadhani'* published from Hyderabad - were baseless. Then, he appointed me as Commissioner of Information, Public Relations, Cinematography and Cultural Affairs and ex-officio Secretary to the Government.

On the day of the posting, the Chief Minister told me, "Prasad garu, we have total confidence in you. We have come to power because of our image and individual prestige. We will continue to be in power only so long as our image is intact. That's why, I am placing the responsibility of safeguarding our image in your hands".

Three months earlier, I had been stuck in the Slough of Despond. Now, I was soaring into the skies with NTR's pat. What a great change in so short a time!

Why was I fed up with life just three months ago – Still, why all this – the allegation, the enquiry, the animosity, agony and explanation – There must be some reason. Perhaps, it was the price I had to pay for some shortcoming of mine in the service of the Lord.

29

MARRIAGES ARE STILL MADE IN HEAVEN

Only hours before he tied the sacred *"thali"* in August 1990, the bride's father could see bridegroom Narendra for the first time.

It was an arranged marriage. The elders had gone through the age-old tradition and rituals of the boy's family taking a look at the girl, exchanging horoscopes and deciding on the auspicious moment and the venue of the wedding etc. Yet, the bride's father could see the groom only when he was seated in the marriage pandal.

Mr. Narendra, working as an Associate Professor of Financial Management in the U. S., had been totally opposed to marrying a doctor or an engineer. He was on the look out for a post-graduate who would turn out to be a good housewife. But he found himself marrying a doctor.

Madhavi had ruled out marriage for the next two or three years until she completed Medicine. Even in future, general consensus in the family was to look only for a doctor, under no circumstances a non-resident Indian. But Madhavi had to marry even before she completed medicine and that too a non-resident Indian who had little to do with medicine.

Madhavi is our daughter.

× × ×

One day in 1990, when I was Vizag Port Trust Chairman, the Indian Oil Corporation's (IOC) General Manager, Mr. Appa Rao, came to see me. He had met me many times earlier regarding matters relating to the IOC terminal at the port. But that day he came on a different mission.

"If you feel like performing your daughter's marriage, there is a good alliance, Sir", he started broaching the subject. I laughed. "Marriage for our daughter? Now? She has not yet completed two years of her medicine in Madras. Until she completes her studies and house surgeonship, we don't intend to perform her marriage. Leave the subject. What else is happening?" I said trying to scotch the marriage proposal.

Mr. Appa Rao did not exert any great pressure. But he would not go without saying what all he had on his mind.

"Our Executive Director, Mr. Venkoba Rao, called me from Madras. He comes from a good, traditional Madhwa family. A nephew of his, who has done doctorate in Finance, is working as an Associate Professor in the U. S. Some one had told them about your family. In case you have any plans about your daughter's marriage, Mr. Venkoba Rao would like to talk to you about his nephew".

I cut short the discussion by pointing out, "Marriage is not at all on our minds. Please make it clear to Mr. Venkoba Rao and the boy's people". There was no point in discussing something impossible.

He would not take a "no" for an answer. "It is the boy's maternal uncle who spoke to me. The boy's father, a Chartered Accountant, is the Managing Director of Ennore Foundries. The boy has been in India on a 20-day visit. His parents are keen on finalising an alliance when the boy is around. Anyway, I will pass on what you have told me to Mr. Venkoba Rao", he said. He once again talked about the family background and traditions of Mr. Venkoba Rao, and how good this alliance would be and finally said, "In case you think of an alliance for your daughter, remember Mr. Venkoba Rao and his nephew". I smiled, saying "Okay", because I knew perfectly that it was not in the realm of possibility.

Our daughter Madhavi was about 20 years old. It would take three to four years for her to complete MBBS and house surgeonship. My wife Gopika and I had firmly decided that we would wait until then and look out for a doctor son-in-law. If the husband and the wife belonged to the same profession, they would mix well and lead a harmonious life, we felt. Against such a backdrop, the marriage proposal that popped up concerned a boy in the U. S. and was not a medical doctor. The proposal was, therefore, a non-starter, I felt.

I briefed Gopika about the offer when I went home that evening. She commented, "The alliance may be good; but marriage is not on our minds. Moreover, the bridegroom you are talking of is not the type we would be looking for".

"I too told Mr. Appa Rao that the proposal need not be pursued". For what it was worth, we took Madhavi into confidence. She had come to Vizag for that week-end. Without evincing any interest, she ended the discussion by asking, "Where is the urgency for marriage. We will talk about it after my studies are over".

That night, an uncle of Gopika called her from Madras. Gopika casually informed him of the marriage proposal for Madhavi. The moment she said the bridegroom was a nephew of Mr. Venkoba Rao, her uncle certified it was a very good alliance. "If the boy does not measure up to our expectations or if the time is not opportune, let us leave it. But if you think of marriage, it is a very good alliance", he opined.

My wife and I decided, "Let us drop the subject at this stage; we can think of it when the girl finishes her studies."

× × ×

The next day happened to be Sunday and *"ekadasi"*. For the previous few years, Gopika and I had been observing total fast on *'ekadasi'*, touching not even water. Early in the morning there was a call from Madras when I was in 'puja". Though annoyed over the disturbance, I took the call. It was from Mr. Vasudeva Rao, Managing Director of Ennore Foundries. It concerned the marital alliance for his son, broached by Mr. Appa Rao the previous day.

Mr. Vasudeva Rao said: ".... There is a small communication gap. Mr. Appa Rao seemed to have told you yesterday that our son Narendra would be in India for 20 days. But it is not correct. My son has been in India for the last 20 days and is leaving for the U. S. tomorrow. Since your daughter is in Madras, we would like to take a look at her today, if you would not mind. Of course, only if you are interested".

Without any equivocation, I told him what Gopika and I had decided the previous night. I went one step further and said, "Whenever we perform the marriage, we want to look for a doctor bridegroom for our daughter. Your son has specialised in Finance." With these words, I thought he would end the subject.

"Anyway, it is up to you", Mr. Vasudev Rao said and added, "Initially, our son too had been totally opposed to marrying a doctor or an engineer. But after a visit to Tirupati a couple of days ago, he changed his mind so far as an alliance with your family is concerned. That too, only if all other aspects are satisfactory". I could not make out the link between their Tirupati visit and the boy's second thoughts on the girl's profession.

Mr. Vasudeva Rao's desire to see the girl that day was impossible. Madhavi happened to be with us at Vizag right then and not in Madras as thought of by Mr. Vasudeva Rao. She was scheduled to board the train that afternoon, and reach Madras only at 6 the next morning. By then, Mr. Vasudeva Rao's son should be boarding the Madras-Delhi flight on his way to the U. S. The question of Madhavi flying to Madras did not arise as there was only one flight from Vizag to Madras every day at 8 a.m. and it should have left by then or be leaving in another 15-20 minutes.

Explaining all this to Mr. Vasudeva Rao, I underlined one more point: "Vasudeva Rao garu, we are not planning to perform our daughter's marriage for the next three years. Even then, we would like to have a doctor son-in-law. Let us, therefore, drop the subject here. Irrespective of the outcome of your proposal, I am happy to get acquainted with you. Let us meet when I visit Madras. May I have your telephone number? Bye. "

I could make out that he was deeply disappointed. But there was little that anybody could do. He gave me the telephone number and hung up.

Once the call was over, Gopika, Madhavi and son Sanjiv (16), who had been watching me, entered into a discussion on whether I had communicated our viewpoint correctly and whether I should have told Mr. Vasudeva Rao some thing more. It was 8 a.m. Sanjiy put an end to the discussion, commenting, "It may be *"Ekadasi"* for you; but don't starve us of our breakfast". As Gopika went into the kitchen, I got up saying, "Since the marriage is not destined to take place, the call landed at the wrong time. There could have been some remote possibility if Madhavi were to be in Madras that day. There was no way we could have left for Madras". As I was about to resume my disrupted *'puja'*, the phone rang again.

× × ×

The caller identified himself as one representing some company in Madras and said: "Sir, I tried to speak to you yesterday; but I was told you were busy. I am now at the airport but the flight to Madras is delayed by three hours. If you please permit me, I would like to see you at your residence just for five minutes".

It would take him at least half an hour to come from the airport to our bungalow in Harbour Park. Thinking that I could finish my *'puja'*, I told him "yes" rather reluctantly.

The moment I put down the receiver, all of us were buffeted by tumultuous thoughts. The caller was a total stranger. Any one who had work with the Vizag Port Chairman or who knew my background would not try to meet me at my bungalow. A bitter experience I had gone through a couple of years back at Hyderabad made me not to receive official visitors at home.

× × ×

One evening, in November, 1987, a leading liquor magnate, Mr. Magunta Subbarami Reddy, dropped in at my residence in Banjara Hills, Hyderabad, when I was Excise Commissioner.

Mr. Subbarami Reddy had met me at office twice or thrice earlier. But he did not have any work that was to be transacted at my level. Lower-level officials normally attended to his work.

Terming his visit as a purely courtesy call, Mr. Subbarami Reddy presented me a packet of Pulla Reddy sweets as Diwali gift. He left saying it was time he left for the airport, as he was on his way to US.

Twenty or thirty minutes after he left, our son Sanjiv returned from school. Apparently feeling hungry, he grabbed the sweets packet he sighted on arrival and opened it. What tumbled out were not sweets – but currency bundles. I was shell-shocked. My father, wife Gopika and children Madhavi and Sanjeev too were all stunned.

Those who knew me would not have played such a dirty trick. But why did Mr. Subbarami Reddy act this way? He did not inform me about the money – Is it because he felt I would spurn a packet of currency? Was that his idea? Or had some one instigated him? Or did he handover the 'wrong packet' to me instead of the regular sweet packet.

When my wife queried, "Why are you wasting your time? Do something quickly", I came back to my senses. I immediately called up the Chief Secretary, DGP and IG, ACB. An ACB team rushed to my home and seized the Rs.1 lakh currency in the packet while another team rushed to the airport and arrested Mr. Subbarami Reddy, who was about to board the flight. I learnt much later that an official facing charges for indiscipline and corruption had Mr. Subbarami Reddy to do this, convincing him that I would accept the money as I was badly in need of money. Later, he could approach me through Mr.Reddy to sort out his matters.

Since then, I had stopped private individuals, stepping into my residence, on official work.

× × ×

Why did this stranger call me on a Sunday and wanted to come to my residence all the way from the airport for a five-minute talk? I doubted his bona fides initially. Since what he wanted to discuss was a routine port matter and since he came from a far off place, I saw no reason to deny his request. Driving 20 km from the airport into the city for a small job did not make sense. He was simply wasting his time and money. But what intrigued me was his harping on the Madras flight being delayed by three hours. A short while earlier, I had told Mr.Vasudeva Rao the flight would have taken off.

What did the new piece of information signify? Why did I get '*that*' information then? Was the flight delay incidental or willed by God? Sanjeev joked, "Daddy, perhaps this also is God's wish", making all of us turn to the nearby Srinivasa statue (presented by friends at Tirupati) and then looked at each other.

Breaking the silence, I finally asked Madhavi, "What do you say? There is still time for the flight. They want to see you". Hesitating a little, Madhavi said, "I won't mind seeing the boy so long as my studies are not disrupted ....". Although she did not complete the sentence, I could make out her feelings.

Gopika intervened, "When the boy's people on their own want to have a look at the girl, what is there to object? It does not necessarily mean that the marriage is round the corner". Surprisingly, there was a sudden transformation in our attitudes.

Without losing time, I called up the airlines and enquired about the Madras flight and the availability of tickets. The airlines confirmed the flight was delayed by three hours but said the Madras flight was fully booked. Our enthusiasm evaporated in no time.

I tried to pull Sanjeev's leg, "Sanjeev, you mention that the delay of the flight is God's wish - but we can't get tickets now". He retorted with a grimace, "You maintain that if something is destined to happen, it will, because Lord Srinivasa will take care of everything. Why do you then taunt me about tickets?".

Right at that moment, Mr. Tirupati Raju, Port Manager (Operations) dropped in. Anybody who was somebody in Vizag knew who Port Triupati Raju was. He had such extraordinary public relations. The moment he heard me, he said, "Sir, let me try once." and made umpteen telephone calls. Ten minutes later, he said he could get one ticket confirmed. But how could Madhavi go alone? Gopika and I had to accompany her

Mr. Tirupati Raju once again spoke to Indian Airlines staff and made them contact their Calcutta office to ascertain whether tickets could be had from that end. He did not succeed. Not one to give up, he said he would go to the airport to make one more attempt. Asking us to get ready meanwhile, he rushed to the airport.

In fact, I did not have adequate cash on hand to pay for the airfares of three persons. It being a Sunday, banks remained shut. Even if some functioned, they would not open until 10 a.m. I had already taken Mr.Tirupati Raju into confidence about the cash aspect. Before he left for the airport, he had spoken to some travel agent and arranged for the issuance of tickets on credit. He called up from airport after an hour, "Sir, with great difficulty, I could get one more confirmed ticket ...". That meant only two of us could go to Madras. Gopika suggested that I accompany Madhavi. But thinking over all aspects, I told her it would be appropriate for the mother to accompany the daughter. She nodded reluctantly.

× × ×

Immediately, I got in touch with the Madras Port Trust Chairman, Mr. Balraj (my IAS batch-mate), and arranged for the stay of Gopika and Madhavi and their local transport. When I called up Mr. Vasudeva Rao in Madras and told him of the arrangements I had made, he was pleasantly surprised and very happy. He exclaimed, "God is great. He seems to have engineered all this." In the next hour, Madhavi and Gopika were on their way to Madras.

By 7 that evening, Gopika anxiously called me from Madras and broke the news: "The boy and the girl like each other. What shall we do now?"

The fast-paced developments sounded incredible. Barely twelve hours ago, there was no intention even to discuss about marriage. What a metamorphosis within a short span!

Gopika said the boy and the girl spoke to each other for an hour before they agreed to marry. But Mr. Vasudeva Rao would like Gopika and Madhavi to call on the boy's grandfather once. But for that formality, the alliance was almost confirmed. "What do you want me to do now?", Gopika asked me.

"You had better take Madhavi to the boy's grandfather", I said.

"Do you want me to go without you? You have not seen Narendra at all? Without your seeing and speaking to him, what is the point in my saying 'yes'? Is it not your responsibility as father?" I could visualise the pace of events. But how could I see Narendra? Narendra was leaving for the U. S. via Delhi the very next morning.

The only way I could meet Narendra was to be in Delhi by the next evening. Poring over air and train timetables for half an hour, I concluded it was not impossible. But how could the alliance be confirmed, as Gopika asked, without my seeing the boy and talking to him?

I pondered: "What is all this fuss about my seeing the boy? The boy likes the girl; and the girl likes the boy. Their family's customs and traditions and economic and social status and the boy's education and employment have all appealed to us. And they are very keen on the marriage once they have seen the girl. What difference does it make if I do not see the boy? Moreover, Gopika too is in favour of the alliance and has nothing against".

Since there was no prospect of my seeing the boy in flesh and blood before he left for the U. S., I spoke to him over the phone, at length.

At 8-30 in the night, I told Mr. Vasudeva Rao: "Since the boy and girl had agreed and all others present are favourably inclined, I also agree. But, I have faith in astrology. Therefore, I would like to show the horoscopes of the boy and the girl to an astrologer. If they match, we can settle the alliance. What do you say?"

Mr. Vasudeva Rao felt a little uncomfortable. Apparently, it would be embarrassing if horoscopes derail the hitherto successful journey. His tone betrayed his feelings. But my faith in astrology is borne out of a series of experiences. When I was a child ....

× × ×

My father, Mr. Patri Krishna Rao was a schoolteacher in Siripuram village of Guntur district. Mr. Baljepalli Kama Sastry was the headmaster of the school. Dr. Chandavarapu Subba Rao was the doctor in the Local Fund Ayurvedic Dispensary in the village. All of them were good friends. Mr. Kama Sastry's son, Siva Sankara Sastry, Mr. Subba Rao's son, Madhava Rao, and I were classmates. Headmaster Kama Sastry was a good astrologer. One day my father rushed home enthusiastically to share with us what Mr. Kama Sastry had to say of my future. He was said to have foretold the future of Sankaram and Madhava also.

The thrust of Mr. Kama Sastry's forecast was that Siva Sankara Sastry would join the uniformed services probably police service and I, the IAS, and that Madhava Rao would become a writer (journalist). All in the family felt as if I had already become an IAS Collector. As time passed, we forgot the forecast in the course of time.

When I was working as a university lecturer at Raipur in Madhya Pradesh after finishing post-graduation and law, my father reminded me of Mr. Kama Sastry's forecast and asked me to take the civil services examination. I followed my father's advice and saw myself joining the Indian Administrative Service.

Mr. Kama Sastry's forecast turned out to be true in the case of my other two classmates also. Siva Sankara Sastry, Mr. Kama Sastry's son, was selected to the Indian Police Service. He worked in Kerala and retired as Director General of Police. Madhava Rao served as a journalist for The Indian Express and The Hindu at Vijayawada for many years and earned the Best Journalist award. He later served as the Political Specialist at the American Consulate General for South India in Madras.

Astrology appeared to me to be a dependable science going by the forecasts of events in my life since childhood. Astrological forecasts might go wrong if the astrologer was not competent but astrology as a science could not be faulted.

That was why I insisted on the horoscopes being referred to an astrologer when I spoke to Mr. Vasudeva Rao. He could not say a 'No'.

× × ×

Gopika brought Narendra's horoscope as she returned from Madras. We showed the horoscopes of the boy and the girl to an astrologer, who commended them as matching and excellent. Marriage was now a certainty. Gopika all of a sudden asked, "Do you recall that Daivagna Sarma of Hyderabad had forecast that Madhavi would join medicine but her marriage would precede her completion of studies?" True. Six years earlier,

Basara Saraswati *'upasaka'* Daivagna Sarma made the forecasted based on numerology.

The marriage *'muhurat'* was fixed for August 23, that was 40 days later. Mr. Vasudeva Rao wanted to perform the marriage in Madras and I in Vizag. Circumstances compelled both of us to opt for the Tirupati venue.

Then only, I confronted the real issue. Except for the house and car I had acquired with Government loans, and the land given to my wife by her father, I did not readily have on hand the money needed to perform daughter's wedding. The balance in the bank was Rs.8000. All that I could raise from the General Provident Fund was Rs.25000. Unless I had Rs.2.5 lakh or more, I would not be able to perform the marriage in Tirupati. I had to borrow. From whom and how?

Thinking over the matter all through the morning, I left for Hyderabad en route to Delhi on some official work. Even on the flight, my mind mulled over money for marriage. Finally, I told myself: " Why should I worry so much? The Lord who has brought the matters to such a head will definitely provide a solution to this problem also. Why not I leave the matter to Him". I let go the problem. As I disembarked at the Hyderabad airport, our Port Trust Manager Subba Rao (based in Hyderabad) informed me that one Mr. Gulam Dastagiri wanted to buy a site of mine in the Sanathnagar industrial estate. Oh! that site – it was another story.

× × ×

One day during 1980-81, Mr. Raja Reddy, Joint Director, Industries, Hyderabad, came to see me when I was TTD Executive Officer. (He was Deputy Director Industries when I was Khammam Collector). As Joint Director, he was on deputation to develop a big private industrial cooperative society at Sanathnagar in Hyderabad. All the promoter-directors of the industrial cooperative society, being devotees of Lord Srinivasa, named their society after Lord Venkateswara. Mr. Raja Reddy and the society directors called on me to request that Lord Venkateswara take the first Rs.100 share. When I said it was not possible, they requested me, the "first servant of the Lord," to take one share at least. I bought the first share.

Two years later, I received a letter from the society saying that the industrial plots were ready and that I as a shareholder could give my willingness for an industrial plot by depositing Rs. One lakh and the allotment of plots will be decided by a draw of lots from out of all those shareholders who paid the deposits. I informed the society that I had neither the capacity nor the inclination to set up an industry. Some months later, the society decided to dispose of few odd-size plots through a lottery and offered me a 200-yard-strip of land for Rs.9000. I could pay the amount in three installments and that the registration would cost another Rs.1000. When I received a notice seeking the payment of the last installment of Rs.3000, I visited Sanathnagar to take a look at the plot. I was disappointed to see the plot. It was an odd piece of land. Lying between an industrial plot and a narrow road, a long strip of uneven breadth, the maximum being nine feet at one point. I felt I had already wasted the money by paying two installments and declined to pay the third instalment. But the society secretary would not relent. Reluctantly, I paid Rs.4000 towards the last instalment and registration. The registration took place during 1985-86. It was a dead investment. Neither I could construct anything there, nor would anybody be interested in purchasing it – I was prepared to sell it off if anybody was willing to pay Rs.10,000/-, the cost of the plot. No one was willing.

× × ×

Mr. Subba Rao told me at the airport that one Mr. Dastagiri wanted to buy that Sanathnagar plot of mine.

"How much is he prepared to offer?"

"Rs.50000, Sir".

"I need immediately more than Rs.2 lakh, Mr. Subba Rao for the marriage. Ascertain the prevailing market rates by visiting the society once". So saying, I left for Delhi.

By the time I landed back in Hyderabad from Delhi, Mr. Subba Rao had collected valuable information and met me at the airport. Mr. Dastagiri had two plots in the industrial estate — one abutting my uneven piece of land and the other across the road. Mr Dastagiri was keen on joining his two plots by acquiring my piece of land and annexing the road, which served no one else.

As Mr. Subba Rao explained the situation, Mr. Dastagiri came to the airport to meet me as per the advise of Mr.Subba Rao. He straightaway made an offer of Rs.75,000/-. I mentioned about the prevailing market prices and informed him that I was expecting about Rs. 3 lakhs. Mr. Dastagir immediately offered Rs.2 lakhs.

"Dastagiri garu, you know how site values have escalated. Your offer of Rs.2 lakh is not fair. Give me Rs.2.5 lakh". (I could queer the pitch because I knew the value of the plot to him. But if I were to sell the piece of land on my own, no sane person would have come forward to buy the uneven site).

Mr. Dastagiri replied: "Sir, I am also a religious person. Neither you nor I should feel the deal was unjust. That's why, let us settle for Rs. 2.25 lakh. Don't say 'no'." I said OK but requested that the money be paid immediately.

Mr. Dastagiri straightway paid me an advance of Rs.50000. He obliged me further by paying the total of Rs.2.25 lakh in three or four installments before the marriage. It was a god sent windfall for me – unexpected. In fact, one had to go through a lengthy and tedious procedure for registration of society plots. Yet, Mr. Dastagiri parted with the entire money without waiting for registration on my handing over my title deeds and the possession. It took six years after Madhavi's marriage for the registration to take place — that too in the name of his son, Mr. Sami as Dastagiri had passed away by then.

× × ×

Madhavi's marriage took place as per tradition at Tirupati on August 23, 1990. I saw my son-in-law Narendra for the first time only during the wedding.

Mrs. M.S. Subbalakshmi singing a song invoking the blessing of the Lord at the time of Madhavi's marriage.

As the money at my disposal was limited, I had planned to perform the marriage as simply as possible. But all the people whom I had invited and those whom I could not invite but who knew me also attended the wedding out of their affection. Many colleagues, friends and well-wishers ranging from TTD's Vedic scholars and priests to mirasidars and Nadaswara vidwans took up responsibilities on their own and conducted the wedding as members of a family. Dr. Bhaskara Rao got the wedding card designed with Srinivasa Kalyanam as the motif. A ll those – who render service to the Lord's kalyanostavam – Purohits, archakas, nadaswaram vidwans, TTd employees – all were there performing the service voluntarily.

Peshkar Krishnaswamy, Seshadri, Santhanam, Dr. Surya Rao, Garden Superintendent Thammanna, engineer Jaggarao, Janardhana Naidu, catering Sastry, Raghavan, TTD Union leader Chenga Reddy, Dr. A. K. V. S. Reddy, Museum Officer (present Director, Salar Jung Museum) N. Dhilleswara Rao, G. Valleeswar, Tirupati Rao, B. Ramachandraiah, Dr. Subbarayudu, my old personal assistants Narayana and Viswamurthy, duffedar Subrahmanyam, driver Gopal were among the many who shouldered marriage responsibilities. I could not forget the cooperation extended by the then Executive Officer, Mr. M. V. S. Prasad – The Endowments Minister, Sri Ravindra Nath Choudhary, who attended the marriage reportedly commented that he was surprised over so many TTD employees spontaneously rendering voluntary service in the marriage of the daughter of an Executive Officer who left the TTD almost a decade earlier. Who inspired all of them! I still wonder!!!

Renowned vocalist Bharat Ratna M. S. Subbulakshmi lent grandeur by not only attending the wedding but also volunteered to sing mellifluously rendering two "*kirtanas*" (standing) during "*mangalya dharana*". I had no occasion to feel the legendary burden of a father performing a daughter's wedding.

× × ×

After the marriage, the newly wed were taken to Tirumala. All of us had darshan of the Lord and performed "*kalyanotsavam*". I expressed my feelings of gratitude, which mere words could not convey, to the Lord. I thought to myself: "Two months earlier, marriage was not at all on our minds. Now, we are in Tirumala after the marriage. What a miracle? How has this happened?" The two-month-long events raced across my mind as in a movie. Unable to restrain myself, I conveyed my feelings to the boy's father, Mr. Vasudeva Rao, who was sitting by my side, participating in the Lord's kalyanam.

Mr. Vasudeva Rao picked up the thread: "Have I not told you? On the look out for a suitable alliance for Narendra, we came here and performed "*kalyanotsavam*". We left the wedding issue in the lap of the Lord. Before we left the temple, the temple priest told me that you had a daughter of marriageable age, now doing medicine in Madras, and asked me to try for that alliance. My son who was particular in not wanting to marry a doctor or engineer had second thoughts about the prospective bride's profession after the "*kalyanotsavam*"..... He agreed". As Narender had hardly one day to leave for States, we contacted, through Mr. Appa Rao — Oh ... What a miraculous sequence and events", he said bowing to the Lord in his '*kalyanotsavam*' 'glory.

I could visualise what was going on in Mr. Vasudeva Rao's mind as I am sure, he is having the same thoughts as I have been having— Neither he, nor I had performed this marriage—-

Hare Sinivasa!!!

Son Sanjeev, Son-in-law Narender, Daughter-in-law Srilekha, P.V.R.K. Prasad, Gopika and Daughter Madhavi.

30

THE INVISIBLE HAND THAT GUIDES

This happened in the first week of April 2003.

There was a function at the IAS Officers' Association building to bid farewell to the outgoing Chief Secretary, Mrs. Sati Nair, and welcome the incoming Chief Secretary, Mr. Mohan Kanda.

Mrs. Sati Nair and I belonged to the 1966 IAS batch. Our batch mates and all others IAS Officers, seniors and juniors were among those attending the meeting. Some of us began travelling down memory lane. We started to recall our experiences when we first joined the Lal Bahadur Shastri Academy at Mussorie. As we exchanged notes, sharing of one experience led to another and old memories.

Replying to the farewell felicitations, Mrs. Sati Nair too travelled 37 years back in time. Recalling the enthusiasm and happiness with which we joined the IAS training and the pranks we played, she cast a glance at me. The moment she saw me in the incarnation of a 'chandasa' (pucca, traditional) Madhwa Brahmin, she commented, "Those days, Prasad did not look anything the saint he is today. Never had we imagined that we would see him one day in his present avataar".

Those who knew Prasad of those days smiled. I too recalled "those days" as well.

× × ×

It was past midnight, but I could not sleep because of the noises being made by room-mate Sarat Kapila on a drinking spree. I could not sleep. I felt quite annoyed, "Sarat, drinking this way is no good", I told him. Switch off the lights and go to bed; we have to get up early and go for horse riding".

Sarat cast a pitiful glance at me. Of course, my appearance invoked such a look. With a clean-shaven head (fresh from Tirupati), I looked every inch a traditional orthodox south Indian country lad, I had a smattering of Hindi and my horrible diction. In contrast, he personified modernity of Delhi's St. Stephen's fame. Naturally, he regarded me as an object for pity. He provoked me saying, "Prasad, you talk like this only because you are an ignoramus so far as drinking is concerned. You don't know the kick you can get out of drinking. Have a drink first and then convince me, that drinking is bad". He was in no mood to listen, however soft my tone was.

He said that I, being jealous, who could not stand the pleasure of his drinking. He accused me of preaching morals for want of courage to drink. He went non-stop in that vein and roused my indignation.

"Sarat, don't tell me about brandy or whiskey. They are not new to me. I have fathomed their depths long back. To prove a point, I don't have to drink again to convince you." I thought I had reprimanded him enough but had not anticipated the repercussions. My words only served to instigate him further. "Is that so? You say you have fathomed their depth of drinks. Show me now how much you can drink. Can you consume one peg? Half a peg? At least a spoonful?"

I could not contain myself. The rest of the night, I competed with Sarat in drinking liquor. My bout with Sarat made me break a solemn commitment that I had made to my father.

× × ×

I had never bargained for making such a promise to my father, Sri Patri Krishna Rao a school teacher-turned-Insurance Agent. But a curious set of circumstances had led me to that. On the eve of my joining the Indian Administrative Service training at the Academy, my friends at Guntur had organised a beer party. Those days, prohibition was in force in the State. With great difficulty, we procured beer bottles and drank to our capacity. Of course, drinking was not new to me.

Staying away from home and living at Nagpur to do M. A. and working at Raipur (then in Madhya Pradesh) as a college lecturer, I had acquired all the virtues of sophistication. A story

I heard during childhood mirrored my status on the eve of my joining the Academy.

A Brahmin is on the look out for a marriage alliance for his daughter. He runs into a middleman who says that he has a "good alliance" for the girl. The girl's father is anxious to check the boy's background, and so asks some questions.

"I hope, the boy does not have any vices"

"He doesn't have any. Only occasionally, he puffs a cigarette".

"Ah, is he addicted to smoking?"

"No, he does not smoke all the time. He does so only when he chews tobacco

"Ah, is he given to chewing 'tobacco?"

"Normally, he doesn't. Only when he eats chicken or mutton".

"Alas, does he eat meat also?"

"That also only when he takes a drink".

"Does it mean that he is addicted to drinking?"

"Only when he gets some good 'company'"

"......"

Unfortunately, my background in 1966 was notorious. Returning home from the beer party at Guntur, I chewed four or five pans and sprayed myself with perfume so that I would not smell. But the moment I stepped into the home my father could make out. He did not shout at me, as he would have done earlier because I had just then returned home after a four-year stint as lecturer.

"Look, Prasad, you belong to a lower middle class family. You have experienced what poverty means. I wanted you to join the IAS so that you could devote your life for bettering the lot of those who are poor. But those with vices cannot earn credibility The prohibition is in force, but you thirst for a drink. What sort of service can you render to the public? How can you preach morals when you are immoral yourself". Although he couched his words softly, their sharpness and bitterness rendered me speechless.

"If only you wanted a kick out of drinking, I myself would have given you that". That was his parting shot. I felt ashamed.

"Never again would I indulge in it", I mumbled and walked into our home. But all through the night, I agonised over his warning "If one who joins the highest service is addicted to vices, one does not enjoy credibility of the public". That very night, I resolved not to touch liquor again.

I reached Mussorie with such a firm determination. That was where I had to reckon with my roommate Sarat Kapila.

× × ×

I used to be very active in the Academy. I was elected Chairman of the Officers' Club. I was always in the forefront whether in fighting the Academy management on behalf of the trainees or in organising cultural events. In no time, I became popular. Or so notorious that friends began to bet on me. "I will pay you a hundred bucks if you show a photograph of Prasad without a cigarette in his hand".

Smoking was the worst vice I had acquired during my M. A. studies. At the Academy, I used to puff about 70-80 cigarettes a day. My fast-paced life earned me the epithet of a 'hedonist' or happy-go-lucky fellow.

To be fair, I could not blame my vices on the environment back at home. I was brought up in a devout Madhwa Brahmin family wedded to age-old customs and traditions. Mother Subhadradevi is an ardent follower of the devotional path of the Gowdiya mutt. My only brother, younger than me, now a Colonel in the Army, is not given to smoking or drinking or eating non-vegetarian food even to this day. But I fell a prey to circumstances during my days as a college student and lecturers. Not that I did not have faith in God. I invariably offered a mini prayer and 'pranam' to God once in the morning after the shower. I used to go to temple and break a coconut before and after exams. On selection to the IAS, I went to Tirupati to offer my hair to the Lord and joined the Academy with a tonsured head. Like any other average Hindu boy, my devotion to and understanding of God were limited.

Once I completed the training at Mussorie and joined as Assistant Collector trainee in West Godavari district, I acquired the additional habit of playing cards, thanks to the then District Judge.

Judicial training is part of Assistant Collector training. It is the District Judge who gives a certificate on successful completion of training. The training is not just routine. The District Judge at Eluru was a lover of the 'rummy'. But he would not play in the club. He, therefore, invited close friends to his home and indulged in his favourite pastime. "If you don't learn rummy, I will not issue the certificate", he used to say. Although he said that in jest - when he repeated it twice or thrice, I went to his bungalow, learnt rummy from him and started playing with him.

My life partner Gopika, who joined me when I was Bhuvanagiri Sub-Collector, was flabbergasted when she observed my habits. Belonging to a more traditional Madhwa Brahmin family than mine, she could not initially stand these aspects of my personality and expressed her revulsion in many ways. But, she reconciled herself to my behaviour after observing my seniors sporting smoke pipes, and whiskey pegs as ornaments in social get-togethers. Reluctantly, she seemed to have told herself "Perhaps the job demands such behaviour". Even as she tried to transform me, I succeeded in teaching her rummy. Subsequently, I was posted as Project Officer of the Small Farmers' Development Agency, Nalgonda, Secretary to Chief Minister P. V. Narasimha Rao, as Director of Sugars and as Collector of Khammam district.

Although I could not keep my commitment to my father on giving up my habits, I tried to take his words of wisdom seriously "You should join the IAS to bring a ray of light and hope to people who are poor and deserve help. His inspiring words which enabled me to occupy certain key positions with distinction. One of them was working with the Chief Minister, at a very early stage in my career.

x x x

While I was Project Officer of the Small Farmers' Development Agency, Nalgonda, the Collector, Mr Obayya, called me over the phone one day and directed me to go to Hyderabad as the Chief Minister wanted to see me immediately. Neither he nor I knew why the Chief Minister had summoned me.

I was baffled: Had I committed any indiscretion? Had I rubbed the Chief Minister's political followers on the wrong side? Had I spoken unwittingly against the Chief Minister anywhere? The Collector found himself in greater bewilderment. An SFDA Project Officer held the rank below that of a Deputy Secretary. What could be the reason for the Chief Minister to call a junior official to Hyderabad?

I landed in Hyderabad, confused and worried. Before meeting the Chief Minister, I inquired in the Chief Minister's office as to why I had been sent for. No one knew. My anxiety grew. Less than 30 years old, I was very emotional. "Let me see; he may after all accuse me of committing some indiscretion or the other". I prepared thoroughly about my project and primed myself for any possible questions.

At our meeting, the Chief Minister came straight up the subject. He said, "The Prime Minister talked about your Nalgonda SFDA in the Chief Ministers' conference..."

At once, I understood what he was referring to. The Nalgonda Small Farmers' Development Agency primarily used to give subsidies to small farmers, arrange loans for well digging and provide wage employment through a works programme for farm workers. It was the first pilot project in the country. Land - owning small and marginal class farmers were the target families for being pushed above the poverty line.

But as the lands cultivated by many small farmers in a district like Nalgonda were 'inam' lands, no bank gave them loans against such lands for the digging of wells. Although the SFDA programme was meant to help the economically backward farmers, the objective could not be realized here as most farmers did not have clear pledgable titles.

I mustered courage and carried out an experiment. I pooled farmers owning less than two and half acres each in contiguous area and persuaded them to excavate community wells. They were paid wages for the excavation under the works programme. The SFDA withheld 50 percent of their wages as their share towards the purchase of a motor and gave the remainder of the amount as subsidy. They got half wages for excavating their own well and water for irrigating the lands. In course of time, they could eke out their livelihood as farmers instead of as workers. I felt that rather than providing wage employment just for one season as labourers digging the well, they would be left with an asset (well & pumpset) which would provide employment during the work period. But the programme as envisaged by Government of India would not permit any flexibility. Only tanks and roads were recognized as community works under the works programme but not wells. Still, I got more than 300 wells excavated, contravening the regulations, as I was convinced that the spirit of the programme was to help the poor to get employment. What was the point in providing wage employment and create assets, which would benefit big farmers. Here, the irrigation well with the pumpset would provide employment to group of marginal farmers throughout the year.

An Additional Secretary of the Government of India, Mr. Ramakrishnayya (who subsequently worked as NABARD Chairman and RBI Deputy Governor), visited the project. He was a very practical administrator and a visionary. He commended my idea. He, however, underlined the contravention of regulations and said the matter had to be discussed at a higher level by the High Powered Committee as I was creating assets in private lands – technically they could not be classified as community works – though they would be benefiting many poor families. Prime Minister Indira Gandhi was taking personal interest in this pilot project.

Coming to the point, the Chief Minister said: "Mrs. Gandhi feels that the community well programme in Nalgonda district although it is contrary to regulations, is innovative and captures the spirit of the Project. I was not aware of it until the Prime Minister told me that 'it is happening in your Andhra Pradesh'. She has now directed that the experiment be extended to all

States under The Million Community Wells' programme. I felt very happy...". That led to the million wells programme in the country.

I sighed in relief. After talking in that vein for some more time, he suddenly said, "I am looking for some one for my office. Join me as my Secretary".

× × ×

Gopika appreciated my line of thinking and style of functioning both moulded by my father's motto in every position I occupied. But she could not condone my habits (although they had been on the decline by then). Against that background, I took over as the Tirumala Tirupati Devasthanams Executive Officer in 1978 in my 37th year. The major change in me between the Bhuvanagiri days and the TTD joining of the TTD was the farewell to smoking. A story hangs by that.

× × ×

When I was Sub-Collector at Bhuvanagiri, around midnight one day I learnt that Naxalites had hacked to death a Deputy Collector from Hyderabad on a visit to his native place in Nalgonda district. The Deputy Collector's driver ran to Bhuvanagiri to convey me the message. I rushed to the spot along with the Deputy Superintendent of Police immediately. As we went through the formalities and were about to send the body to his family, we received information about the movement of the naxalites. Immediately, the DSP and I, along with the police party, began scouring the forests in the neighbourhood traveling through hills and valleys, we called off the mission after 36 hours as we sighted no naxalites. Immediately on return home, I asked Gopi, "Where are the cigarettes?"

Gopika retorted, "How many packets did you carry when you left the day before?"

I recalled that I did not take any packets. Perhaps, I had gone with the cigarette in hand, I told her.

"What did you smoke in the forests?"

Then I realised that I had not smoked a single cigarette during the previous one and half days. Gopika then followed up, "After all, you could do without even thinking of smoking for two days. Give up smoking altogether now. Let us see what happens". I was lost in thought.

"You can quit. All you need is will power. After all you would have noticed in the last two days that the pleasure you get out of smoking is the same as the one you get without smoking. Why do you harm your health by smoking? If you firmly decide, you can stop smoking. You are capable."

The arrow she unleashed at my willpower worked. From that day onwards, I quit smoking. Prasad, minus the vice of smoking, took over as TTD Executive Officer.

× × ×

Even after joining the TTD, my habits haunted me occasionally for few days. But when I had *'darshan'* of Lord Srinivasa for the first time after I took over as Executive Officer, a transformation began to take place.

I went into a trance as I saw Lord Srinivasa shimmering in light thrown up by oil wick lamps in all His resplendent glory and appearing as the protector of all humanity of divine rays that incinerated all sins. I had visited Tirumala many a times and seen the Lord in the past. But only when I stood reverently before Him as Executive Officer, I felt every cell in my body electrified.

I shut my eyes and prayed, "Oh Lord, enable me as your servant to serve your devotees".

Gopika had during the course of an argument the previous day, pointedly asked me. "If you can't shed your vices totally even when you work in the Lord's precincts, how can you serve His devotees? Listen to me. Such habits do not befit the first servant of Lord Srinivasa".

As Gopika's words repeatedly reverberated in my ears, I strongly resolved in the Lord's presence "I won't touch liquor or meat or play cards as long as I am in Tirumala Tirupati".

The idea, which germinated during the 'darshan' of Lord Srinivasa, struck roots to such an extent that in a few months I gave up these habits even when I was not in Tirupati. That single *'darshan'* catapulted me onto a satvic path.

× × ×

As TTD Executive Officer, I had to go to Bangalore once with Gopika. My father-in-law, Mr. Susarla Srinivasa Rao, called me from Kakinada to suggest that we call on Sri Satya

Pramoda Teertha Swamiji of Uttaradi Mutt who happened to be in Bangalore then.

The *'swamiji'* whom I saw at Bangalore, captivated me with his radiant face, simplicity in speech and disciplined demeanors.

Thanks to the TTD, I had developed affinity with a number of *'swamijis'* and *'peethadhipathis'*. Like the Kanchi and Sringeri *'peethadhipatis'*, Ahobila *'mutt'* and Parakala *'mutt' jeeyars,* the senior and junior Narayana *Jeeyars* of Andhra Pradesh and the *'Jiyyangars'* of Tirumala.

I had the privilege of having close associations with Pejawar Swamiji, other Udipi *'peethadhipatis'*, Swamiji of and heads of Uttardi *'mutt'*, Vyasaraya *'mutt'*, Sripada raja *'mutt'* of Mulabagal, and Raghavenda Swami *'mutt'* of Mantralayam. I had good contacts with spiritual Masters like Puttaparthi Satya Sai Baba, Chinmayananda Swami, Swami Chidananda of Sivananda Ashram, Swami Ranganathananda (Ramakrishna *'mutt'*), Vidya Prakasananda Swami of Suka Brahmashram, Master Ekkirala Krishnamacharya of World Teachers' Trust, the Swamijis of Vyasashramam and representatives of Brahmakumari Eswariya Vidyalayam. I became close to the Swamijis of Ramachandra Mission, Hare Krishna movement, *'Adwaita'* proponents of Karnataka, Lingayat Swamijis and gurus of Radha Swami Satsanga.

These acquaintances and relationships went to such an extent that I used to take part in most of their spiritual meetings at Tirumala and Tirupati. The TTD job conferred on me such a rare privilege (Who made it possible?).

With the guidance of so many Hindu *'dharme'* leaders, preachers and heads of institutions, I took up a number of *'Hindu Dharma Rakshana'* activities. The people who visited me seemed to feel that the Executive Officer should be a great spiritual scholar and philosopher, thanks to the scholarly Executive Officer's foreward (though not necessarily mine) in hundreds of books published by the TTD.

Ranging from the pocketsize *'Bhagavatgita'* written by our Public Relations Officer Ravula Suryanarayana Murty to the heavy compendium of Hindu thought brought out under the series of *'Arsha Vignana Sarvasam'* by Professor Raghunathacharya, we published hundreds of books. We published life stores of sages, saints, and mythological characters under the *'Balabharati'* series to put children on the devotional path, books on householder's responsibilities and on *Vedic* teachings for senior citizens. We brought out the *Vedas* in Telugu and got the Vedas audio-recorded. Publication of spiritual literature went on like a campaign. Among the litterateurs who fuelled the campaign with their talent and erudition were: *'Karuna Sri'* Jandhyala Papayya Sastry, *'Saraswati Putra'* Puttaparthi Narayanacharylu, eminent scholars like Malladi Chandrasekhara Sastry, Sribhashyam Appalacharya, Nanduri Ramakrishnamacharya, Balantrapu Rajanikantha Rao, Rani Narasimha Sastry, Pannala Radhakrishna Sarma, Dr. Arka Somayaji, Ushasri, Samudrala Laksmaiah, Rammurthy Sarma, Professor Ramaraju, Vadlamudi Gopalakrishnayya and N. C. V. Krishnamcharyulu. Prof. Raghunathacharya coordinated such literary activities.

The campaign resulted in devotional literature reaching the masses. The response to the publication campaign was so overwhelming that we had to reprint many works repeatedly. They sold lakhs of copies during the Godavari and the Krishna 'Pushkarams'. As the devotional literature penetrated every nook and corner, people began to mistake the Executive Officer for another "Paramahamsa", as every book contained a foreword by the Executive Officer.

Only then the question cropped up in me: I had been promoting so much of spiritual literature. I had been taking Hindu *'dharma'* into midst of people and giving lot of advice to the householders to acquire knowledge, bhakti and exhorting them to imbibe the knowledge of sastra and follow the path of kerma. I had been discussing spiritual matters with so many *'pethadhipatis'*, *'mathadhipatis'* and *'swamijis'*. But what was the spiritual path I myself should follow as an individual? Was I doing what I was advising others to do?

I posed this question to myself in front of Lord Srinivasa when I was taking part in *'arjita seva'* in the temple one day. "What is the *'dharma'* that I should follow? Who will enlighten me and when?" As usual, the Lord would not respond. But as I returned home, I had the phone call from my father-in-law concerning Sri Satya Pramoda Teertha Swamiji at Bangalore.

× × ×

That was how I happened to see Sri Satya Pramoda Teertha Swamiji. The moment I saw the Swamiji with a glow on his face, an inexplicable wave of devotion swamped me. I was humbly waiting for his blessings.

Mr. P.V.R.K. Prasad with his Guru H.H. Sri Satya Pramoda Tirtha Swamiji

Suddenly, he called me near him and blessed me. Along with *'mantraskhitas'*, a *'krishnaginam'* (deer skin) and a *'devatarchana'* box. I realised that accepting the box meant doing daily worship. How could I, who was not even given to doing *'Gayatri japam'* once a day, worship the Lord every day in a traditional way? The Swamiji, I was told, would not take kindly to the householder who, having accepted the box, did not offer daily worship. The rumour was that if the Swamiji, on a surprise visit, found the disciple not offering worship, he would take away the *'saligramam'* and statuettes of Gods. I had neither been accustomed to daily ritualistic worship nor was I interested in making a new beginning. How should I face the situation? I hesitated to accept the box.. The Swamiji's disciples and followers present looked askance at me. In their view, receiving the *'mantrakshatas'* (sacred rice) themselves from the Swamiji was a great blessing. Unless one was destined by one's good deeds, one would not be fortunate to receive *'Sudarsana saligrama'* from him. If he gave the *'saligramam'* itself it was an extraordinary, auspicious blessing. If, in addition, he gave a statue of Krishna, *'Vasudeva saligramam'*, *'sankhu'*, *'Vishnu padas'*, *'chakrankitas'* and a box containing statuettes of *Hanuman, Garuda, Garutmanth and Adisesha,* it was a considered an act of compassion possible only with great *'Poorva Janma sukruta* (result of great pious action in the earlier lives). All of them felt such a fortune was awaiting me. Standing behind me, they whispered, 'Please accept, accept".

I could not muster the requisite courage. Was he giving this blessing because I was the TTD Executive Officer. If I were to accept the *'pooja'* box, I should offer daily worship. But I did not have the self-confidence that I would.

The Swamiji smiled. As if he had read my mind, he said "We don't know why, but we felt like giving this *'devatarchana'* set to you. May be, it is God's will. It is not because you are the TTD Executive Officer, we are giving it to you. Had you not been eligible, the idea would not have struck to us. If you can't do justice by doing daily prayers in the prescribed manner, the fault is guru's. We take the blame, if there is any infraction. Accept the box and let us know your experience after some time."

His sweet words hypnotised me. I was filled with a new inspiration. As I kept seeing him, I began to feel, "Here is my guru". The doubts, clouding my mind till then, vanished.

The Swamiji went on to explain in simple language, the duties of a householder. The secular responsibilities one discharged as an employee were different from those of an individual. He expounded what a householder should and should not do and what a Brahmin, according to the *'varnasrama dharma'*, should do and should not do. One has to do his individual *'sadhana'* as prescribed for his *'swadharma'*.

"...Swadharmo nidhanamsreyah, paradharmo bhayavaha"

-Bhagavatgita

I shut my eyes for a moment and recalled Lord Srinivasa. By the time I opened my eyes, the Swamiji had laid the *'devatarchana'* set in my hands.

After returning to Triupati, I used to offer *'aarti'* to the *'devatacharchana'* box every day for some time. Beyond that, I did nothing.

Some time later, I was shifted from the TTD. I stayed in England for a year. While in England, I sent the *'devatacharchana'* box to my father-in-law's place at Kakinada, where my mother-in-law Mrs Shanta Bai, a pious lady, arranged for *'puja'* by a priest. Gopika reminded me of the box when I returned from England. The Swamiji's benign face and words flashed across my mind. "If you can't do daily *'devatacharchana'*, we will take the blame upon ourselves".

I reviewed the past and realised that the series of events were a sequel to my request to Lord Srinivas. Thereafter, I did not tarry. Since that day, for the last twenty years or more, I have been trying my best to practise the do's and don'ts prescribed for the gruhasta (householder), as advised by the Guru.

× × ×

The daily routine activities, which I now carry out with Guru's blessings and wife Gopika's cooperation, have become elaborate.

The *'anusthana karma'* with *'Sandhyavandana'* and *'Gayatri japa'* and a mini *'devatacharchana'*, which I began with the blessings of Guru Sri Satya Pramoda Teertha Swami, whetted my appetite for *'Vaidika dharma'*. In the past 20 years, I received the blessings of innumerable *'swamijis'* in many new forms.

Sri Prasad with the Present pontiff of Sri Uttaradi Muth, Sri Satyatma Tirtha Swamiji

When I was working as Media Advisor to Prime Minister P. V. Narasimha Rao in Delhi (1992-96), Sri Viswesa Teertha Swamiji of Pejawar *'Mutt'* presented me the rarest of the rare *'Vyasa saligramam'* which he had brought from Badrinath. Shortly after I began offering worship to that *'saligramam'*, I was transferred to Hyderabad where I began studying the *'sastras' and Vyasa Sahitya* under Pundit Sri Nagendra Prasad. Thereafter, I was lost in the study of Sri Veda Vyasa's *Brahmasutras* as interpreted by Sri Madhwacharya, with Sri Teekacharya's and Sri Raghavendra's commentaries, the *Mahabharata*, the *Bhagavata*, the *Upanidshads* etc.with the commentaries of Madhwa.

Sri Satyatma Teertha Swami of Uttaradi Mutt (the successor of Sri Satya Pramodathirtha Swami) initiated me in *'Astha mahamantra Japa'* and presented me statues of

'Srikrishna and Srinivasa'. The Swamiji of Raghavendra Swami Mutt presented me with *'Sudarsana saligramam'*. Palimar *Mutt* Swamiji of Udipi Srikrishna *Mutt* initiated me in *'Krishnamantra japa'*. Pundit Nagendra Prasad gifted me a *'Trivikrama'* statue when we completed the study the *'Brahmasutra bhashyam'*. Pundit Vyasakare Prabhanjanachari taught *'Sri Vishnutatwa vinirnayam'* and gave me a *'simsumara'* statue. With all these blessings, my lifestyle underwent considerable change. Now, my daily schedule includes *'sandhya vandanam'*, *'mantra japam'*, *'devatarchana'*, *'naivedyam'*, *'vaiswadeva homam'*, *'hastodakam'*, *('brahma yagnam')*, and *'baliharanam'* – an elaborate systematic ritual had become part of my daily two-and-half-hour-long routine. By the time my father passed away in 1997, after these daily rituals, for the past eight years, we had an hour's lesson in sastra by Pd. Nagendra Prasad.

My wife and I have been following the *'grihasta dharma'* and discharging the duties prescribed by sastra observing *'Nirjala'* (without even taking water) fast on every *'ekadasi'* and *'Krishtastami' 'chaturmasa vrata'* for four months in a year for the past ten years. Gopika and I felt that we should spend at least nine hours a day in spiritual pursuits by the time I retired. So far, I have been indulging more in *'karma'* ritualistic (worship) but not much on *'jnana'* activities (acquiring knowledge – except the one hour lesson). In the *'jnana'* pursuit, my wife has overtaken me. Occasionally, Gopika remarks that I, who once did not spend any time on worship, am today spending too much time on rituals and neglecting *'jnana karyam'*.

True, I am far behind many in abiding by the do's and don'ts of *'grihastasrama dharma'* and in pursuing the *'jnana'* path. But there has been a perceptible change in my appearance as part of the *'swadharmacharana'* prescribed by gurus. My forehead now sports *'Gopichandana' 'akshata'* and *'angaram'*. A *'sikha'* adorns my head.

Perhaps it was looking at my appearance that prompted, my friend, the retiring Chief Secretary Mrs. Sati Nair comments "none of us expected the hedonist Prasad of those days would be transformed like this".

I have no doubt now as to the inspiration for my transformation. It is from the very power which turned me away from habits like smoking and drinking into the *'bhakti'* path, used me as an instrument to do some good deeds in the TTD, showed me the right guru and made me understand and practise my *'dharma'*, as per my *'Yogyata'* - constantly reminding me that 'I am not the doer, 'He' does – However, whatever we seem to be doing and achieving, is made possible only because of His grace.

Naham Karta Hari Karta

Tatpuja Karmachakhilam

Tadhapi Matkruta puja

Twat Prasadena na anyadha

'Hare Srinivasa'

Hoping that every individual, reposing faith in God wishing to realise the ultimate goal of life, will follow the path of *'dharma'* and *'bhakti'* which help him travel even to the other world in peace...gnana, bhakti vairagya and ultimately the blessings (*Anugraha*) of the Lord – paving the way for salvation (*Moksha*) as per his *'yogyata'* (entitlement).

——PVRK Prasad

INDEX